Low-Code Development with Xomega.NET

Generate .NET Apps for Blazor, MAUI, WPF, ASP.NET, and TypeScript

Serghei Sarafudinov

Apress®

Low-Code Development with Xomega.NET: Generate .NET Apps for Blazor, MAUI, WPF, ASP.NET, and TypeScript

Serghei Sarafudinov
Princeton, NJ, USA

ISBN-13 (pbk): 979-8-8688-1789-2 ISBN-13 (electronic): 979-8-8688-1790-8
https://doi.org/10.1007/979-8-8688-1790-8

Copyright © 2025 by Serghei Sarafudinov

This work is subject to copyright. All rights are reserved by the Publisher, whether the whole or part of the material is concerned, specifically the rights of translation, reprinting, reuse of illustrations, recitation, broadcasting, reproduction on microfilms or in any other physical way, and transmission or information storage and retrieval, electronic adaptation, computer software, or by similar or dissimilar methodology now known or hereafter developed.

Trademarked names, logos, and images may appear in this book. Rather than use a trademark symbol with every occurrence of a trademarked name, logo, or image we use the names, logos, and images only in an editorial fashion and to the benefit of the trademark owner, with no intention of infringement of the trademark.

The use in this publication of trade names, trademarks, service marks, and similar terms, even if they are not identified as such, is not to be taken as an expression of opinion as to whether or not they are subject to proprietary rights.

While the advice and information in this book are believed to be true and accurate at the date of publication, neither the authors nor the editors nor the publisher can accept any legal responsibility for any errors or omissions that may be made. The publisher makes no warranty, express or implied, with respect to the material contained herein.

> Managing Director, Apress Media LLC: Welmoed Spahr
> Acquisitions Editor: Ryan Byrnes
> Editorial Assistant: Gryffin Winkler

Cover designed by eStudioCalamar

Cover image designed by Pexels

Distributed to the book trade worldwide by Springer Science+Business Media New York, 1 New York Plaza, New York, NY 10004. Phone 1-800-SPRINGER, fax (201) 348-4505, e-mail orders-ny@ springer-sbm.com, or visit www.springeronline.com. Apress Media, LLC is a Delaware LLC and the sole member (owner) is Springer Science + Business Media Finance Inc (SSBM Finance Inc). SSBM Finance Inc is a **Delaware** corporation.

For information on translations, please e-mail booktranslations@springernature.com; for reprint, paperback, or audio rights, please e-mail bookpermissions@springernature.com.

Apress titles may be purchased in bulk for academic, corporate, or promotional use. eBook versions and licenses are also available for most titles. For more information, reference our Print and eBook Bulk Sales web page at http://www.apress.com/bulk-sales.

Any source code or other supplementary material referenced by the author in this book is available to readers on GitHub. For more detailed information, please visit https://www.apress.com/gp/services/source-code.

If disposing of this product, please recycle the paper

To my mother, who always believed in me.

Table of Contents

About the Author xi

About the Technical Reviewer xiii

Acknowledgments xv

Introduction xvii

Chapter 1: Getting Started with Xomega 1

   Create Xomega Solution 1

      Xomega Solution Template 1

      Xomega Solution Configuration 3

      Blazor Solution Structure 5

      Reviewing the Initial Application 7

   Model Project Structure 11

      Xomega Generators 11

      Import Model from Database 13

      Application Model Files 15

   Xomega Model Overview 16

      General Model Structure 16

      Logical Types 20

      Domain Model 25

      Service Model 34

      Presentation Model 40

      Summing It Up 53

   Generate CRUD Views 54

      Adding CRUD Operations 54

      Default CRUD Operations 55

TABLE OF CONTENTS

    Search and Details Views 55

    Generating Application Code 56

  Review Search/Details Views 58

    Sidebar Menu 58

    Search Results Grid 59

    Search Criteria 61

    Details Screen 65

  Summary 66

Chapter 2: Building Out a List View 69

  Refine Search Result Columns 69

    Update Read List Output 69

    Configure Column Labels 72

    Review the Results 73

  Use Static Enumerations 74

    Define Enumerations 74

    Define Enumeration Types 75

    Update Field Types 76

    Review the Results 76

  Custom Search Result Fields 78

    Add Custom Result Field 79

    Custom Field Population Logic 80

    Configure Key Field and Links 81

    Review the Results 82

  Using Child Subobjects 83

    City/State Result Field 84

    Entity Model Diagrams 85

    Subobject As a Child List 88

    Reading Subobject Fields 91

    Review the Result 93

Extend Generated Entities 94
    Why Not a Subobject 95
    Customize Generated Entities 97
    Customize Entity Configuration 99
    Use Enhanced Entity 101
    Review the Results 102
Summary 103

Chapter 3: Configuring Search Criteria 105

Add or Remove Criteria 105
    Removing Useless Criteria 106
    Adding Non-field Criteria 107
    Review the Results 108
Configuring Operators 108
    Configure Default Operator 109
    Remove Criteria Operators 111
    Custom Range Operators 113
    Custom Operator Logic 116
Multi-value Criteria 122
    Configure Multi-value Control 123
Dynamic Enumeration 126
    Configure Dynamic Enumeration 127
    Custom Criteria Implementation 129
    Auto-complete for Multi-value 131
    Statically Displayed Criteria 133
    Customizing Criteria Object 135
Cascading Selection 138
    Country Dynamic Enumeration 139
    Adding Country Criteria 140
    Configuring Cascading Selection 142
Summary 145

TABLE OF CONTENTS

Chapter 4: Building Out a Details View 147
Displaying Child Lists 147
Removing Fields and Actions 148
Adding the Pay History Child List 153
Department History Child List 160
Summary 165
Configuring Panel Layout 166
Grouping Fields into Panels 166
Organizing Panels with Tabs 167
Laying Out Fields and Panels 171
Fields from Related Objects 175
Fields from the Person Object 175
View and Edit Phone Number 193
Person Phone Subobject 194
Master-Detail Layout 203
Dynamic View Title 203
Master-Detail Employee View 205
Add/Edit Related Objects 208
Displaying Home Address 208
Address Details Screen 214
Add and Edit Employee Address 220
Lookup Selection Form 229
Generating a Lookup View 229
Employee Address Lookup Link 233
Employee Address Validation 235
Computed UI Fields 239
Adding Current Pay Info 239
Adding Current Department 248

Working with Hierarchies	256
Adding the Manager Field	257
Adding Direct Reports	270
Summary	275

Chapter 5: Implementing Security 277

Implement Password Validation	278
Password Validation Service Logic	278
Remove Default User and Password	279
Review Email-Based Login	280
Populate User Claims	281
Enhancing User Info for Claims	282
Reading User Info for Claims	283
User Info Conversion to IPrincipal	284
Claims IPrincipal Extensions	289
Define Application Permissions	292
AppPermissions Enumeration	293
Application Permission Rules	294
Securing Business Services	295
Securing Operation Access	296
Row-Level Security	302
Secure Sensitive Data	305
Secure UI Views and Fields	314
Secure Editing on the UI	315
Hiding Sensitive Data	322
Securing Page Access	332
Summary	340

Index **341**

About the Author

Serghei Sarafudinov is a software developer, architect, and entrepreneur with more than 25 years of experience building large-scale enterprise applications for leading North American telecommunications and transportation companies using .NET, Java, and Typescript.

He currently serves as a Senior Software Specialist at Princeton Consultants and is the President and CEO of SIS Consulting. He holds a master's in Applied Mathematics from the Moscow Institute of Physics and Technology and a US patent on Extensible Business Object Modeling and Generation of System Artifacts.

He is the visionary behind the Xomega.NET low-code platform and the open source Xomega Framework, helping .NET developers to build quality enterprise systems faster. Visit xomega.net for more information.

About the Technical Reviewer

Vladislav Bilay is a DevOps Engineer with professional experience in fields such as designing and delivering Cloud-Native IT solutions, improving software development processes, managing UNIX-based systems, supporting Big Data services, and configuring production CI/CD tools and pipelines. He is certified as an AWS Solutions Architect and Salesforce System/Application Architect.

Acknowledgments

I'd like to extend my sincere thanks to **Richard Campbell** and **Carl Franklin** for creating the ever-inspiring show *.NET Rocks!* and for the honor of joining them as a guest to talk on Xomega. Their enthusiasm and deep curiosity made the experience unforgettable.

A big thank-you to **Ryan Byrnes** for inviting me to author this book on Xomega and for his continued encouragement. Many thanks as well to the incredible team at **Apress**, whose expertise and dedication made this book possible—from concept to publication.

Finally, to my **amazing wife and children**: your unwavering support, gentle nudges, and steadfast belief in me were the true driving force behind this journey. This book owes its heartbeat to you.

Introduction

To stay competitive, companies around the world need to build or modernize an ever-increasing number of business applications each year. Microsoft provides one of the largest development ecosystems for building such applications, centered around their .NET platform, which includes a range of technologies—from legacy ASP.NET WebForms in .NET Framework to state-of-the-art Blazor and MAUI frameworks.

While there is an abundance of excellent documentation and tutorials on these technologies, including those from Microsoft, each technology may require a separate and potentially steep learning curve, as they use different architectures and frameworks for building applications.

Although each framework in the .NET ecosystem provides the basic building blocks, creating large enterprise applications that follow best practices for architecture and software development remains quite manual and, often, tedious. Combined with the steep learning curve, this can significantly increase the costs and delay the timelines of such development projects.

What Is Xomega

The Xomega platform is designed to help you quickly create solutions for your application using a .NET architecture of your choice, with clean separation between application layers. This separation provides immense benefits for maintenance and any future modernization of your application.

As a low-code platform, Xomega allows you to define your domain, service, and presentation models and then generate high-quality application code from those models, while still letting you customize the generated code for your specific needs. Best of all, you can easily update the models and regenerate all the code without losing your customizations.

At its core, the Xomega platform consists of the following components:

- **Xomega.Net** – A Visual Studio extension that provides a special Xomega model project for defining and editing your application models and for running code generators on those models.

- **Xomega Solution wizard** – A Visual Studio wizard that helps you select and configure components of your application architecture and then creates an initial solution preconfigured for the selected architecture.

- **Xomega modeling technology** – An extensible XML-based modeling technology that allows you to define your application's domain, service, and UI models in a simple yet powerful way.

- **Xomega generators** – A set of extensible code generators that transform your models into source code, database scripts, technical documentation, or other artifacts for all application layers.

- **Xomega Framework** – An open source framework that powers your application, taking care of common functionality for enterprise-grade applications, and helping you write clean, reusable, and maintainable code that follows industry best practices.

About This Book

To help you learn .NET development with Xomega, this book will walk you through building a full-fledged Blazor Server or WebAssembly application using Microsoft's sample AdventureWorks database. This database covers many facets of an enterprise information system for a mid-size company, from Human Resources and procurement to production and sales.

In this book, we will focus on the Human Resources module and build a powerful list screen for browsing and searching employees, as well as a complete details screen for viewing and editing employee information. Finally, we will secure our application with password-based authentication and a robust security model to control access to application functionality and data.

What You Will Learn

After reading this book, you will have a solid understanding of Xomega model concepts and the development process with Xomega. You will learn how to implement common use cases for typical business applications, specifically how to

- Configure and create a new Blazor solution using the Xomega Solution wizard.
- Import an existing database schema into the Xomega model.
- Generate default search and details views for the imported entities.
- Model and generate a powerful custom search screen for browsing your entities.
- Model static data and dynamic lookup data for your application.
- Write platform-independent custom code, preserved after regeneration from the updated model.
- Model CRUD operations and generate a complete details screen for your entities.
- Secure functionality and data in your application using a multi-layered approach.

You will see that the Xomega model, development process, and most of the code in Xomega applications are largely platform-agnostic, which can help you use what you learn in this book to build applications not just with Blazor but with any of the other supported .NET technologies, such as MAUI, WPF, ASP.NET, etc.

Clear layer separation and writing or generating platform-independent code will also help you future-proof your application and easily adapt it to new technologies or alternative frameworks, including the following:

- Using different architectures, where the same business services can be called directly (e.g., Blazor Server), through a REST API (e.g., Blazor WebAssembly), or via another communication protocol, such as gRPC
- Reusing client objects and logic with different UI technologies, such as MAUI, WPF, or ASP.NET
- Generating UI views with different .NET component libraries, such as Syncfusion, MudBlazor, etc.

We will also discuss how the Xomega platform can leverage Generative AI to further speed up the development process and improve efficiency and productivity.

INTRODUCTION

Who This Book Is For

This book is primarily intended for .NET developers who want to learn how to build modern data-driven applications using the Xomega low-code platform. It will also be useful for architects and technical leads who want to understand how to use Xomega to create robust, maintainable, and future-proof applications.

You should be familiar with XML syntax and standard .NET and Microsoft technologies, such as Blazor, ASP.NET Core, Entity Framework Core, REST API, and SQL Server.

Code Snippets

As part of building out the functionality of our application in this book, we will use code snippets that show you the changes we make to previous code or model files. For context, the code snippets will include the method name or the relevant parent XML elements in the model but may use ellipses (...) to skip over any irrelevant parts.

To communicate the changes made to the code, the code snippets will include deleted lines that start with a dash (-) and use strikethrough font, as well as added lines that start with a plus (+) and use bold font, as shown in the following example.

```
  public void MethodBeingUpdated()
  {
      // This is a highlighted line of existing code
      ... // other code skipped for brevity
-     // This is a line of code that was removed from the method
+     // This is a new line of code added to the method
  }
```

Any existing lines of code that we want to highlight will use bold font without any special markers at the beginning of the line.

Prerequisites

To practice the steps for building and running the application in this book, make sure you have the following installed on your machine:

- Visual Studio 2022 Community Edition or higher
- Xomega.Net extension for your version of Visual Studio
- A valid Xomega license
- The sample Microsoft database AdventureWorks installed on your local or network SQL server

Note In this book, we used version 2022 of the sample database installed from the published backup AdventureWorks2022.bak. If you use a different version of the database, you may see some differences from this book.

Full Source Code

The source code for this book is available on GitHub via the book's product page, located at www.apress.com/ISBN.

Note The full source code is for the final application, which you can build and run. You can still use it as a reference when going through the steps in this book, but it may not match the code snippets exactly, as we will be building the application step by step.

CHAPTER 1

Getting Started with Xomega

In this chapter, you'll get an overview of the Xomega platform and will be able to generate a .NET Blazor application with default search and details views from an existing database with no coding whatsoever.

You will also get familiar with the main concepts and elements of the Xomega model, which will help you to better follow the material in subsequent chapters.

Create Xomega Solution

The Xomega.Net Visual Studio extension adds a new project template that allows you to create and configure your solution tailored to specific architecture. So, let's start by creating a new Blazor solution for our application in Visual Studio using Xomega.

Xomega Solution Template

To create a new Xomega Solution, select the *New Project* option in your Visual Studio, and then pick *Xomega* project type or enter *Xomega* in the search box to find the *Xomega Solution* template, as shown in Figure 1-1.

CHAPTER 1 GETTING STARTED WITH XOMEGA

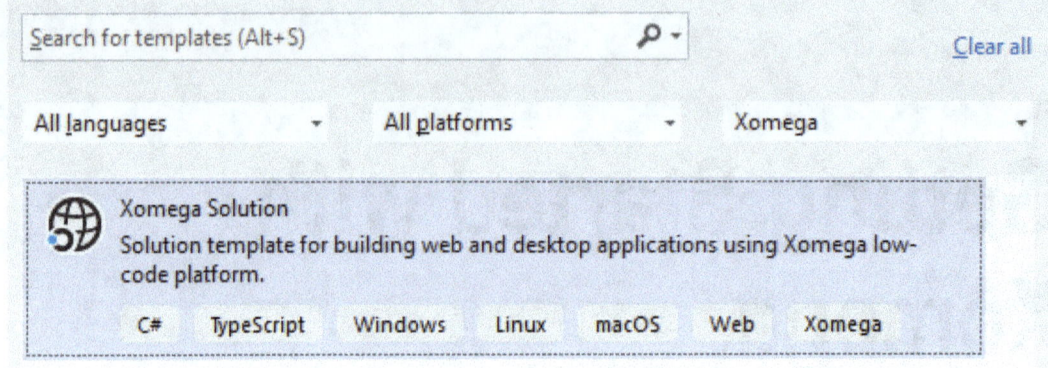

Figure 1-1. Xomega Solution template

Select the *Xomega Solution* template, and click *Next* to get to the screen in Figure 1-2.

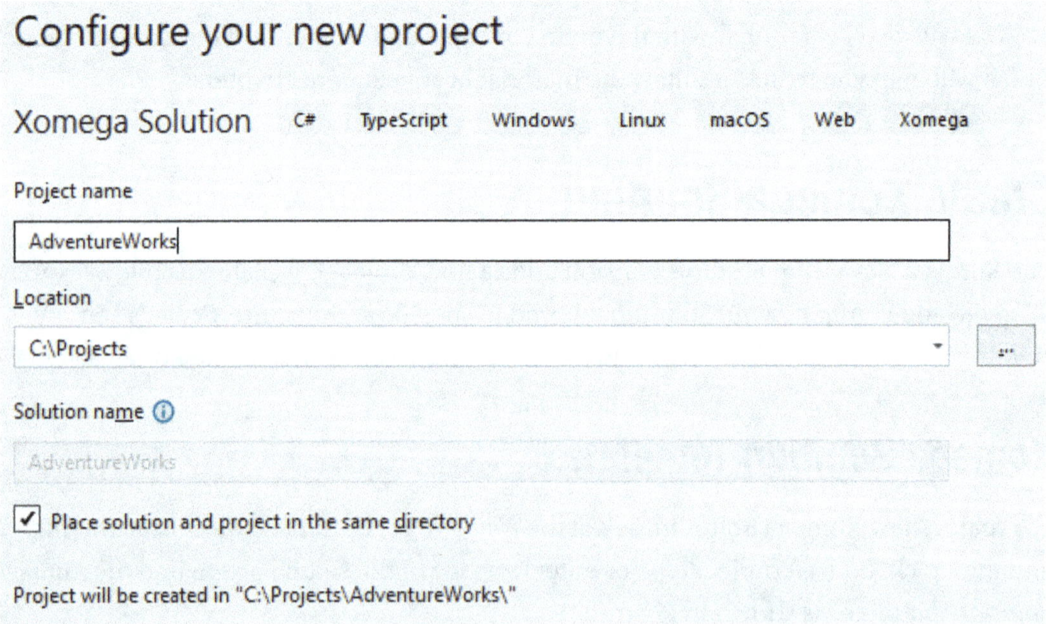

Figure 1-2. Creating AdventureWorks Xomega Solution

Set *AdventureWorks* as the project name, select the location to create the solution, check the checkbox to place the solution and project in the same directory, and click *Create*.

> **Note** If you are using Xomega for the first time, you may get asked to supply an Xomega license file here. If you haven't done it yet, you'll need to download the license file from your order and then select that file in the next dialog.

Xomega Solution Configuration

You should see an *Xomega Solution Configuration* screen, which allows you to select an authentication option, as well as to pick and configure client-side and server-side technologies and projects that you want to use in your solution. Any other projects that are required for your selection will be automatically included in the solution as well.

As you'll see in a later chapter, we'll use custom data stored in our sample database for authentication, which means that we should keep the default *Password (Custom)* as the authentication option. Let's select the *ASP.NET Core Blazor* project for the client-side technology, as well as a project for *Entity Model Diagrams* to help us visualize the model, as shown in Figure 1-3.

CHAPTER 1   GETTING STARTED WITH XOMEGA

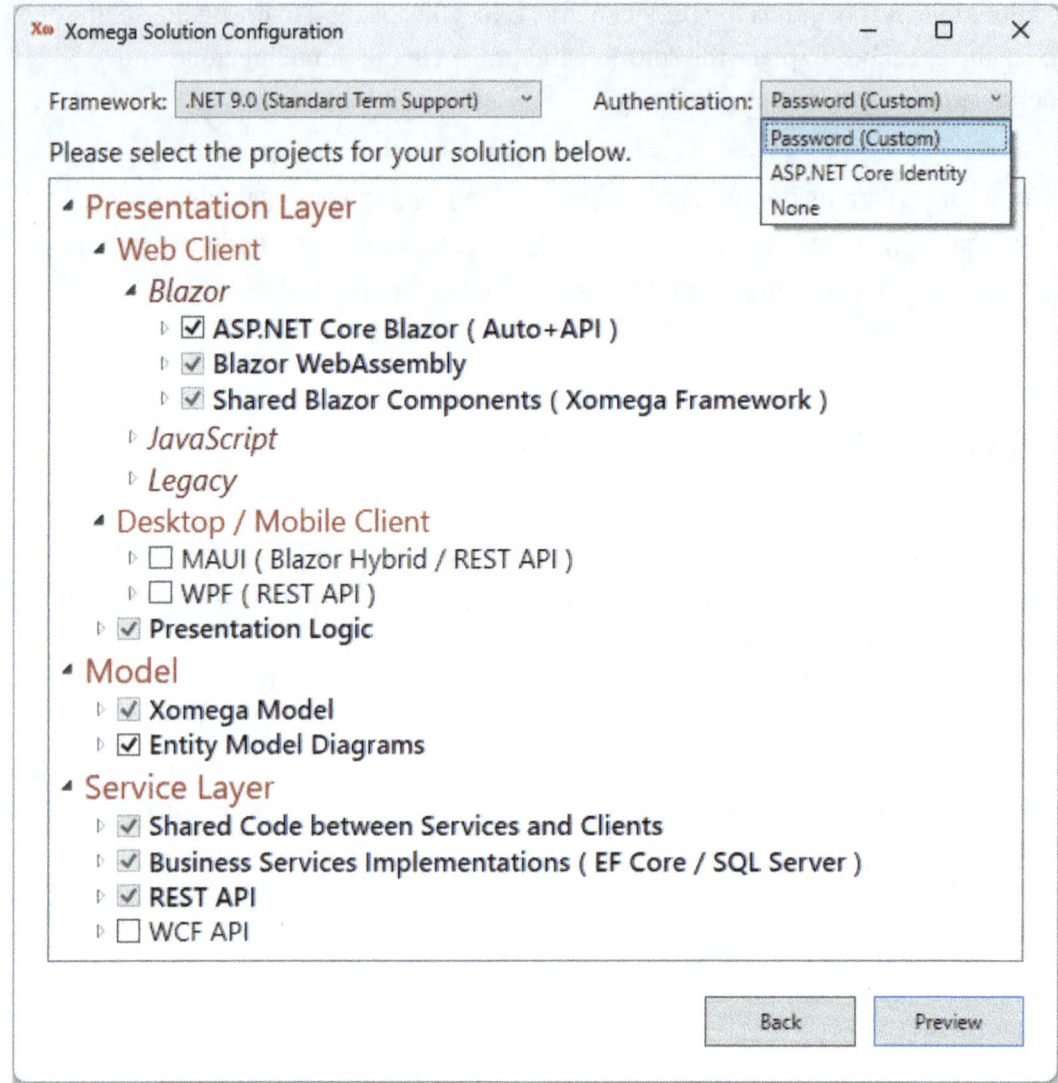

Figure 1-3. Xomega Solution wizard

You'll notice that all required projects with common logic and services will be automatically selected. The WebAssembly project will also require a REST API to access the business services.

Note   If you want to target several technologies at the same time, such as WPF, you can select additional projects here, and they'll share most of the presentation and business logic of your solution.

CHAPTER 1 GETTING STARTED WITH XOMEGA

Once you select the projects for your solution, click *Preview* to view and update the configuration of the selected projects. You can customize the name of each project and specify project-specific options, such as which Blazor components to use, as shown in Figure 1-4.

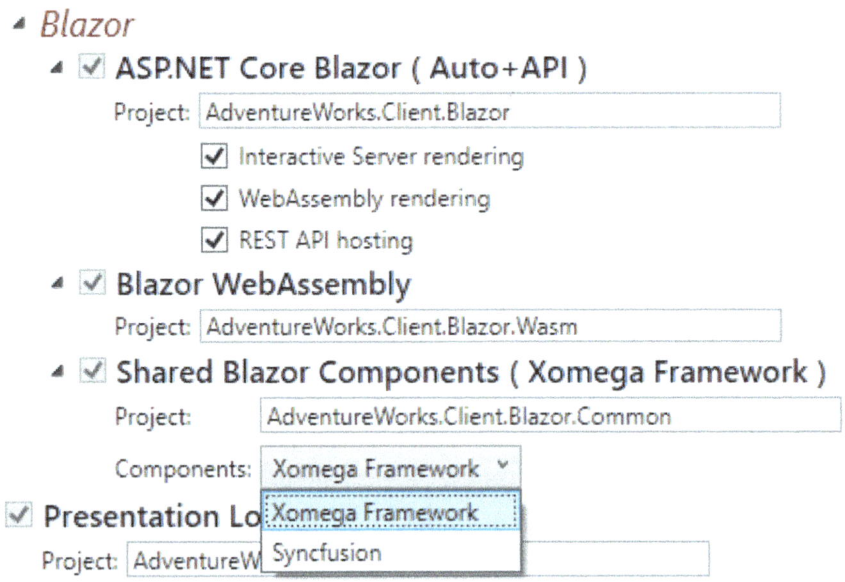

Figure 1-4. Configuring Xomega projects

Tip You can also specify this configuration for each project on the previous screen by expanding the corresponding projects.

We will use the default configuration that includes both Blazor Server and WebAssembly interactive rendering using the Auto mode and hosts the REST API right in the Blazor project, so that you don't have to run a separate project for it. Therefore, you can just go ahead and click the *Create* button.

Blazor Solution Structure

Creating a solution with all the projects may take a while as all the dependency packages are being restored, and the projects are being configured, but once the dust settles, you can collapse all projects and see the following nine projects created in your solution (see Figure 1-5).

5

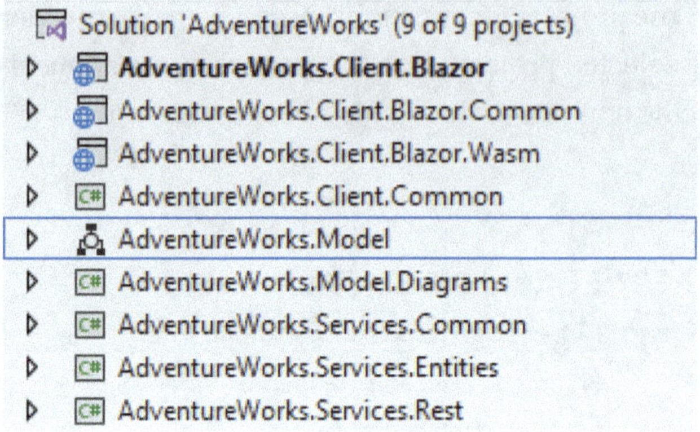

```
Solution 'AdventureWorks' (9 of 9 projects)
▷  🌐 AdventureWorks.Client.Blazor
▷  🌐 AdventureWorks.Client.Blazor.Common
▷  🌐 AdventureWorks.Client.Blazor.Wasm
▷  C# AdventureWorks.Client.Common
▷  🔷 AdventureWorks.Model
▷  C# AdventureWorks.Model.Diagrams
▷  C# AdventureWorks.Services.Common
▷  C# AdventureWorks.Services.Entities
▷  C# AdventureWorks.Services.Rest
```

Figure 1-5. Xomega Blazor solution structure

- **AdventureWorks.Model** is the project that will contain your XML domain and service models for the application and various generators that perform model transformations and code generation.

- **AdventureWorks.Model.Diagrams** project allows you to create diagrams that will help you visualize your entity model and associations between the entities.

- **AdventureWorks.Services.Common** project will have all interfaces and data contracts (DTOs) for your service model, as well as other classes that are shared between the client and the services layers.

- **AdventureWorks.Services.Entities** project will contain the back-end domain object classes based on Entity Framework, as well as implementations of the services that use these domain objects.

- **AdventureWorks.Services.Rest** project will contain Web API controllers that expose the services via the REST interface.

- **AdventureWorks.Client.Common** project will contain Xomega Framework C# data objects for the presentation layer, as well as view models for different views, and will encapsulate a significant part of the client logic. These objects and view models are not specific to any client and are reused by all C# based clients, such as WPF clients, Blazor Server, or WebForms. This is why they are configured to have their own project.

CHAPTER 1   GETTING STARTED WITH XOMEGA

- **AdventureWorks.Client.Blazor.Common** project will contain Blazor views and components that are shared between the Blazor Server and WebAssembly projects.

- **AdventureWorks.Client.Blazor.Wasm** project contains the Blazor WebAssembly client.

- **AdventureWorks.Client.Blazor** project is the main application project for the Blazor client.

Reviewing the Initial Application

Now that you understand the solution structure, let's build the solution and run the application that we got out of the box. Our solution template created an empty application that is secured with a username and password, so you should see a Login screen, as shown in Figure 1-6.

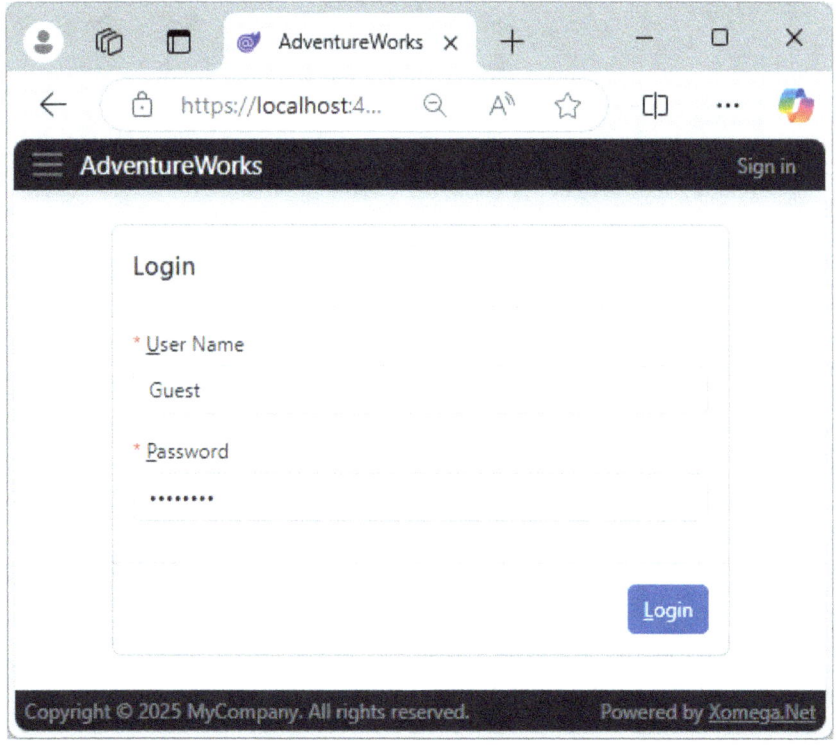

Figure 1-6. *Default password login form*

7

CHAPTER 1 GETTING STARTED WITH XOMEGA

> **Caution** The template also added some code to **pre-populate the username and password** with some default values to make it easier for you to run the app during the development. You should **remove this code** after you implement proper security for your app.

The login screen has been generated from the model as a details view, so you can immediately see some standard features of the details views that you get for free.

For example, all required fields are automatically marked with a red asterisk in front of their labels. Any invalid fields will be highlighted in red, with the validation message displayed right below the field. And if you try to submit an invalid form, the summary of all validation errors will be also displayed at the top, as illustrated in Figure 1-7.

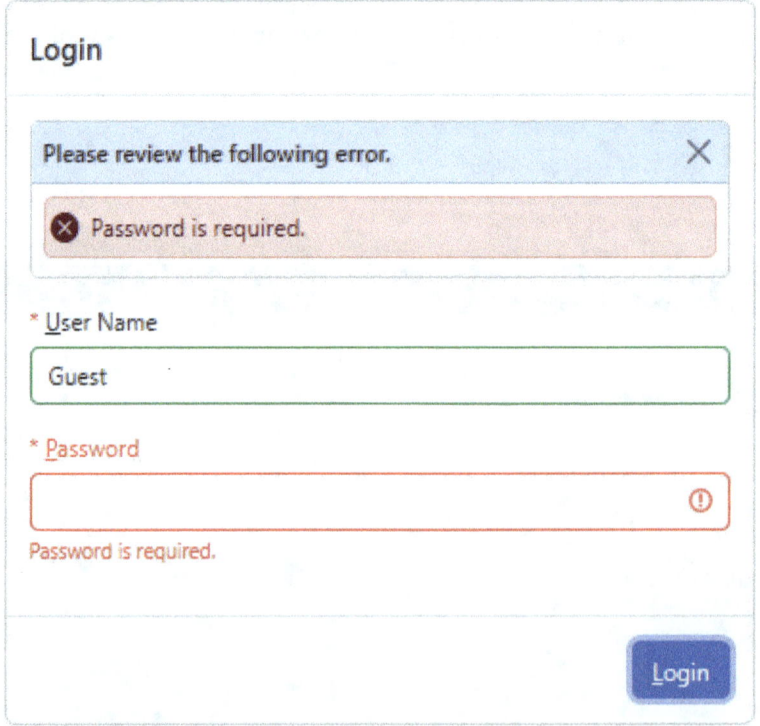

Figure 1-7. *Login field validation*

Furthermore, the initial solution template has set up all the plumbing for checking the security, where you just need to implement the last bit of the actual validation of the username and password in a special login service, which you will see how to do later in this book.

CHAPTER 1 GETTING STARTED WITH XOMEGA

By default, the login service allows any username and the word "password" as the password. If you enter a different password, you'll see the following error from the login service (see Figure 1-8), which gives you an idea of how an invalid login will look like in the real app.

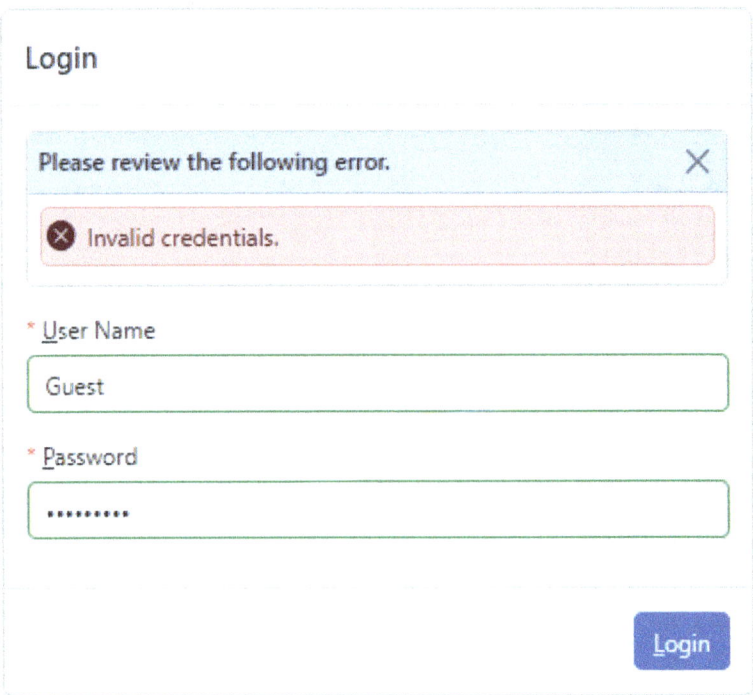

Figure 1-8. *Login credential validation*

If you enter the default username and *password*, then you should get to a blank *Home* screen with a (rather empty) sidebar menu, as illustrated in Figure 1-9.

9

CHAPTER 1 GETTING STARTED WITH XOMEGA

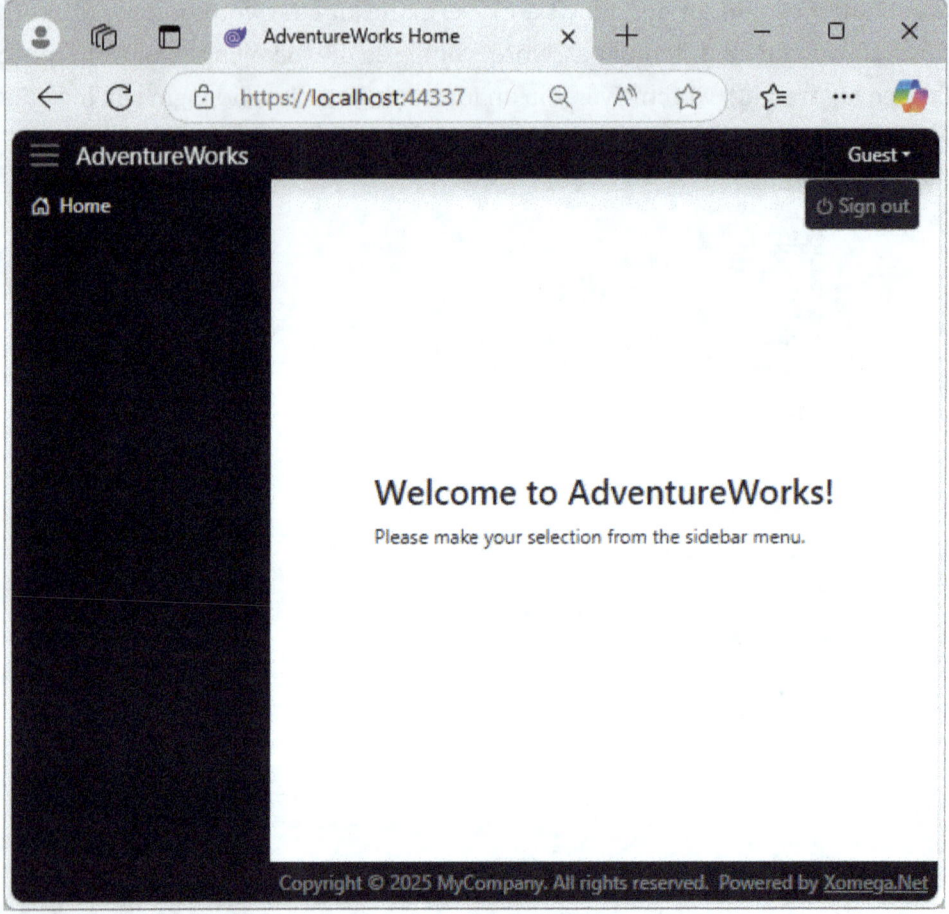

Figure 1-9. *Default home screen after authentication*

Note Take note of the logged-in user's name in the top right corner, as well as a *Sign out* menu, which will log you out and will take you back to the *Login* screen.

Now that we have reviewed the blank initial Blazor application that we created, let's import our Xomega model from a sample database, so that we can build it out further.

CHAPTER 1 GETTING STARTED WITH XOMEGA

Model Project Structure

Right in the middle of the solution, you will find the `AdventureWorks.Model` project that contains a set of application model files and their configurations, as well as generators for generating code and other artifacts based on the Entity, Service, and Domain models defined in the model project. Figure 1-10 illustrates the structure of a model project.

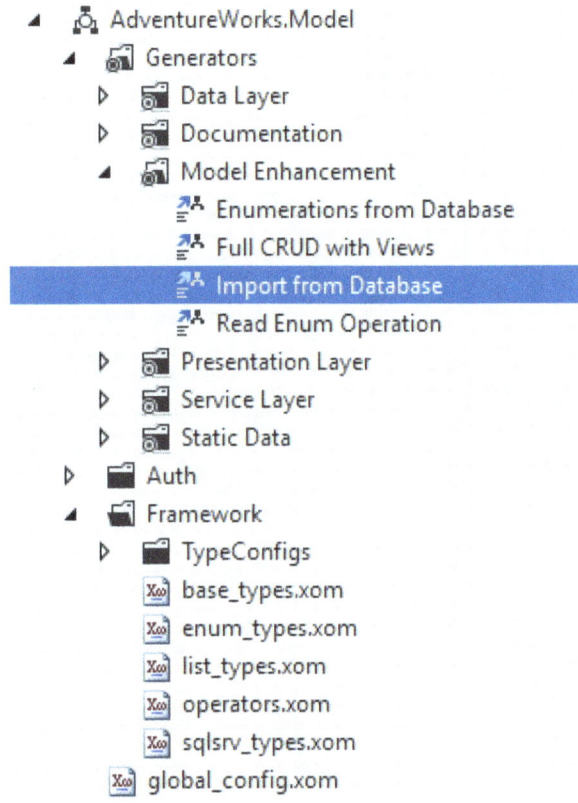

Figure 1-10. Xomega model project structure

Xomega Generators

As you can see from Figure 1-10, all the generators in the model project are nested under the *Generators* node and are further grouped by their functionality in their respective folders, such as the *Model Enhancement* folder shown in the picture, which groups generators that help you to enhance the model itself.

11

CHAPTER 1 GETTING STARTED WITH XOMEGA

To configure generator parameters, you can right-click on the generator node and select *Properties* from the context menu (or hit F4), which will open the generator properties dialog, as shown in Figure 1-11.

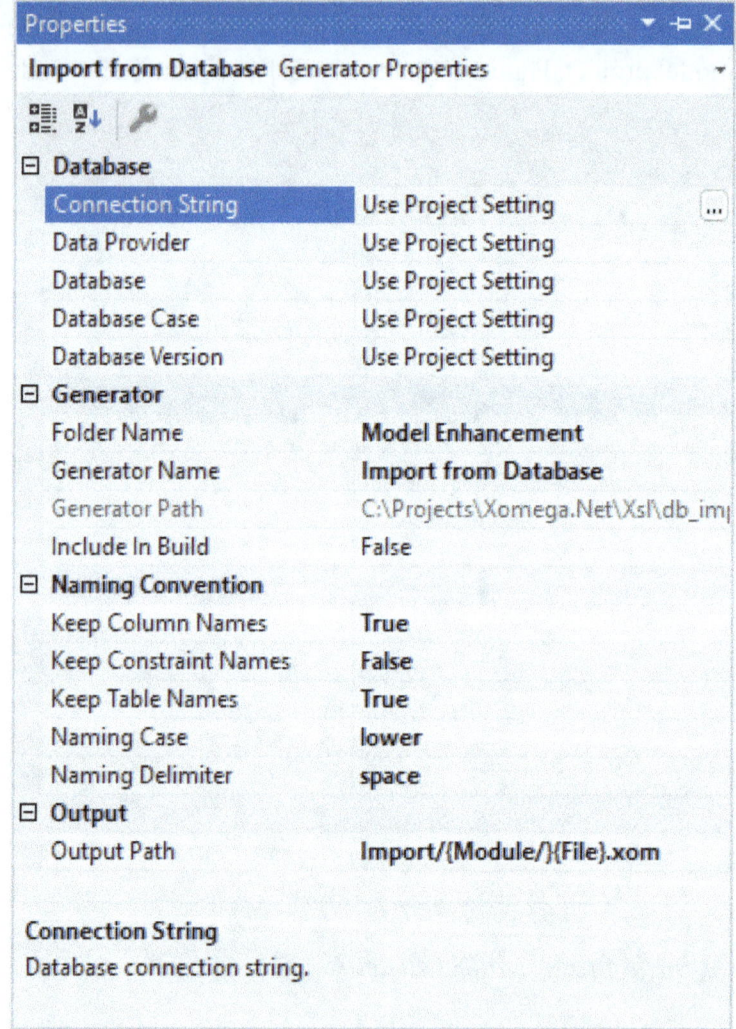

Figure 1-11. *Xomega generator configuration*

Note To rename the generator or to change its folder in the project, you can update the *Generator Name* or the *Folder Name* properties, respectively.

The properties are grouped into categories and show a detailed description at the bottom when you select the property. The property description may include possible values, format, or the meaning of any placeholders used in the value.

Output Path Property

For example, the *Output Path* property of the *Import from Database* generator shown in Figure 1-11 specifies that the generated model files will be saved in the *Import* folder and then grouped into folders by their module and individual objects, as indicated by the {Module} and {File} placeholders.

You can configure the output path for your own needs and group it based on your preferences. If you remove the {File} placeholder, then all the output will be placed in one file per module. If you also remove the {Module} placeholder, then everything will be output into a single file. This will reduce the number of files generated but will make them larger and possibly harder to read and navigate.

Include In Build Property

You can run any generator by right-clicking on it and selecting *Generate* from the context menu. However, each generator also has an *Include In Build* property that you can set to True or False. If you right-click on the Model project and select *Build*, *Rebuild* or *Clean* from the context menu, then only the generators with the *Include In Build* property set to True will be executed.

This allows you to control which generators are run automatically when you build the project and which ones you want to run manually. For example, you want to run the *Import from Database* generator only when you need to import the model from the database, and not every time you build the project.

Import Model from Database

Now that you are familiar with Xomega generators, let's import our model from the AdventureWorks sample database. For that, we first need to configure the connection parameters for that database by clicking on the *Connection String* property of the *Import from Database* generator.

This will open the *Connection Properties* dialog, where you can specify the connection parameters, as shown in Figure 1-12.

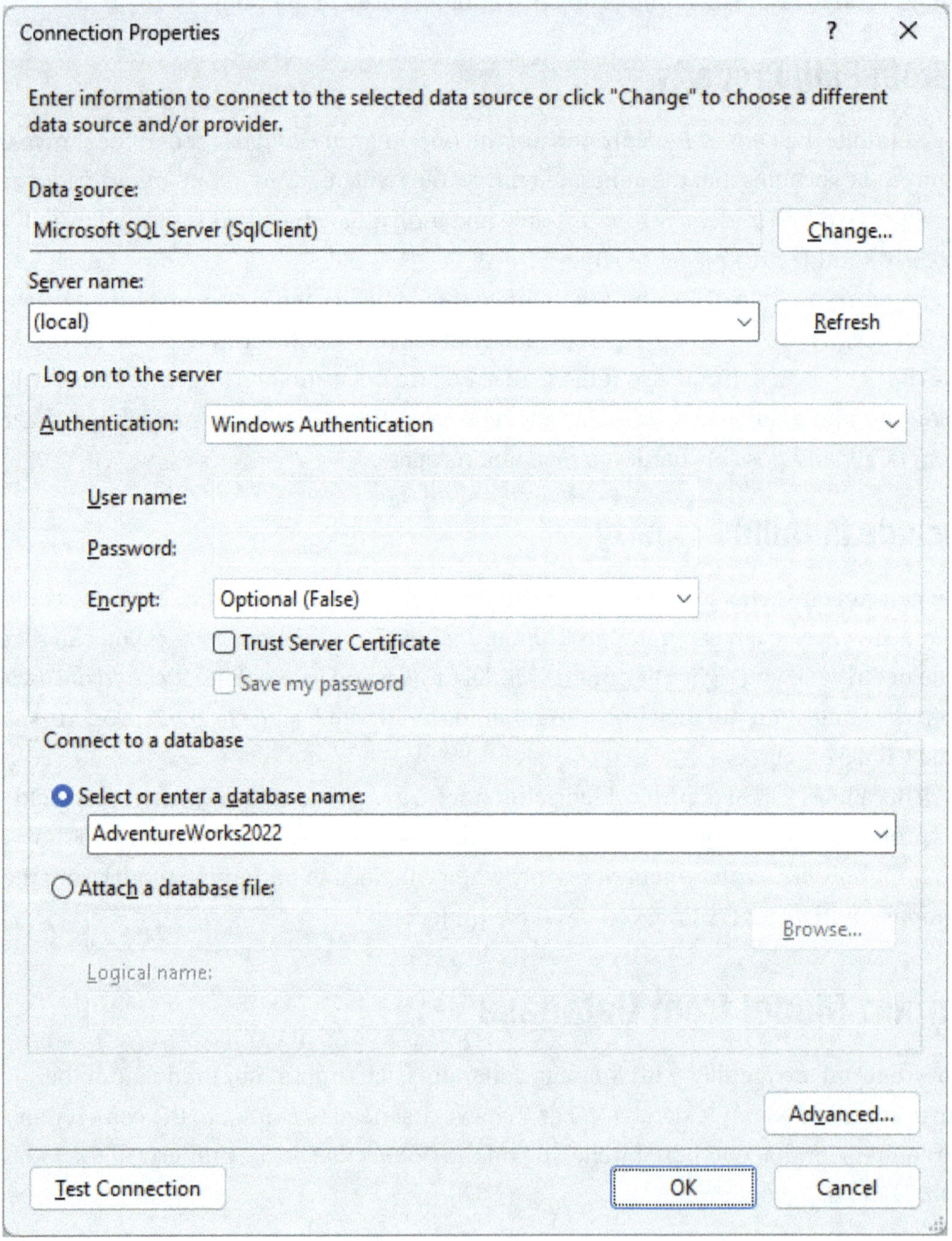

Figure 1-12. Import from Database connection properties

CHAPTER 1　GETTING STARTED WITH XOMEGA

Once you click OK, you'll be prompted on whether you want to save this configuration as the default for the Model project rather than specific to this generator. If you choose to save it as the default, then other generators that require a database connection will be able to use the same connection properties.

Application Model Files

After you configure the connection properties, let's run the *Import from Database* generator by right-clicking on it and selecting *Generate* from the context menu. This will generate the model files based on the database schema and place them in the specified output folder, as illustrated in Figure 1-13.

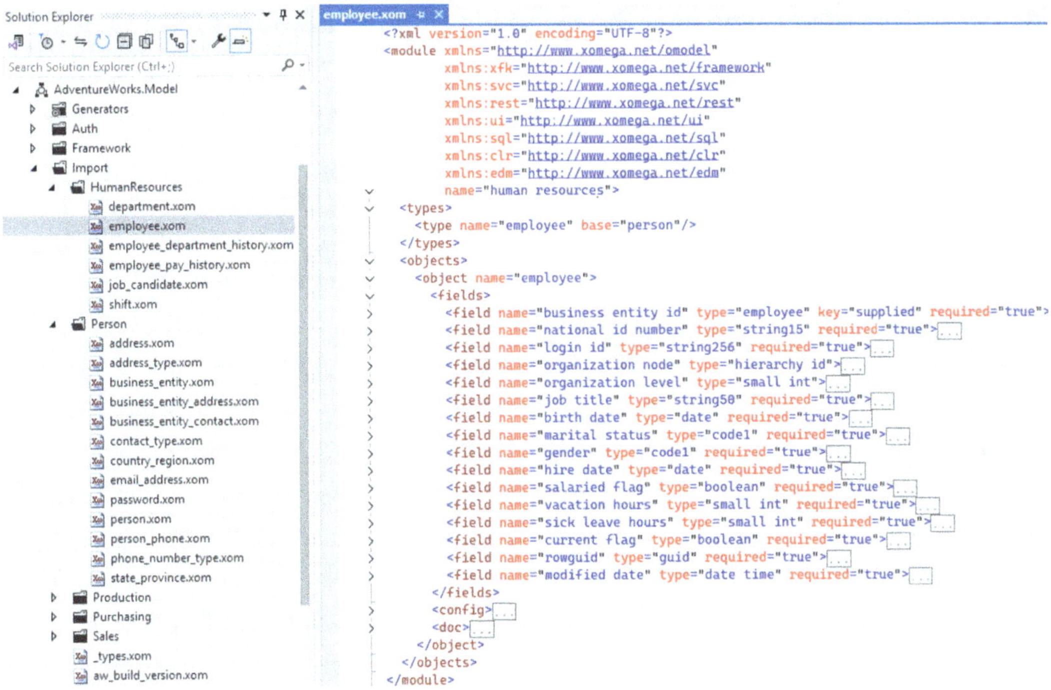

Figure 1-13. Model files and their structure

Notice that the import process defined a domain object for each database table and used its database schema as the module for that object. Following the structure of the *Output Path* property, it placed each such object in a separate file under the module folder, which in turn are placed under the top-level *Import* folder.

15

To better understand the structure of the Xomega model, keep on reading the next section, where I provide an overview of the model's structure and elements.

Xomega Model Overview

Xomega model allows you to model your domain entities, services, and the presentation layer, from which you can generate code and other artifacts for all layers of your application.

In this section, you will learn the basic concepts of the Xomega model, as well as the meaning and the purpose of the most important model elements. This section is packed with good info, which will help you better understand subsequent sections. However, don't worry if you don't fully get all the concepts right away, as you will have many chances to see them in action throughout this book.

General Model Structure

Xomega model uses an easy to read and navigate XML format for describing different types of the model elements. The structure of the Xomega models is defined by extensible XSD schemas, which govern what elements and attributes are allowed in the model within each element, what order these elements go in, the types of allowed values, as well as specific enumerations for attributes that allow values only from a strict list.

The core model is defined in the `http://www.xomega.net/omodel` namespace, which covers the general structure of the model, and includes basic domain and service model elements. This is usually the default namespace that is used without a prefix in the model.

In addition to the core model elements, Xomega allows layer-specific or custom extensions that are defined in separate namespaces and would require their own prefix. Those are also defined by separate XSD schemas.

Modules

To help you better organize your model, Xomega uses a top-level module element in each file for all model elements except for the global configurations. Each module can have a name attribute, signifying the name of the module. If the name attribute is missing, the elements will be in the "default" module.

> **Note** Xomega modules are **not hierarchical**, and you cannot nest them within each other. They also **don't serve as namespaces**, so any names you use for model elements must be globally unique. All modules do is provide a simple way for grouping related model elements.

Modules can be used to output generated artifacts under separate folders for each module, which helps you better manage the generated code. In certain cases, modules can also be adapted to represent **microservices** so that the generated artifacts for each module would go into their own individual microservice.

Listing 1-1 shows the structure of the module element with descriptions of each child element. While any of the child elements can be omitted there, when present, they should follow the specified order.

Listing 1-1. Structure of the module element

```xml
<module xmlns="http://www.xomega.net/omodel"
        xmlns:xfk="http://www.xomega.net/framework"
        xmlns:ui="http://www.xomega.net/ui"
        name="my module">
  <doc>[...] <!-- allows you to provide some documentation for the
              module. -->
  <types>[...] <!-- definitions of logical types -->
  <fieldsets>[...] <!-- definitions of reusable field-sets -->
  <enums>[...] <!-- static data enumerations -->
  <structs>[...] <!-- definitions of reusable structures for service
                  operations -->
  <objects>[...] <!-- definitions of domain objects and their
                  operations -->
  <xfk:data-objects>[...] <!-- Xomega Framework data objects used as view
                          models -->
  <ui:views>[...] <!--definitions of UI views in the model-->
</module>
```

Element Documentation

Most model elements have an associated child element doc to allow you to maintain good documentation for any such element right in the model.

You can provide a short description for the element under the nested summary tag and have more detailed documentation in plain text in the remainder of the doc element, as shown in Listing 1-2.

Listing 1-2. doc elements in the model

```
<enum name="operators">
  <properties>
    <property name="multival" default="0">
      <doc>
        <summary>1 if the additional property can be multi-valued, 0
        otherwise.</summary>
        The name should be in synch with the constant AttributeMultival
        defined in the OperatorProperty class.
      </doc>
    </property>
  </properties>
  ...
</enum>
```

Note This is like the documentation that you provide on regular C# elements.

These descriptions can be displayed in the model editors as tooltips on the corresponding references or when selecting them via IntelliSense drop-down lists or in the *Symbol Browser* view, which can help you better understand your model as you browse or edit it.

They are also output as C# documentation on the generated classes, which would help you when using those generated classes in your custom code or when debugging the generated code.

Finally, you can also generate technical design docs from the model that will use the documentation you provided. This will allow you to communicate the model design with other developers or stakeholders and make sure such documentation is always up to date.

Element Configuration

All essential elements in the Xomega model have a dedicated child node `config`, where you can specify additional specific configurations from a custom namespace, which can be used by different generators.

For example, a logical type `money` may have an additional custom configuration with a mapping to the corresponding SQL type, the Xomega Framework property, and a UI display configuration, as shown in Listing 1-3.

Listing 1-3. config elements for logical types

```xml
<type name="money" base="decimal">
  <config>
    <sql:type name="money" db="sqlsrv"/>
    <xfk:property class="MoneyProperty"
                  namespace="Xomega.Framework.Properties"
                  tsModule="xomega"/>
    <ui:display-config typical-length="12"/>
  </config>
  <usage generic="true"/>
</type>
```

Similarly, an `address` object may be mapped to a specific database table using a `sql:table` configuration, as shown in Listing 1-4.

Listing 1-4. config elements for objects

```xml
<object name="address">
  <fields>[...]
  <config>
    <sql:table name="Person.Address"/>
  </config>
</object>
```

> **Note** The `config` nodes also serve as extension points where you can supply your own configuration for your custom generators.

Global Configuration

The Xomega model also allows a single top-level `config` node, where you can specify a global model configuration that is not tied to any element. By default, it is defined in the `global_config.xom` file and allows various configurations for individual extensions in their respective namespaces.

The global model configuration is used to provide a configuration that needs to be shared between multiple generators, as well as a complex configuration that cannot be easily specified by a generator property.

Logical Types

Logical types are defined under the `types` element of the `module` and constitute one of the core elements of the Xomega modeling, allowing you to freely model your application on the logical level without being restricted by any physical types of any specific technology or platform. This, in turn, helps you make your application consistent across all layers and, therefore, easy to learn and maintain.

The logical types do eventually map to specific physical types in various layers to allow Xomega to generate an actual application for you, but you should always try to define your logical types on a conceptual level for your domain model rather than just mirroring a set of physical types from one platform or another.

For example, you may have a logical type `user` that represents a user of your application and is mapped to a physical type that is used to store the user ID, such as `integer`. If, later, you decide to switch the physical type for the user ID to a `string`, then it will be an easy change, as opposed to refactoring it across all layers of your entire application.

Separately, you can also define two logical subtypes `internal user` and `external user` that would map to the same physical type and may even provide no additional configuration initially. Now, whenever you need to define a field that stores a user ID, such as `create_user`, you can decide whether to set its type to the `internal user`, `external user`, or just a generic `user` type based on your specific domain.

Even though either choice will result in the same application being generated, this information will be captured in your Xomega model on the logical level, and you will always be able to easily modify it later to add certain validations, specify special formatting rules, or restrict a list of allowed values in the UI, as needed.

Type Configuration

Logical type definitions for string-based types may include a `size` attribute, which would be used as a maximum length for the corresponding database columns, or also for validation on the service or client side, or for restricting user input on the UI.

Any additional configuration of the logical type's definition comes from the nested `config` element, which may contain various technology, platform, or layer-specific configurations defined in other namespaces, as shown earlier in Listing 1-3.

These configurations include mapping the logical type to a physical database type, EDM type, or a C# type, specifying the Xomega Framework property or UI controls to use for displaying and editing fields of this type in various UI frameworks, as well as any other additional configurations.

Note Logical types allow you to maintain **consistency within your application** both horizontally, where different fields of the same type will have the same lengths, physical types, and edit controls, as well as vertically, where you ensure that physical types, validations, and UI controls for the same field are consistent across different layers.

Type Inheritance

Similar to class inheritance in C#, you can specify a `base` type for any logical type in the base attribute, and your type will inherit all configurations from the base type or any of its own base types. You can override any of the base type's configurations in your type in addition to adding new configurations.

For example, in Listing 1-5 the `employee` type is a subtype of `person`, which eventually has the `integer` as the root base type.

Listing 1-5. A chain of type inheritance

```xml
<types>
  <type name="integer">
    <config>
      <sql:type name="int" db="sqlsrv"/>
      <clr:type name="int" valuetype="true"/>
      <xfk:property class="IntegerProperty"
                    namespace="Xomega.Framework.Properties"
                    tsModule="xomega"/>
      <ui:display-config typical-length="6"/>
    </config>
  </type>
  <type name="integer key" base="integer">
    <config>
      <xfk:property class="IntegerKeyProperty"
                    namespace="Xomega.Framework.Properties"/>
    </config>
  </type>
  <type name="business entity" base="integer key"/>
  <type name="person" base="business entity"/>
  <type name="employee" base="person"/>
</types>
```

So the employee type will inherit all configurations from the integer type except for the xfk:property, which it will inherit from the integer key since it's overridden there.

Caution You cannot inherit a type from multiple base types that are not part of the same hierarchy. If you need to combine configurations from multiple types, you may need to set one of them as the base type and just add the missing configurations from the other base type to your own type.

Enumeration Types

If the values of your logical type should be restricted to a certain enumeration, or if you want to configure a list of possible values when selecting the value, then you can associate that logical type with a static or dynamic enumeration that is also defined in the model, as described below.

Static Enumerations

If you have a static enumeration defined in your model, then you can associate a logical type with that enumeration using a nested enum element, where you set the ref attribute to the enumeration name, as shown in Listing 1-6.

Listing 1-6. Associating a logical type with a static enumeration

```
<module xmlns="http://www.xomega.net/omodel" name="framework">
  <types>
    <type name="operator" base="enumeration">
      <enum ref="operators"/>
    </type>
  </types>
  <enums>
    <enum name="operators">[...]
  </enums>
</module>
```

> **Tip** You want to use this configuration when the values for your logical type come from a static list, which does not change from one release of your app to another and, therefore, can be specified in your static data model.

Dynamic Enumerations

If the possible values for the type are not static but are sourced from a service operation that is configured with xfk:enum-cache element, then you can also associate such a dynamic enumeration with your logical type, much the same way you do it with static enumerations.

CHAPTER 1　GETTING STARTED WITH XOMEGA

You just need to use the dynamic enumeration's name from the enum-name attribute of the xfk:enum-cache element when you set the enum's ref attribute on your type.

In the example shown in Listing 1-7, the dynamic enumeration product is sourced by the read enum operation of the product object and is associated with the type product.

Listing 1-7. Associating a logical type with a dynamic enumeration

```xml
<types>
  <type name="product" base="integer enumeration">
    <enum ref="product"/>
  </type>
</types>
<objects>
  <object name="product">
    <fields>[...]
    <operations>
      <operation name="read enum">
        <output list="true">
          <param name="product id"/>
          <param name="name"/>
          <param name="is active" type="boolean" required="true"/>
          <param name="list price"/>
        </output>
        <config>
          <xfk:enum-cache enum-name="product"
                          id-param="product id"
                          desc-param="name"
                          is-active-param="is active"/>
        </config>
      </operation>
    </operations>
  </object>
</objects>
```

Domain Model

Xomega allows you to model your business domain following Domain Driven Design principles. The main elements of an Xomega domain model are domain objects with their fields, which map to Entity Framework entities with their properties and to database tables with their columns.

It also includes reusable fieldsets that you can define only in the Xomega model to help you create a domain model, but they don't have a direct representation in any generated code.

Fields and Fieldsets

Fieldsets are named groups of fields that you can define in the Xomega model under the `fieldsets` element nested within the `module` element, which you can then reference in the definitions of your domain objects. This allows you to easily add certain facets to your domain objects in an aspect-oriented way that would be consistent across your domain.

For example, if all or most of your domain objects must have a set of standard audit fields, such as the user who created or modified it, as well as the creation and last modification time stamps, then you can just define such a fieldset in your model, as shown in Listing 1-8.

Listing 1-8. Defining a fieldset for audit fields

```xml
<module>
  <fieldsets>
    <fieldset name="audit fields">
      <field name="create date" type="date time" required="true"/>
      <field name="create user" type="user" required="true"/>
      <field name="modified date" type="date time" required="true"/>
      <field name="modified user" type="user" required="true"/>
    </fieldset>
  </fieldsets>
</module>
```

When you add this fieldset to individual objects, they will automatically have those audit fields. If later you will need to include any additional fields to the audit, e.g., the ID of a program or application that created or updated the object, then you'll be able to add them to that fieldset, and they will be automatically included in your domain objects.

Another common usage for fieldsets is to allow defining composite object keys, as you will see later.

Domain Objects

You can define domain objects in the Xomega model with an `object` element either under the `objects` node of the top-level `module` element or within the `subobjects` element of its parent aggregate object. The object's `name` should be unique either globally or within its parent object.

Listing 1-9 shows the object's possible elements in the order they must be listed, when present, provided that you cannot have more than one element of each kind.

Listing 1-9. Structure of the object element

```xml
<module xmlns="http://www.xomega.net/omodel"
        name="my module">
  <objects>
    <object name="my object">
      <fields>[...] <!-- fields and fieldsets of the object-->
      <operations>[...] <!-- operations supported by the object -->
      <config>[...] <!-- additional object configuration -->
      <doc>[...] <!-- object documentation -->
      <subobjects>[...] <!-- subobjects of an aggregate object -->
    </object>
  </objects>
</module>
```

A domain object is defined by its `fields` element, which should contain a list of fields or fieldsets that make up the object, as illustrated in Listing 1-10.

Listing 1-10. Defining fields for a domain object

```xml
<object name="sales order">
  <fields>
    <field name="sales order id" type="sales order" key="serial"
    required="true"/>
```

```
    <field name="order date" type="date time" required="true"/>
    <field name="customer id" type="customer" required="true"/>
    <fieldset ref="audit fields"/>
  </fields>
</object>
```

Simple Primary Key

As illustrated in Listing 1-10, for domain objects with a simple primary key, the key field should be marked with a key attribute, which can be set to one of the following values:

- `serial` - The key is auto-generated by the system, usually by incrementing the values.

- `supplied` - The key is manually supplied by the user when creating new objects.

- `reference` - The key is just a reference to another object's primary key.

Xomega model requires you to use a **dedicated logical type** for your key fields. More specifically, it validates that the logical type of a `serial` or `supplied` key field cannot be used on more than one object, which allows Xomega to uniquely identify the object by just the logical type of its key.

This, in turn, allows you to easily establish an **implicit relationship** with your domain object from any other object by simply using the key's logical type, or its subtype, on any field of the other object. If that field also needs to be a key field of the other object, then you would set the `key="reference"` attribute on it.

Note You cannot have more than one field marked with a key attribute. If your object has multiple keys, then read the following section on composite primary keys.

Composite Primary Key

For domain objects with a composite primary key that consists of more than one field, you must define a **dedicated fieldset** with those fields and add it to the object with a key attribute set to one of the following values:

- `supplied` - The key is supplied by the user when creating new objects.
- `reference` - The key is a reference to another object's composite primary key.

In Listing 1-11, we define a fieldset `email address`, which we then use as a key on the `email address` object.

Listing 1-11. Defining a composite primary key

```xml
<module xmlns="http://www.xomega.net/omodel"
        name="person">
  <fieldsets>
    <fieldset name="email address">
      <field name="business entity id" type="person"
             required="true"/>
      <field name="email address id" type="integer"
             required="true"/>
    </fieldset>
  </fieldsets>
  <objects>
    <object name="email address">
      <fields>
        <fieldset ref="email address" key="supplied"
                  required="true"/>
        <field name="email address" type="email"/>
        <field name="rowguid" type="guid" required="true"/>
        <field name="modified date" type="date time"
               required="true"/>
      </fields>
    </object>
  </objects>
</module>
```

CHAPTER 1 GETTING STARTED WITH XOMEGA

Just like with the simple primary keys, Xomega requires that any `supplied` key fieldset is only used on one object, which allows Xomega to uniquely identify that object by that fieldset alone. So, to add a reference to your object from any other object, you just need to add its key fieldset to the other object's fields, and this will establish an implicit relationship between them.

Tip A lot of domain objects with composite keys typically represent subobjects of another aggregate object in your domain model. If you define such objects as **subobjects** in the Xomega model, then they'll automatically include the parent's object key, which could minimize the need to use composite keys in your domain objects.

Associations Between Objects

Xomega domain model is structured in such a way that you don't need to explicitly specify associations between domain objects. Any associations are automatically inferred from the logical types or fieldsets that you use on your domain objects. Yet, you do have the ability to configure the details of the corresponding database foreign keys.

Simple Associations

As we discussed above, the logical type on a simple key field of a domain object cannot be used on a key field of any other domain object, which allows Xomega to uniquely identify an object by just the logical type and establish an implicit association to it from another object whenever you use that type, or its subtype, on one of its fields.

Listing 1-12 illustrates how the key field `customer id` of the `customer` object uses a dedicated type, also named `customer`, while the `customer id` field of the `sales order` object below it also uses this type, thereby referencing the `customer` object.

Listing 1-12. Defining a simple association

```
<types>
  <type name="sales order" base="integer key"/>
  <type name="customer" base="integer key"/>
</types>
```

29

```xml
<objects>
  <object name="customer">
    <fields>
      <field name="customer id" type="customer"
             key="serial" required="true"/>
      <field name="account number" type="char string10"
             required="true"/>
    </fields>
  </object>
  <object name="sales order">
    <fields>
      <field name="sales order id" type="sales order"
             key="serial" required="true"/>
      <field name="order date" type="date time"
             required="true"/>
      <field name="customer id" type="customer"
             required="true"/>
    </fields>
  </object>
</objects>
```

Note If you define a subtype of the `customer` type, e.g., `internal customer`, and use that subtype on the `customer id` field, then Xomega will still define an association to the `customer` object unless, of course, that subtype is also used on a key field of another object.

Complex Associations

Like simple associations, Xomega automatically establishes an implicit association to a domain object with a complex key whenever you use its key fieldset in another domain object. This is possible because fieldsets that are used as keys on one object cannot be used as a key on another object, as we discussed above.

CHAPTER 1 GETTING STARTED WITH XOMEGA

Listing 1-13 shows how the `special offer product` object has a composite key implemented by the corresponding fieldset with the same name, and the `detail` subobject of the `sales order` object uses that fieldset, thereby referencing the `special offer product` object.

Listing 1-13. Defining a complex association

```
<fieldsets>
  <fieldset name="special offer product">
    <field name="special offer id" type="special offer"
           required="true"/>
    <field name="product id" type="product" required="true"/>
  </fieldset>
</fieldsets>
<objects>
  <object name="special offer product">
    <fields>
      <fieldset ref="special offer product"
                key="supplied" required="true"/>
    </fields>
  </object>
  <object name="sales order">
    <fields>[...]
    <subobjects>
      <object name="detail">
        <fields>
          <field name="sales order detail id"
                 type="sales order detail"
                 key="serial" required="true"/>
          <field name="order qty" type="small int"
                 required="true">
          <fieldset ref="special offer product"/>
        </fields>
      </object>
    </subobjects>
  </object>
</objects>
```

31

Subtype Associations

If a simple primary key of your domain object has an association with another object, then it's modeled in Xomega by using a subtype of the referenced object's key type as the key type of your object.

To illustrate this concept, let's consider that you have three domain objects: `business entity`, `person`, and `employee`, where each type of domain object defines a subset of the previous type of object, i.e., `employee` objects are a subset of `person` objects.

What you need to do is to define a logical type for each type of domain object and inherit them from each other, as shown in Listing 1-14.

Listing 1-14. Hierarchy of key types

```xml
<types>
  <type name="business entity" base="integer key"/>
  <type name="person" base="business entity"/>
  <type name="employee" base="person"/>
</types>
```

Now, when you use these types on the key fields of the corresponding domain objects, as illustrated in Listing 1-15, you will establish implicit associations to the base type's object, i.e., the `employee` object will have a reference to the `person` object from its key, which will, in turn, have a reference to the `business entity` object from its key.

Listing 1-15. Objects with subtype associations

```xml
<object name="business entity">
  <fields>
    <field name="business entity id" type="business entity"
        key="serial" required="true"/>
    ...
  </fields>
</object>
<object name="person">
  <fields>
    <field name="business entity id" type="person"
        key="supplied" required="true"/>
    ...
```

```
    </fields>
  </object>
  <object name="employee">
    <fields>
      <field name="business entity id" type="employee"
             key="supplied" required="true"/>
      ...
    </fields>
  </object>
```

Subobjects and Aggregates

Following the best practices of Domain Driven Design (DDD), Xomega allows you to define some domain objects as subobjects of the parent aggregate object. The top-level object is called an *aggregate root* in DDD.

Subobjects are defined under the `subobjects` element of its parent object and have the same structure as any other objects, including being able to have their own subobjects. Subobjects do have the following differences from aggregate roots:

- The subobject name must be unique only within its parent object, but its full unique name starts with the full name of its parent.

- The subobject's primary key automatically includes the primary key of its parent.

- The subobject has an implicit association with its parent object.

In Listing 1-16, the `sales order` object has a list of `line item` subobjects, which in turn includes a list of options for each line item defined by its subobject `option`.

Listing 1-16. Defining subobjects

```
<object name="sales order">
  <fields>
    <field name="sales order id" type="sales order"
           key="serial" required="true"/>
    <field name="customer id" type="customer" required="true"/>
  </fields>
```

```xml
<subobjects>
  <object name="line item">
    <fields>
      <field name="product id" type="product"
             key="reference" required="true"/>
      <field name="quantity" type="integer"
             required="true"/>
      <field name="line total" type="money"
             required="true"/>
    </fields>
    <subobjects>
      <object name="option">
        <fields>
          <field name="option code" type="product option"
                 key="supplied" required="true"/>
        </fields>
      </object>
    </subobjects>
  </object>
</subobjects>
</object>
```

The presence of the key field(s) in subobjects indicates that the aggregate object can have a list of such subobjects, and Xomega will automatically define a one-to-many association between the parent object and the subobject.

If the subobject has no key fields, then it will be considered to allow no more than one such subobject, and the primary key of the subobject will be the same as the parent object's key. In other words, the subobject will have an optional one-to-one association with its parent object.

Service Model

Xomega service model consists of **service operations** defined for your domain objects, as well as various **service structures** that are used in those operations. You can define these structures either inline within the operation or another structure that it's used in, or as an independent, reusable named structure that you can include by reference from multiple places.

CHAPTER 1 ■ GETTING STARTED WITH XOMEGA

Note These structures represent what is known as *data transfer objects* (DTO) or *data contracts* in WCF.

Service Structures

You can define reusable named structures using `struct` elements inside the `structs` child of the `module` element. The `struct` element for the top-level structure must have a globally unique `name` attribute and contain an array of `param` or `struct` elements for its parameters and nested structures, respectively, followed by `config`, *usage*, and doc elements as needed.

Inside the structure, you should use `param` elements for parameters of a primitive type (or a list of primitive types) and `struct` elements for complex structures or a list thereof (e.g., tables). Listing 1-17 demonstrates what a service structure consists of and provides some descriptions of its elements.

Listing 1-17. Anatomy of a struct element

```
<structs>
  <struct name="my structure">
    <!-- an array of param/struct elements with unique names within the
    structure -->
    <param name="scalar value" type="my type"
           required="true"/>
    <param name="scalar array" type="my type" list="true"/>
    <struct name="referenced structure"
            ref="top level structure"/>
    <struct name="referenced table"
            ref="top level structure" list="true"/>
    <struct name="nested structure">[...]
    <struct name="nested table" list="true">[...]

    <config>[...] <!-- extensible additional configuration of the
    structure -->
```

35

```
      <usage>[...] <!-- usage specification on top-level structures only -->
      <doc>[...] <!-- documentation on top-level structures only -->
   </struct>
</structs>
```

The `config` element is available on any level and allows you to supply additional configuration for its parent `struct` element.

If your structure must have an array of scalar values or other structures, you just need to set the `list="true"` attribute on the child `param` or `struct` element, respectively.

Nested Structures

Xomega allows you to define arbitrarily deep and complex nested structures. You have the following two ways to define them, which you can mix and match to best suit your service model design:

- Define **inline structures** nested inside the parent structure.

- Define a **named standalone structure**, and reference it from your structure.

Tip Defining nested inline structures is very convenient when it's very specific to your current structure, and you don't need to reuse it in any other structures.

Inferring Parameter Types

If most of your structure parameters represent fields of some domain object, then you can specify the dot-separated fully qualified name of the object on the structure, e.g., `object="sales order.line item"` for the `line item` subobject of the `sales order` parent object.

In that case, for any parameters that have a field with the same name in the specified object, Xomega will be able to infer the logical type and the required flag from that field, so you won't need to specify them separately on the structure, as shown in Listing 1-18.

Listing 1-18. Inferring parameter types from a reference object

```
<struct name="credit card info" object="credit card">
  <param name="credit card id"/>
  <param name="card number"/>
  <param name="expiration" type="string"/>
</struct>
```

You would still need to specify the logical type on any parameter that doesn't match any of the object's fields or if you want to explicitly override the type or the `required` flag on that parameter.

> **Note** For inline structures nested inside a service operation, by default Xomega will use the fields of the operation's parent object to infer the parameter's types.

Object Operations

Domain services are defined by a set of operations that you can define on any domain object under its `operations` element. The operations can be defined both on aggregate root objects, as well as on subobjects. You can provide additional service configuration under the object's `config` element. Listing 1-19 illustrates the standard CRUD operations for an object.

Listing 1-19. Defining CRUD operations for a domain object

```
<module xmlns="http://www.xomega.net/omodel">
  <objects>
    <object name="sales order">
      <fields>[...]
      <operations>
        <operation name="read" type="read">[...]
        <operation name="create" type="create">[...]
        <operation name="update" type="update">[...]
        <operation name="delete" type="delete">[...]
        <operation name="read list" type="readlist">[...]
```

```
      </operations>
      <config>[...]
    </object>
  </objects>
</module>
```

> **Note** Domain services line up well with the REST standards, where a domain object represents a resource, and the operations correspond to various methods for reading or updating its state.

Operation Input and Output

The `input` and `output` of the operation have the same structure as the regular structures, where you list parameters and nested structures inline. The current object that contains the operation will serve as a reference object for the inline structures, meaning that for any parameter that has an object field with the same name, Xomega can infer its type and required flag, so you don't need to specify them explicitly, unless you want to override them with a different value.

For example, the `update` operation in Listing 1-20 has input parameters and structures listed right under the `input` element, and its `data` parameter has its own parameters and referenced structures.

Listing 1-20. Defining input and output structures for an operation

```
<operation name="update">
  <input>
    <param name="sales order id"/>
    <struct name="data">
      <param name="status"/>
      <param name="account number"/>
      <struct name="customer" ref="customer update"/>
      <struct name="payment" ref="payment update"/>
    </struct>
  </input>
```

```
<output>
  <param name="revision number"/>
  <param name="modified date"/>
</output>
<config>[...] <!-- additional configuration for the operation -->
<doc>[...] <!-- operation documentation -->
</operation>
```

When you specify input parameters, as shown in Listing 1-20, the generated service method will have two separate arguments - `sales order id` and `data`. If, instead, you want Xomega to use a structure with these parameters as a single argument of the service method, then you need to set the name of the argument in the `arg` attribute as shown in Listing 1-21.

Listing 1-21. Defining a single input argument for an operation

```
<input arg="input">[...]
```

> **Tip** Keeping separate input arguments works better for exposing services via REST since you can map some parameters to the URL path or query and designate a single structure argument for the request body.

Instead of defining input and output structures inline, you can also define them as regular structures and then reference them on the `input` or `output` elements of any operation using a struct attribute, as shown in Listing 1-22.

Listing 1-22. Referencing structures for input and output

```
<operation name="read list">
  <input struct="sales order criteria"/>
  <output struct="sales order row" list="true"/>
</operation>
```

Whether you use a referenced or inline structure, if your operation returns or accepts a list of objects, then you need to set the `list="true"` attribute on your `output` or `input` elements, respectively, just like you do on regular structures or parameters, as illustrated in Listing 1-22.

> **Note** The operation output must always be a structure or a list of structures, even if it has a single parameter. You cannot return a scalar value or a list of values from an operation.

Presentation Model

Xomega presentation model describes UI views, their view models, and the underlying presentation data objects that they are composed of. All these presentation model entities have corresponding supporting classes in the Xomega Framework, which powers the application generated from the model.

The unique feature of Xomega modeling is that you build your presentation model on top of the structure of your service model, which not only eliminates the need for you to manually build out the elements of your views and view models, but it also automatically ties your views to the corresponding service operations and therefore allows Xomega to generate a fully functional application with minimal effort.

The views that you define in the presentation model can be used in your application both as individual screens or as building blocks for more complex screens and workflows.

Data Objects

Xomega Framework data objects serve as data models for some parts of your view, such as a panel or a data grid, which get bound to the data object and its properties. This means that any changes in the data properties, including their states, such as visibility or editability, get automatically reflected in the bound UI controls, and any updates that you make in the editable bound controls are automatically applied to the data properties.

Data objects can contain other child objects, which is typically mirrored on the UI, where a panel bound to the parent object contains subpanels or data grids bound to its child objects. This allows you to build out the general structure of your UI view by defining composable parent and child data objects.

You can declare data objects in your model using `xfk:data-object` element under the `xfk:data-objects` node, which should go at the end of the top-level `module` element. You must set the `class` attribute to a unique class for the data object and set the `list="true"` for list objects that represent tabular data and are typically bound to a data grid.

CHAPTER 1 GETTING STARTED WITH XOMEGA

If you want to use a custom subclass of the generated data object, where you can override methods and add functionality, then you can add a `customize="true"` attribute to the data object declaration, and Xomega will create such a custom subclass for you, which will be preserved whenever you regenerate data objects.

Listing 1-23 illustrates declarations of data objects, as well as their possible content elements, which should follow the order they are listed here.

Listing 1-23. Declaring data objects

```
<module xmlns="http://www.xomega.net/omodel"
        xmlns:ui="http://www.xomega.net/ui"
        xmlns:xfk="http://www.xomega.net/framework">
  ...
  <xfk:data-objects>
    <xfk:data-object class="MyList" list="true"/>
    <xfk:data-object class="MyObject" customize="true">
      <xfk:summary>[...] <!-- optional description of the data object -->
      <!-- an array of child data objects, if any -->
      <xfk:add-child name="child" class="ChildObject"/>
      <xfk:add-child name="list" class="ChildList"/>
      <ui:display>[...]  <!-- configuration of the UI display of the
                             object -->
      <!-- an array of object links to other views, if any -->
      <ui:link name="view1" view="SomeView"
               child="true" mode="popup">[...]
      <ui:link name="view2" view="AnotherView"
               child="true" mode="inline">[...]
    </xfk:data-object>
  </xfk:data-objects>
</module>
```

If you declare a new data object, as illustrated in Listing 1-23, the Xomega model will show you a warning that your data object doesn't have any properties. However, you may have noticed that the definition of a data object in the model doesn't really support the ability to list its data properties explicitly. Instead, those are included in the data object implicitly based on your service model, as explained below.

41

CHAPTER 1 GETTING STARTED WITH XOMEGA

Data Object Properties

To add data properties to a data object, you need to pick one or more structures defined in the model and add xfk:add-to-object config element to it, where you set the class attribute to the class of your data object, as shown in Listing 1-24.

Listing 1-24. Adding data properties to a data object

```
<struct name="customer info" object="customer">
  <param name="customer id"/>
  <param name="store id"/>
  <param name="store name" type="string" required="false"/>
  <param name="person id"/>
  <param name="person name" type="string" required="false"/>
  <param name="account number"/>
  <param name="territory id"/>
  <struct name="billing address" ref="address key"/>
  <struct name="shipping address" ref="address key"/>
  <config>
    <xfk:add-to-object class="SalesOrderCustomerObject"/>
  </config>
</struct>
```

This will add all param elements of the structure as data properties of your data object. Any inline struct elements though, such as the billing address and shipping address from the above example, will not be included in the data object.

Note The structure element that you add to your data object can be defined anywhere in the model, including standalone structures, nested inline structures, or input/output structures of your service operations.

The specific class of each data property will be determined by the xfk:property configuration of the parameter's logical type or inherited from its base types, as shown in Listing 1-25.

Listing 1-25. Configuring a property class for a logical type

```
<type name="enumeration" base="selection" size="25">
  <config>
    <sql:type name="nchar" db="sqlsrv"/>
    <clr:type name="string"/>
    <xfk:property class="EnumProperty"
                  namespace="Xomega.Framework.Properties"
                  tsModule="xomega"/>
  </config>
</type>
```

As mentioned before, you can add properties to a data object from multiple various structures that are defined in your service model. Parameters with the same name in different structures would correspond to the same property, which means that they should map to the same property class and must have consistent list attributes that indicate if this is a multi-value property.

Caution You won't get model validation errors if parameters with the same name in different structures are added to the same object but map to different property classes or have inconsistent list attributes. Instead, you will only get the errors when you run the *Xomega Data Objects* generator, which is included in the Model build.

Data Object Operations

In addition to adding properties to the data object, specifying xfk:add-to-object inside inline operation structures or in any structures referenced by the operation structures tells Xomega about the service operations that the data object is involved in so that the generated data objects could include methods that call the corresponding service operations.

When calling the service operation, such a method first populates its input structure with the values of the data object's properties that map to the corresponding input parameters, then calls the service, and finally populates the data properties (or the entire list object) from the output of the service call, if it's mapped to that object.

For example, let's consider a typical update operation for a `sales order` object, where the input parameters consist of the `sales order id`, which will be part of the URI path when called via REST API, and a separate data structure that will be passed in the body of the REST request.

In order to make sure that **all** input parameters are populated with the values of the data object's properties, you need to add the `xfk:add-to-object` config element to **both** the `input` element and the nested `<struct name="data">` element, as shown in Listing 1-26.

Listing 1-26. Adding operation's input parameters to a data object

```
<operation name="update" type="update">
  <input>
    <param name="sales order id"/>
    <struct name="data">
      <param name="status"/>
      <param name="purchase order number"/>
      <param name="comment"/>
      <config>
        <xfk:add-to-object class="SalesOrderObject"/>
      </config>
    </struct>
    <config>
      <xfk:add-to-object class="SalesOrderObject"/>
    </config>
  </input>
  <output>[...]
  <config>
    <rest:method verb="PUT"
                 uri-template="sales-order/{sales order id}"/>
  </config>
</operation>
```

The update method may internally update the sales order's `revision number` and `modified date` and return them as output parameters. To make sure those sales order properties get populated with the new values, you also need to add the `xfk:add-to-object` config to the `output` structure, as shown in Listing 1-27.

Listing 1-27. Adding operation's output parameters to a data object

```xml
<operation name="update" type="update">
  <input>[...]
  <output>
    <param name="revision number"/>
    <param name="modified date"/>
    <config>
      <xfk:add-to-object class="SalesOrderObject"/>
    </config>
  </output>
  <config>[...]
</operation>
```

When you set a proper type attribute on your operations, the generated data object can use it to implement the standard CRUD methods on the base data object, which will, in turn, allow Xomega Framework to take care of the standard supported actions on your views, such as *Search, Save, Delete*, etc.

Also, by adding input and output structures to your data objects, you will ensure that your data object will automatically have all the necessary data properties to supply the input for the operation, store the output of that operation, or both. If you later need to add any input or output parameters to your service operation, then your data object will be automatically adjusted to accommodate those.

Moreover, based on which structures you add to your data object, Xomega can infer how each property should be used. For example, if a data property maps only to output parameters and has no corresponding input parameters, then it will be considered read-only, and Xomega will use a display-only control, such as a data label, to show that property on the view.

UI Field Config

For each data object property, you can configure the options of the corresponding UI field using a ui:field element under the ui:display/ui:fields of your data object, as illustrated in Listing 1-28. Such options include the label for the field, its visibility, editability, and other UI-specific properties.

Listing 1-28. Configuring UI field options for data object properties

```xml
<xfk:data-object class="SalesOrderDetailObject">
  <ui:display>
    <ui:fields field-cols="2">
      <ui:field param="sales order detail id" hidden="true"/>
      <ui:field param="sales order id" hidden="true"/>
      <ui:field param="sales order number" hidden="true"/>
      <ui:field param="subcategory" editable="true"/>
      <ui:field param="product id" label="Product"/>
      <ui:field param="special offer id"
                label="Special Offer"/>
    </ui:fields>
  </ui:display>
</xfk:data-object>
```

Note The `ui:display` element can be also used to control the general layout of the data object's fields and child objects in the bound UI panel.

UI Views

You declare your UI views in the Xomega presentation model using `ui:view` elements under the `ui:views` child at the end of the top-level `module` element. Each view should have a unique name specified in the `name` attribute.

You can also set a custom localizable base title for the view in the `title` attribute. The actual view title may change based on the state of the view. For instance, the title would be "New Sales Order" when creating a new object. For dynamic view titles, you can include some placeholders in the base title, as illustrated by the `SalesOrderDetailView` view in Listing 1-29, but you will need to customize the view model to populate the values.

Listing 1-29. Declaring UI views

```xml
<module xmlns="http://www.xomega.net/omodel"
        xmlns:ui="http://www.xomega.net/ui"
```

```
        name="sales">
  ...
  <ui:views>
    <ui:view name="SalesOrderView" title="Sales Order">[...]
    <ui:view name="SalesOrderListView"
             title="Sales Order List" customize="true">[...]
    <ui:view name="SalesOrderDetailView"
             title="Line Item for Sales Order {0}"
             child="true">[...]
  </ui:views>
</module>
```

If a view should be opened only from another view and not from the top-level navigation menu, then you need to set the `child="true"` attribute. In this case, the view will not be included in the generated navigation menu, which includes only the top-level views that you can open without parameters to start a new workflow.

Note For object details views, the navigation menu will include only the option to create a new object that requires no parameters. The view to open and edit details of an existing object that requires object ID parameters will be invoked as a child view from another view.

The generated view will be for the specific UI framework, such as Blazor, WebForms, or WPF, but they will use common framework-agnostic view models. If you need to apply **UI framework-specific customizations** to a view, then you can add a `customize="true"` attribute to the view, and Xomega will generate a subclass or partial class for the view, where you can add your custom code.

View Model

Inside each view, you need to specify a `ui:view-model` child element, where you must set the main data object for the view in the `data-object` attribute, as shown in Listing 1-30.

Listing 1-30. Configuring the view model for UI views

```
<ui:view name="SalesOrderView" title="Sales Order">
  <ui:view-model data-object="SalesOrderObject"
                 customize="true"/>
</ui:view>
<ui:view name="SalesOrderListView" title="Sales Order List">
  <ui:view-model data-object="SalesOrderList"/>
</ui:view>
```

The generated view models will contain platform-independent logic and actions for the view, as supported by the Xomega Framework. If the main data object for the view has a `list="true"` attribute set, then Xomega will generate a standard *Search View* with an optional criteria panel and a results grid. Otherwise, Xomega will generate a *Details View* for editing object details.

If you need to add or change any behavior for the generated view model, then you can set the `customize="true"` attribute on the `ui:view-model` element, and Xomega will create and use a subclass of the generated view model, where you can add **custom platform-independent code**, or override any of the methods from the generated view model.

Custom View Layout

If you are unable to configure the layout of your data objects or view using the Xomega model to make the generated view look the way you need it to look, you can go ahead and just update the generated markup for the view directly.

However, to preserve your manual markup changes from being erased when the view is regenerated, you will need to set the `custom="true"` attribute on the `ui:layout` element of your view, as shown in Listing 1-31.

Listing 1-31. Marking a view layout as custom

```
<ui:view name="SalesOrderView" title="Sales Order">
  <ui:view-model data-object="SalesOrderObject"/>
  <ui:layout custom="true"/>
</ui:view>
```

When you mark the view layout as custom like that, Xomega will not overwrite your markup or code-behind when generating the views.

CHAPTER 1 GETTING STARTED WITH XOMEGA

Caution Obviously, this also means that your **view will not be automatically updated** if you add new fields or change your model otherwise, so you'll need to update such a view manually.

Tip It's best to **stick to the auto-generated views** as much as possible during the prototyping phase when your model keeps changing and only consider manually customizing the views when the model is stable.

Navigation

Navigation between UI views is modeled in the Xomega presentation model by configuring links to one of the defined views on the appropriate data objects.

Object Links to Views

You can add links to any data object by adding a `ui:link` element, giving it a unique name within the object using the `name` attribute, and specifying the target view in the `view` attribute.

If you want the target view to open as a child of the current view, then you need to set the `child="true"` attribute (see Listing 1-32). Otherwise, the link will open the view in a new workflow and may replace the current view when navigating to the new view. You can also set the `mode` attribute to either `inline` for a master-detail view or a `popup` for opening the view in a popup dialog.

To specify custom localizable text and access key for the link button, you can set the `title` and `access-key` attributes on the nested `ui:display` element as shown in Listing 1-32.

Listing 1-32. Configuring object links to views

```
<xfk:data-object class="SalesOrderList" list="true">
  <ui:display>[...]
  <ui:link name="express" view="SalesOrderView"
          child="true" mode="inline">
    <ui:params>
      <ui:param name="_action" value="create"/>
```

```
    <ui:param name="type" value="EXPRESS"/>
  </ui:params>
  <ui:display title="Add Express Order" access-key="E"/>
  </ui:link>
</xfk:data-object>
```

In order to pass parameters to the target view, you need to add them as `ui:param` elements nested under the link's `ui:params` node, as shown above. For fixed-value parameters, you can set the parameter's name and the fixed value in the corresponding attributes.

Framework parameters, such as `_action`, start with an underscore ("_") and can be selected from a predefined list, along with its possible values.

Caution Xomega does not validate fixed parameter values that you specify. They are just passed to the activation method of the target view, which typically sets them as properties of the underlying data object or criteria object, so the target view may show validation errors for invalid values.

Instead of a fixed value, you can also source the parameter value from one of the properties of the current data object or any of the child or parent objects in its hierarchy. For that, instead of the `value` attribute, you should set the `field` attribute to one of the data object properties and optionally set a `data-object` attribute to the data object's path relative to the current object.

Note Xomega will provide IntelliSense for both the relative paths in the `data-object` attributes and the properties of that object in the `field` attribute. It will also validate those attributes based on the structure of the data objects in the model.

For example, in Listing 1-33, the parameter `type` is sourced from the field `order type` of a sibling data object named `child`, if it exists in the data object hierarchy.

Listing 1-33. Sourcing parameter values from data object properties

```
<ui:params>
  <ui:param name="type" field="order type"
            data-object="../child"/>
</ui:params>
```

Links from a List

When you add a link to a list object and specify any link parameter that uses a list object's property, then the link will be displayed on each row of the bound data grid. Conversely, any links that don't use values from the list object's properties will be displayed as link buttons under the data grid.

You need to specify how to display a link on each row in the ui:display element of the link using one of the following options:

1. Set the on-field attribute to one of the visible properties of the list object. In this case, the link will be displayed as a hyperlink in the corresponding column, using the value of that column as the text.

2. Set the on-selection="true" attribute, which will not display the link but invoke it by default whenever you select a row in the data-bound grid, which is useful for master-details views.

You can also set both attributes, as shown in Listing 1-34, but normally you want to set one or another.

Listing 1-34. Displaying links on each row of a data grid

```
<xfk:data-object class="SalesOrderList" list="true">
  <ui:display>[...]
  <ui:link name="details" view="SalesOrderView"
           child="true" mode="inline">
    <ui:params>
      <ui:param name="sales order id" field="sales order id"/>
    </ui:params>
    <ui:display on-field="sales order number"
                on-selection="true"/>
  </ui:link>
</xfk:data-object>
```

Note If you don't specify any of those `ui:display` attributes, such a link will be displayed on the first visible column of the grid.

Links with Results

In addition to just invoking the target view with parameters, you can also configure a link to handle the results from invoking that view. This is useful when the target view is used for the selection or entering of some data that needs to be returned to the original view.

In this case, you need to add a `ui:result` element to your link, where you map the output parameters of the target view to the fields in the current data object, or any object in its hierarchy, as indicated by the `data-object` attribute relative path. If all fields to be updated are not on the current object, then you can also specify the `data-object` on the entire `ui:result` element.

In Listing 1-35, the `look up` link on the `SalesCustomerLookupObject` invokes a child `CustomerListView` for selecting a single customer and passes its entered values for the store and person name, as well as the default *Contains* (CN) operator. The resulting fields of the selected customer are then copied to the corresponding fields of its parent data object (`data-object=".."`).

Listing 1-35. Configuring links with results

```
<xfk:data-object class="SalesCustomerLookupObject">
  <ui:link name="look up" view="CustomerListView"
           child="true">
    <ui:params>
      <ui:param name="_action" value="select"/>
      <ui:param name="_selection" value="single"/>
      <ui:param name="store name operator" value="CN"/>
      <ui:param name="store name" field="store name"/>
      <ui:param name="person name operator" value="CN"/>
      <ui:param name="person name" field="person name"/>
    </ui:params>
```

```
  <ui:result data-object="..">
    <ui:param name="customer id" field="customer id"/>
    <ui:param name="store id" field="store id"/>
    <ui:param name="store name" field="store name"/>
    <ui:param name="person id" field="person id"/>
    <ui:param name="person name" field="person name"/>
    <ui:param name="account number" field="account number"/>
    <ui:param name="territory id" field="territory id"/>
  </ui:result>
 </ui:link>
</xfk:data-object>
```

Note Xomega will also provide IntelliSense and validation on the result fields based on the structure of the target data object.

Tip Another use case for this could be when you need to select some entity from a list, but it doesn't exist yet. So, the link would open a view for creating a new entity and return the ID and description of the newly created entity back to the original screen.

Summing It Up

In this section, you've learned the most important Xomega model concepts for creating a domain model, a service model and a presentation model for your application. In subsequent chapters, you will see how to use these models to construct and generate a fully functional application.

Note To get additional details on the Xomega model and generators, you can always **refer to the Xomega documentation** (https://xomega.net/docs).

Generate CRUD Views

Now that you have become familiar with the main concepts of the Xomega model, let's enhance the domain model that we have imported from our database and add CRUD operations to one of the objects, as well as the corresponding search and details views for managing these entities.

For our example, we will pick the `employee` object from the human resources module, which will allow the users to search employees, create new employee records, and edit existing employee details.

Adding CRUD Operations

As you may remember, one of the unique concepts of the Xomega model is that the views and view models it defines are based on the underlying service operations and their input and output structures.

Every view that needs to display or update some data requires one or more service operations to get the data or to store it and perform any business logic. In a properly architected application with a separate service layer, you would need to define these operations anyway. So, essentially, Xomega just makes you think about your API first and then helps you generate the UI views based on that API.

The views for editing a certain object require the `create`, `read`, `update`, and `delete` operations, which are collectively known as CRUD operations. The views for searching and listing objects require a `read list` operation.

You can always manually add such operations to your object. However, Xomega makes it easy by providing a flexible *Full CRUD with Views* generator that can add these operations, as well as the corresponding data objects and views, to one or more selected objects.

To add CRUD operations to the `employee` object, let's right-click on the `employee.xom` file in the `AdventureWorks.Model` project and select the *Generate* ➤ *Model Enhancement* ➤ *Full CRUD with Views* option from the context menu, as shown in Figure 1-14.

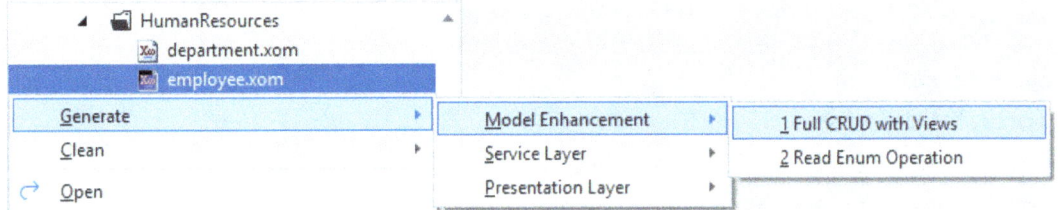

Figure 1-14. Generating CRUD operations and views

Default CRUD Operations

The generator will add standard create, read, update, delete (CRUD) and read list operations to the object, as shown in Listing 1-36.

Listing 1-36. Default CRUD operations

employee.xom
```
<object name="employee">
  <fields>[...]
  <operations>
    <operation name="read" type="read">[...]
    <operation name="create" type="create">[...]
    <operation name="update" type="update">[...]
    <operation name="delete" type="delete">[...]
    <operation name="read list" type="readlist">[...]
  </operations>
</object>
```

Given only the list of object fields as the input, the generated operations will be initially configured to use all those fields in the read and write operations, as well as in the search criteria. You will be able to update them later as needed and regenerate all the artifacts from the updated structure, but the initial CRUD operations can serve as a good point to start with.

Search and Details Views

In addition to the CRUD operations, the generator will define data objects that are based on those operations, as well as search and details views that use these data objects as view models, as shown in Listing 1-37.

CHAPTER 1   GETTING STARTED WITH XOMEGA

Listing 1-37. Search and details views and view models

employee.xom
```
<xfk:data-objects>
  <xfk:data-object class="EmployeeObject">[...]
  <xfk:data-object class="EmployeeCriteria">[...]
  <xfk:data-object class="EmployeeList" list="true">[...]
</xfk:data-objects>
<ui:views>
  <ui:view name="EmployeeView" title="Employee">[...]
  <ui:view name="EmployeeListView" title="Employee List">[...]
</ui:views>
```

The data object `EmployeeObject` will be used as a view model for the details view `EmployeeView`, while the `EmployeeCriteria` and `EmployeeList` data objects will be used as a view model for the search view `EmployeeListView`.

Generating Application Code

Once you have added the CRUD operations and views to the `employee` object, you can build the model project to generate the application code based on the updated model. To do that, right-click on the `AdventureWorks.Model` project in the Solution Explorer, and select the *Build* option from the context menu, as shown in Figure 1-15.

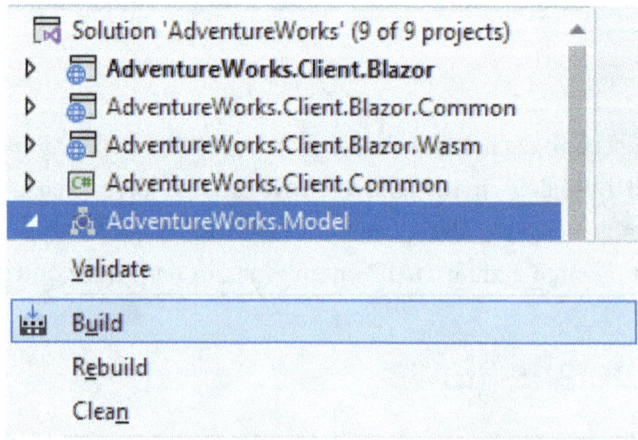

Figure 1-15. *Building the model*

CHAPTER 1   GETTING STARTED WITH XOMEGA

Caution   By default, the Model project is excluded from the solution build configuration. Therefore, you need to build the Model project explicitly to generate the application code, as it won't run automatically if you just build the entire solution.

This will run all the generators in the model that are configured with the *Include In Build* parameter set to True. The output of the model build process will show all the generators that have been run, as illustrated in Listing 1-38.

Listing 1-38. Model build output

Model build output
```
------ Build started: Project: AdventureWorks.Model, Configuration:
       Debug Any CPU ------
         Project Model Schema Validation.
         Project Model Xomega Validation.
         Generating EF Domain Objects.
 warning : Property
Address.SpatialLocation has been skipped,
    since no CLR type is defined for its type "geography"
            ...
         Generating Entity Data Model.
 warning : Property Employee.OrganizationNode has been skipped,
    since no EDM type is defined for its type "hierarchy id"
            ...
         Generating Service Implementations.
         Generating REST Service Clients.
         Generating Service Contracts.
         Generating Web API Controllers.
         Generating Xomega Data Objects.
         Generating View Models.
         Generating Label Resources.
         Generating Blazor Views.
```

```
Generating Lookup Cache Loaders.
Generating Enumeration Data XML.
Generating Enumeration Constants.
========== Build: 1 succeeded or up-to-date, 0 failed, 0 skipped ==========
```

You can also see some warnings produced by each generator, such as the warnings related to the `Employee.OrganizationNode` field. Its database column has a type `hierarchyid`, but the corresponding logical type `hierarchy id` has no EDM type defined for it, so this field cannot be added to the generated entity.

> **Note** If you change the build verbosity to Normal instead of Minimal, you will see more detailed information about each generator and the files it has generated.

Review Search/Details Views

Now that you have built the model project, which generated the code for all application layers from the model, let's build and run our solution to review the screens that we generated.

Sidebar Menu

Let's launch the application by clicking F5; log in using the default credentials on the *Login* screen, and expand the sidebar menu. You will notice that in addition to the *Home* menu, it now contains two new menu options - to create a *New Employee* and to open the *Employee List* screen, as shown in Figure 1-16.

CHAPTER 1 GETTING STARTED WITH XOMEGA

Figure 1-16. *Sidebar menus for new views*

The new menu options are nestled under the *Human Resources* group menu based on the module of those views. The *New Employee* menu will open the Details view for creating a new employee, while the *Employee List* menu will open the search view for searching and listing employees.

Search Results Grid

Let's click on the *Employee List* menu to open the employee search view. The view will display a grid with search results based on the search criteria that you can specify. If you run the search with no criteria, the results grid will show all employees, with a column for every field of the employee object by default, as shown in Figure 1-17.

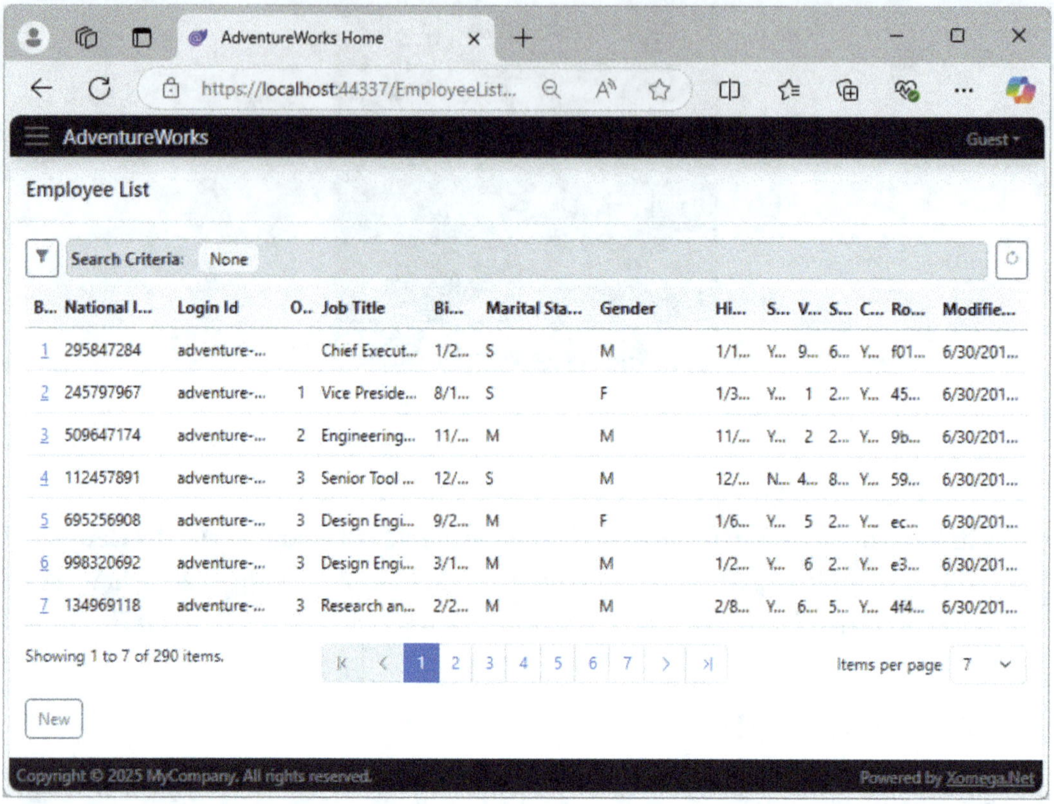

CHAPTER 1   GETTING STARTED WITH XOMEGA

Figure 1-17. Search results grid

Above the grid, you will find a filter button to open the Search Criteria panel, as well as a panel that displays the summary of the currently applied search criteria, and a button to refresh the grid by rerunning the search with the same criteria.

The grid shows paged results with the total number of records in the grid displayed at the bottom of the grid, as well as the ability to navigate between pages and to change the number of rows per page. You can also sort the grid by one or more columns by clicking on the column headers.

You can open the details screen for existing employees by clicking the hyperlink in the first column of the corresponding row in the grid. You can also add a new employer by clicking the *New* button at bottom, which will open a child details view for a new employee object. This would be an alternative to selecting the *New Employee* menu from the sidebar.

CHAPTER 1 GETTING STARTED WITH XOMEGA

Search Criteria

Clicking the button with the filter icon at the top-left corner will open the Search Criteria panel, where you can specify the search criteria to use. To add criteria by a certain field, you will first need to select it from a drop-down list, as shown in Figure 1-18.

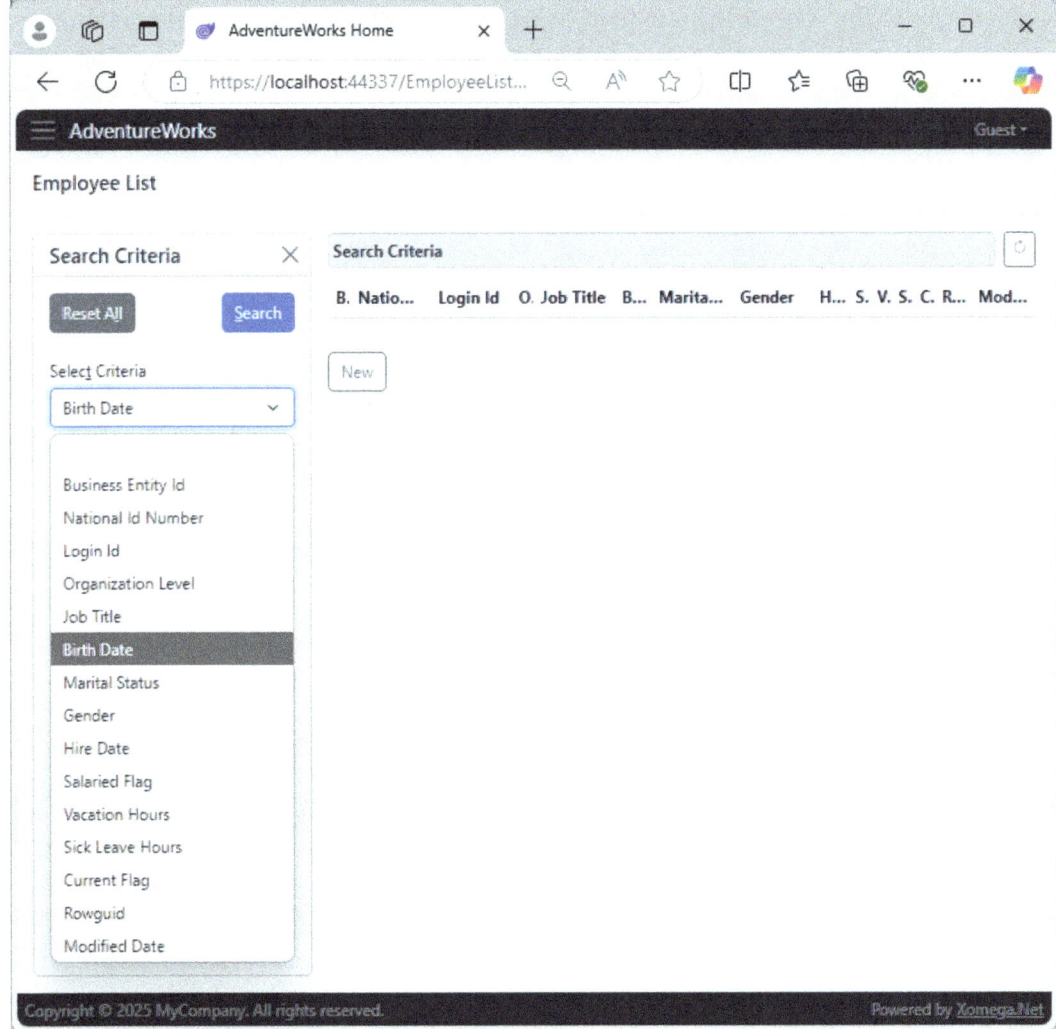

Figure 1-18. *Search criteria selection*

As with the result columns, the search criteria contain all employee object fields by default. Despite a large number of criteria, selecting it from a drop-down list and editing one by one allows the Search Criteria panel to display only the selected criteria, rather than all criteria at once.

61

This design can help make your search screens quite powerful by providing a lot of useful search criteria, while keeping it clean and easy to use, without overwhelming the Search Criteria panel by showing all of them at once.

Search Operators

Once you select the specific criteria field, you can specify the operator to use, as shown in Figure 1-19. The operators available for each field depend on the field's data type and can be configured for each field or for all the fields for maximum flexibility.

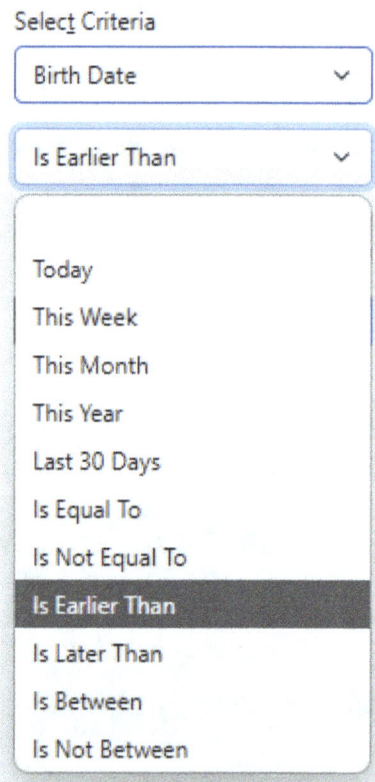

Figure 1-19. Search criteria operators

For example, the operators for date/time fields include the standard comparison operators, such as `Is Later Than` or `Is Between`, as well as some predefined relative date operators such as `Today`, `This Week`, `Last 30 Days`, etc.

CHAPTER 1 GETTING STARTED WITH XOMEGA

Editing Criteria

Some operators such as `Is Null` or `This Month` require no additional input, while others will show an additional control (or a pair of controls for ranges) for you to specify the values to compare against, as illustrated in Figure 1-20.

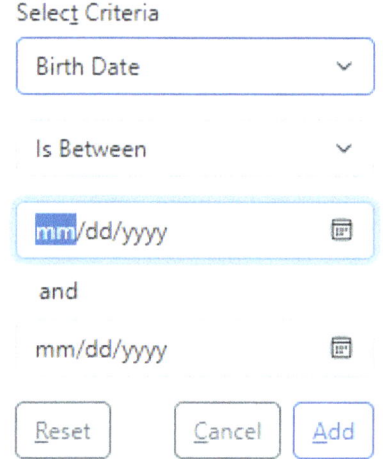

Figure 1-20. *Editing search criteria*

Once you specify the criteria and click *Add*, the criteria will be added to the Search Criteria panel, as shown in Figure 1-21. You can add as many criteria as you need and remove them by clicking the X button next to each criterion.

63

CHAPTER 1   GETTING STARTED WITH XOMEGA

Figure 1-21.   Search criteria display

To edit the values of the selected criteria, you can either select them again in the drop-down list or click on the criteria values in the Search Criteria panel, which will open the same editor that you used to add the criteria.

Applied Criteria

After you hit search, the panel above the grid will display the summary of the applied criteria, as shown in Figure 1-22. This will help the users to always have the context of the data that is displayed in the results grid.

▼	Search Criteria:	Job Title *Contains*	Manager	Birth Date *Is Between*	1/1/1970 and 1/1/1990								⟳
B...	National I...	Login Id	O.. Job Title	Bi...	Marital Sta...	Gender	Hi...	S...	V...	S...	C...	Ro...	Modifie...
3	509647174	adventure-...	2 Engineering...	11/...	M	M	11/...	Y...	2	2...	Y...	9b...	6/30/201...

Figure 1-22.   Summary of applied search criteria

64

CHAPTER 1   GETTING STARTED WITH XOMEGA

Tip   You can also click on any of the values displayed in the Applied Criteria panel to open the Search Criteria panel and edit the criteria.

Details Screen

If you click any of the links in the first column of the Employee List screen, the Employee details view for the selected employee will open as a child pop-up dialog, as shown in Figure 1-23. As usual, the Details view displays all the fields of the employee object by default and provides a *Save* button to save your changes as well as a *Delete* button to delete this object.

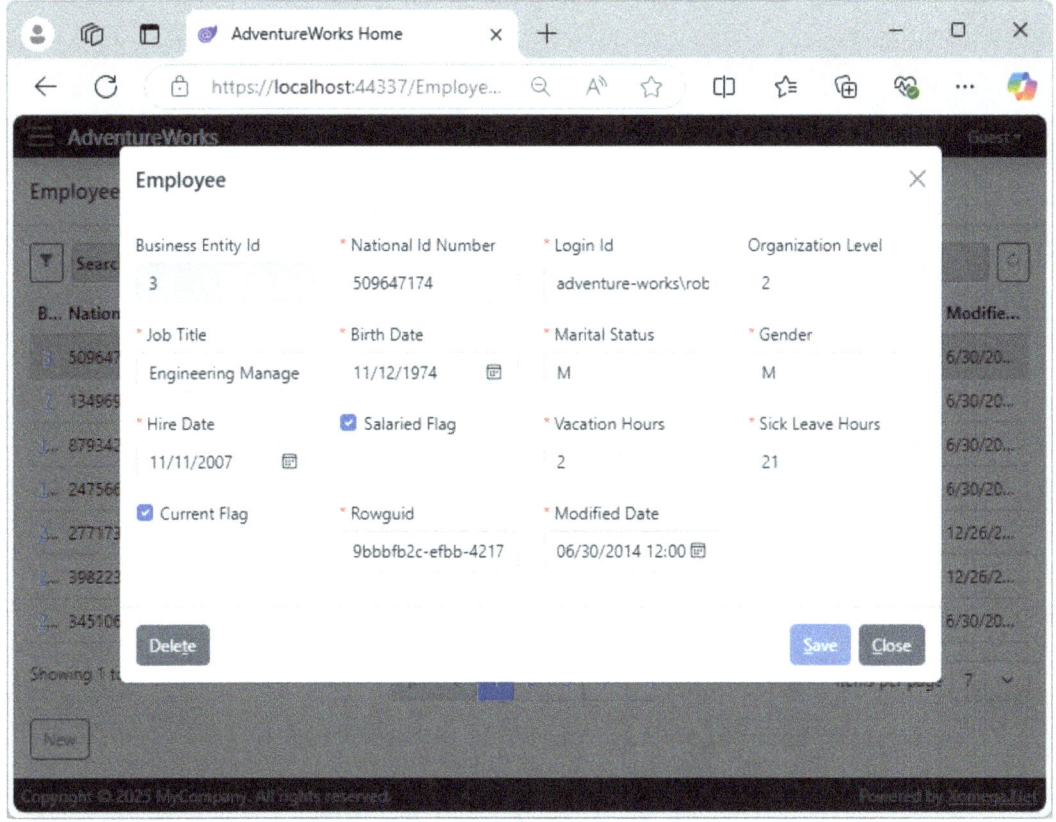

Figure 1-23. *Details view as a child dialog*

65

From Figure 1-23, you can see that the Details view uses appropriate editing controls based on the type of the field, such as a date picker for the Birth Date field. It was even smart enough to make the internal Business Entity Id field read-only, as it's a key field and is not supposed to be edited by the user.

Just like you saw earlier with the Login screen, the labels for required fields on the Employee details screen are automatically marked with a red asterisk. If you leave such a field blank or enter an invalid value, the validation messages will be displayed under that field. Also, any errors during the save operation, including any validation errors, will be displayed at the top of the screen.

By default, the fields of the object are laid out neatly in four columns on the details screen. However, the screen uses a **responsive layout**, which will reduce it to three, two, or even one column as you reduce the width of the screen. This will make sure that the Details view looks good on any device, from a large desktop screen to a small mobile phone screen.

Summary

In this chapter, you have learned how to create a new Xomega Solution using the Xomega Solution wizard and reviewed the structure of the initial application created by the wizard.

Then you learned about the Xomega model project, the generators and model files that it contains, and how to import the initial Xomega model from the AdventureWorks sample database.

You got familiar with the main concepts and elements of the Xomega model, such as logical types, domain objects, service operations, and data objects as view models for the UI views, which will help you to easily follow material in subsequent chapters.

Next, you saw how to quickly generate CRUD operations and views for managing Employee objects in the model and then generate the actual application code and views from the model.

Finally, you have reviewed the functionality of the generated search and details screens for the employee object, which may have helped you appreciate how Xomega allowed you to quickly build a full-featured application with no coding or screen designing so far.

Clearly the default screens that were generated, which just contain all fields of the Employee object, can hardly be used as is, since the functionality they provide can be compared with just a glorified database table editor.

In the next chapter, you will learn how to update the model and provide some minimal coding to make the Employee List view much more useful and tailor it to the specific requirements. Along the way, you will also learn several new concepts and techniques of the Xomega application development process.

CHAPTER 2

Building Out a List View

In the previous chapter, we created a Blazor Xomega Solution and generated a couple of UI views for browsing and editing Employee entities. By default, the generated Employee List view just shows all the properties of the Employee entity, which is not something that would be particularly useful in a real-world application.

In this chapter, we are going to update our model, regenerate the services and the views, and implement any necessary code to make the Employee List display more appropriate and useful results. While at it, you will also learn a few Xomega concepts and development techniques, such as defining static enumerations and subobjects, writing custom code, and extending the generated entities, which we will keep using in subsequent chapters.

Refine Search Result Columns

Since the initially generated Employee List view contains all fields from the employee object, we are going to start by deleting the fields that we don't want to read or display in the result list, such as the internal field `rowguid`, and then rearranging the result columns to be in a desired order. We'll also configure better column labels, where the default ones, which are derived from the field names, are not appropriate.

Update Read List Output

The result columns of the generated Employee List view are driven by the output parameters of the `read list` operation of the `employee` object. Let's delete the parameters that we don't want to return from this operation and therefore display them in the results list of employees, as shown in Listing 2-1.

Listing 2-1. Removing output parameters of a "read list" operation

employee.xom
```
<object name="employee">
  <operation name="read list" type="readlist">
    <input>
      <struct name="criteria">[...]
    </input>
    <output list="true">
      <param name="business entity id"/>
-     <param name="national id number"/>
-     <param name="login id"/>
-     <param name="organization node"/>
      <param name="organization level"/>
      <param name="job title"/>
      <param name="birth date"/>
      <param name="marital status"/>
      <param name="gender"/>
      <param name="hire date"/>
      <param name="salaried flag" type="yesno"
            required="true"/>
-     <param name="vacation hours"/>
-     <param name="sick leave hours"/>
-     <param name="current flag" type="yesno"
            required="true"/>
-     <param name="rowguid"/>
-     <param name="modified date"/>
    </output>
  </operation>
</object>
```

Note Even though we may want to not display the internal `business entity id` field in the `result list`, this is a key field, and we still need to return it from the read list operation to be able to open the corresponding Employee Details view. You will see how to hide it in the UI later in this chapter.

CHAPTER 2 BUILDING OUT A LIST VIEW

To control the order of the columns in the results grid, you can just order the output parameters in the read list operation. Normally, you may want to put more important parameters first and keep related parameters together.

For example, we can move the gender above the marital status parameter and move the birth date parameter down, right before the hire date, as shown in Listing 2-2.

Listing 2-2. *"read list" output after removing and reordering output parameters*

```
<output list="true">
  <param name="business entity id"/>
  <param name="organization level"/>
  <param name="job title"/>
  <param name="gender"/>
  <param name="marital status"/>
  <param name="birth date"/>
  <param name="hire date"/>
  <param name="salaried flag" type="yesno" required="true"/>
  <config>
    <xfk:add-to-object class="EmployeeList"/>
  </config>
</output>
```

Notice that in the config section of the output structure, these parameters are being added to the EmployeeList data object, which serves as the view model for the Employee List view. The definition of this data object in the model allows you to further configure the UI display of the fields and other UI attributes.

Tip You can go to the definition of that data object by right-clicking on the class attribute and selecting the *Go to Definition* context menu.

71

Configure Column Labels

By default, the column headers in the Employee List results grid are derived from the names of the properties of the `EmployeeList` data object, which in turn are based on the output parameters of the `read list` operation. Some of them may use internal names that are not appropriate for the UI labels or names that are too long for a narrow column header, such as "Organization Level" or "Salaried Flag".

You can specify a better label for a data object field in the `ui:display/ui:fields` section of the data object definition in the model, as shown in Listing 2-3. These labels will be used as column headers for the data grid bound to this list object, or as field labels, if the data object is not a list object.

Listing 2-3. Configuring field labels in the model

```
<xfk:data-object class="EmployeeList" list="true">
  <ui:display>
    <ui:fields>
+     <ui:field param="organization level" label="Level"/>
+     <ui:field param="salaried flag" label="Salaried"/>
    </ui:fields>
  </ui:display>
  <ui:link name="details" view="EmployeeView" child="true">[...]
  <ui:link name="new" view="EmployeeView" child="true">[...]
</xfk:data-object>
```

Note Xomega uses these custom labels, as well as the default labels, to generate localizable resources. Therefore, you don't need to set these custom field labels here to merely translate them into a different language. Instead, you should just translate the generated **resources** into the desired language.

CHAPTER 2   BUILDING OUT A LIST VIEW

Review the Results

Now that we have updated the model, let's regenerate all the code by right-clicking on the AdventureWorks.Model project and selecting the *Build* context menu. Then, once you build and run the application and navigate to the Employee List view, you should see the updated results grid, as shown in Figure 2-1.

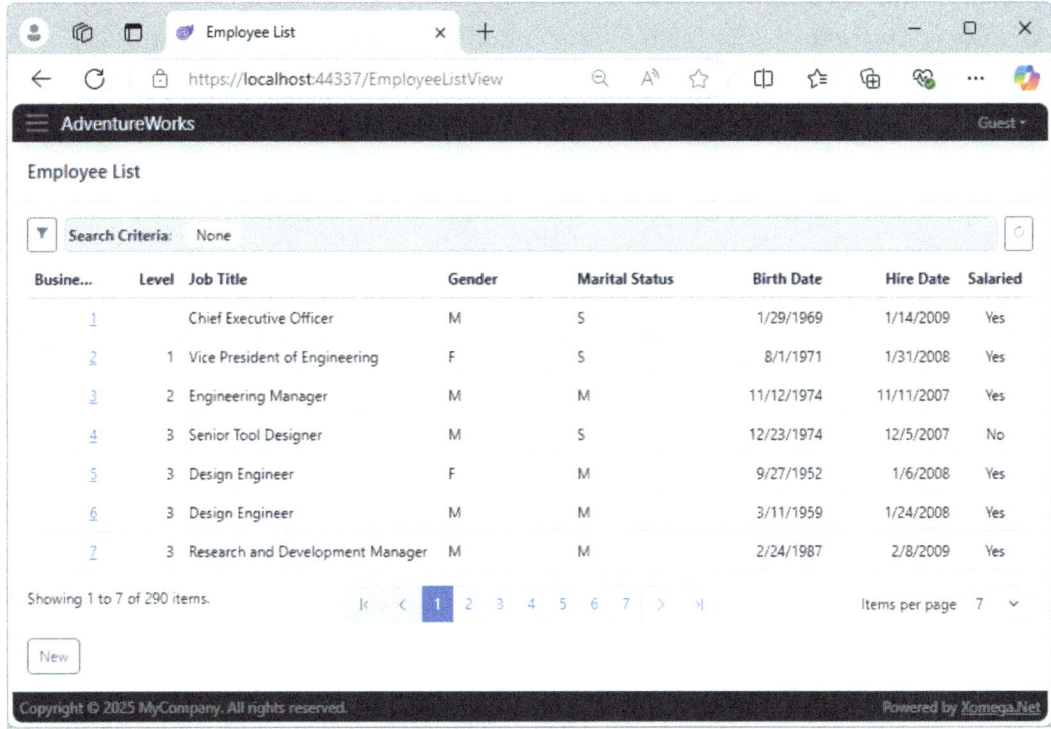

Figure 2-1. *Updated search results grid*

Notice how the results grid displays only the selected fields, in the desired order, and with the custom labels that we have configured in the model.

Note   We didn't bother to set a custom label on the internal business entity id field, since we are planning to hide this column later anyway.

Use Static Enumerations

If you have noticed, the gender and `marital status` fields in the Employee List view are displayed as single letters, e.g., M or F, and edited using standard text controls by default. However, the values in these fields can only be one of the predefined values from a static list that doesn't need to be changed dynamically.

Furthermore, even if we store these fields as short codes in the database to save space, we still want to display them as user-friendly values in the UI. For example, if you expand the doc node on the gender field, you will see the code and description of each allowed value, as shown in Listing 2-4.

Listing 2-4. Allowed gender values and their descriptions

```
<field name="marital status" type="code1"
       required="true">[...]
<field name="gender" type="code1" required="true">
  <config>
    <sql:column name="Gender"/>
  </config>
  <doc>
    <summary>M = Male, F = Female</summary>
  </doc>
</field>
```

To model such cases, Xomega allows you to define static enumerations right in the model. Then, it will be able to leverage those enumerations to decode internal values and show the user-friendly names in the UI, provide a selection control for entering the values, and validate the values against the enumeration.

Define Enumerations

Let's start by defining a couple of enumerations for the gender and `marital status` in the `employee.xom` file, as shown in Listing 2-5.

Listing 2-5. Defining static enumerations

employee.xom
```
<enums>
  <enum name="gender">
    <item name="Male" value="M"/>
    <item name="Female" value="F"/>
  </enum>
  <enum name="marital status">
    <item name="Single" value="S"/>
    <item name="Married" value="M"/>
    <item name="Divorced" value="D"/>
    <item name="Widowed" value="W"/>
  </enum>
</enums>
```

Note While the description of the `marital status` field indicates that it's also limited to just two values (Single and Married), I have added some more values to demonstrate certain examples for larger enumerations. You are also free to add more items to the `gender` enumeration, as needed.

Define Enumeration Types

Next, we're going to define the logical types for gender and `marital status` and will add a reference to the respective enumerations in each type, as shown in Listing 2-6.

Listing 2-6. Defining enumeration types

employee.xom
```
<types>
  <type name="employee" base="person"/>
+  <type name="gender" base="enumeration" size="1">
+    <enum ref="gender"/>
+  </type>
```

```
+   <type name="marital status" base="enumeration" size="1">
+     <enum ref="marital status"/>
+   </type>
  </types>
```

Notice how instead of the original logical type code1 on our fields (see Listing 2-4), the new types extend the enumeration base type, which is compatible with the code type, and set the size="1" attribute.

You need to make sure that you use the appropriate enumeration base type based on the original type of your field. For example, if your enumerated field has a type small int, then you should use small int enumeration as the base type for your new type and use integers as values on your enums.

Update Field Types

Once you have defined new logical types that reference the enumerations and are compatible with the original types, you can update the field definitions in the model to use these new types, as shown in Listing 2-7.

Listing 2-7. Updating field types to use enumeration types

```
<field name="marital status" type="marital status"
       required="true">[...]
<field name="gender" type="gender" required="true">[...]
```

Note We don't need to update the logical type on any of the input or output parameters of the employee object's operations, as they automatically use the type on the corresponding field. However, make sure to update the type as needed on any parameters that specify the type explicitly.

Review the Results

Now that we have updated the model, all you need to do to regenerate the screens and application code is to build the Model project. After that, let's build and run the solution to review the updated screens.

Once you log in and navigate to the Employee List screen, you will see that the *Gender* and *Marital Status* fields now show user-friendly names from our enumerations everywhere, and the corresponding criteria use a drop-down list for value selection, as shown in Figure 2-2.

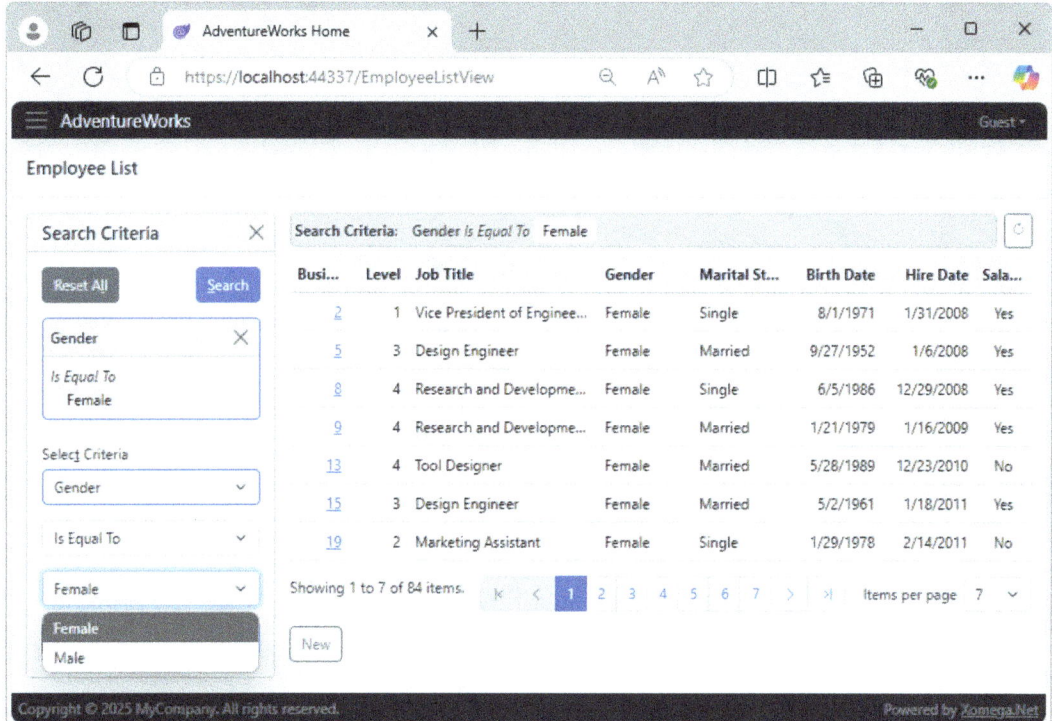

Figure 2-2. *Enumeration values in the results grid and search criteria*

If you open the Details view for any employee, you will see that those fields use drop-down lists with user-friendly names there as well, as illustrated in Figure 2-3.

CHAPTER 2   BUILDING OUT A LIST VIEW

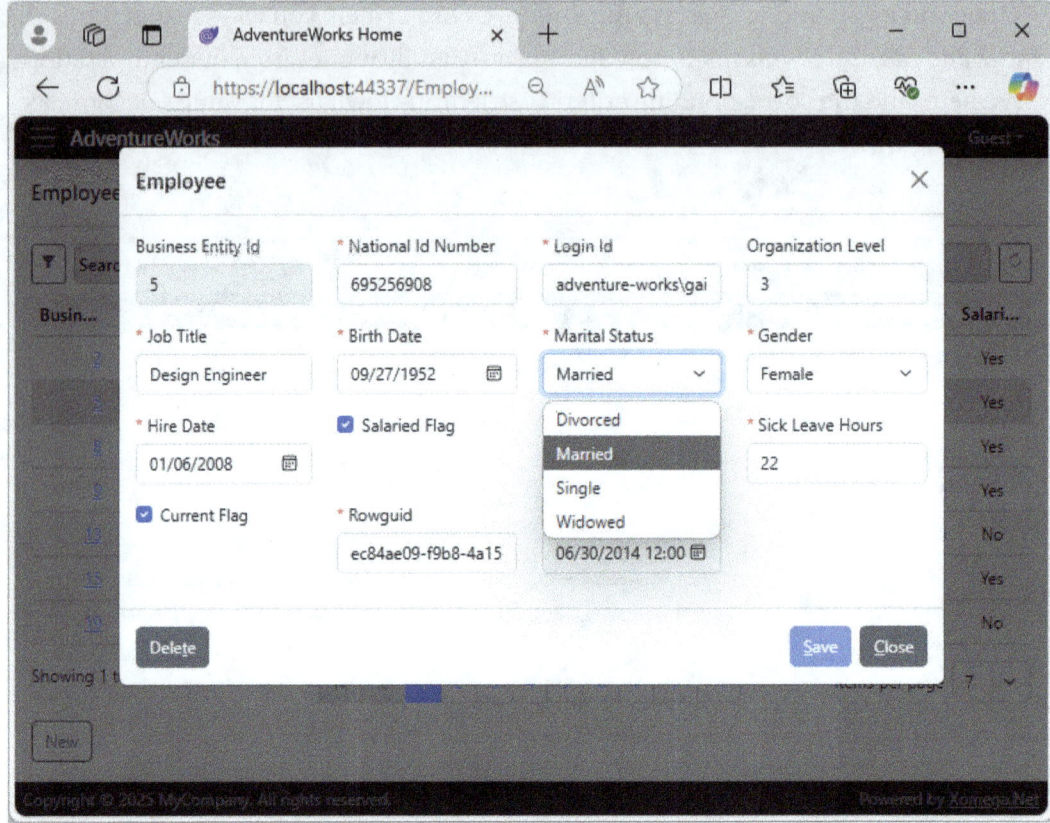

Figure 2-3. *Enumeration values on the details view*

Note   If you were paying close attention, you might have noticed that Boolean output parameters for our `read list` operation, such as the `salaried flag`, use a `yesno` type, which is also a static enumeration. This allows you to display user-friendly values "Yes" and "No" for Boolean fields, instead of "True" and "False."

Custom Search Result Fields

When looking at the list of employees, the first thing you may want to see is the employee's name. However, the Employee object does not contain any fields for employee names in and of itself. Instead, the Employee object has an association to the Person object in the AdventureWorks database, which in turn stores the first and last names of the associated person.

78

In this section, we will add a custom field to the Employee List view that will display the full name of the employee in the search results. We will also configure the Employee List view to provide a link to the Employee Details view on the employee's name, rather than on the internal `business entity id` column, which we will hide from the results grid.

Add Custom Result Field

To add a custom result field to the Employee List view, we need to modify the `read list` operation output in the `employee.xom` file. Let's add a new output parameter called `full name`, as shown in Listing 2-8. Since parameter name doesn't match the name of any employee fields, we need to explicitly set the logical type for it.

Listing 2-8. Adding a custom field to the "read list" operation output

```
<operation name="read list" type="readlist">
  <input>
    <struct name="criteria">[...]
  </input>
  <output list="true">
    <param name="business entity id"/>
+   <param name="full name" type="string"/>
    <param name="organization level"/>
    <param name="job title"/>
    <param name="gender"/>
    <param name="marital status"/>
    <param name="birth date"/>
    <param name="hire date"/>
    <param name="salaried flag" type="yesno" required="true"/>
    <config>[...]
  </output>
</operation>
```

CHAPTER 2   BUILDING OUT A LIST VIEW

> **Note** Because this is a display-only field, and does not require any editing or validation, we can get away with using a generic `string` type on it and not worry about the length of this field.

Custom Field Population Logic

Next, let's build the Model project to regenerate all the code, and then go to the `AdventureWorks.Services.Entities` project, and open up the generated `EmployeeService.cs` file in the *Services > HumanResources* folder.

If you scroll down to the `ReadListAsync` method, you will notice that it does not have the code to populate the `FullName` output parameter. Instead, Xomega added a *TODO* comment asking you to populate this field, which is also wrapped in between the `CUSTOM_CODE_START` and `CUSTOM_CODE_END` comments.

As the reference to the Person object on the Employee object was generated using the `BusinessEntityObject` property, we can use it to set the `FullName` to a concatenation of the last and first names of the associated person, as shown in Listing 2-9.

Listing 2-9. Custom field population logic

EmployeeService.cs
```
public virtual async
  Task<Output<ICollection<Employee_ReadListOutput>>>
  ReadListAsync(
    Employee_ReadListInput_Criteria _criteria,
    CancellationToken token = default)
{
...
    var qry = from obj in src
        select new Employee_ReadListOutput() {
            BusinessEntityId = obj.BusinessEntityId,
            // CUSTOM_CODE_START: set the FullName output parameter of ReadList operation below
-           // TODO: FullName = obj.???, // CUSTOM_CODE_END
```

CHAPTER 2   BUILDING OUT A LIST VIEW

```
+               FullName = obj.BusinessEntityObject.LastName
+                 + ", " + obj.BusinessEntityObject.FirstName,
+               // CUSTOM_CODE_END
                OrganizationLevel = obj.OrganizationLevel,
                JobTitle = obj.JobTitle,
                Gender = obj.Gender,
                MaritalStatus = obj.MaritalStatus,
                BirthDate = obj.BirthDate,
                HireDate = obj.HireDate,
                SalariedFlag = obj.SalariedFlag,
            };
...
}
```

Given that the file we just edited has been generated by Xomega, you may be asking "What will happen to our custom code when we regenerate the code?" The cool feature of Xomega is that **any custom code will be preserved** in the generated files, as long as you put it in between those special comments CUSTOM_CODE_START and CUSTOM_CODE_END, AND the comment following the CUSTOM_CODE_START tag, which contains the output field name and the operation name, remains the same.

This means that if you remove or rename that output parameter, or if you rename the operation, you will lose the custom code that's mixed in with the generated code. Similarly, you may lose this custom code if you decide to clean the generated output by running the *Clean* command on the Model project or the generator, unless you take certain actions to prevent this file from being cleaned, which are described in the header of the generated file.

In any event, I recommend that you **always keep the generated files in a source control system**, such as git, so that you could easily revert your changes or retrieve the custom code, if it gets lost accidentally.

Configure Key Field and Links

Now that we have added the custom full name field to the Employee List view, we can configure the model to hide the existing business entity id key field from the results grid, and to display the details link on the full name field instead.

81

For that, you can go to the definition of the `EmployeeList` data object in the model and set the `hidden="true"` attribute on the `business entity id` field. Then, you need to expand the `ui:link` element for the details link and change the `on-field` attribute to `full name`, as shown in Listing 2-10.

Listing 2-10. Hiding a field and changing a details link

```
<xfk:data-object class="EmployeeList" list="true">
  <ui:display>
    <ui:fields>
+     <ui:field param="business entity id" hidden="true"/>
      <ui:field param="organization level" label="Level"/>
      <ui:field param="salaried flag" label="Salaried"/>
    </ui:fields>
  </ui:display>
  <ui:link name="details" view="EmployeeView" child="true">
    <ui:params>[...]
-     <ui:display on-field="business entity id"/>
+     <ui:display on-field="full name"/>
  </ui:link>
  <ui:link name="new" view="EmployeeView" child="true">[...]
</xfk:data-object>
```

Note Remember that the `business entity id` will still be returned to the client to allow opening the Details view, but there will be no column for it in the results grid.

Review the Results

With these changes made, let's build the Model project once again to regenerate the code, and then run the application to review the results. If you navigate to the Employee List view now and run the search, you will see that the *Full Name* is displayed as the first column now and contains a link to the detail screen, as shown in Figure 2-4.

CHAPTER 2   BUILDING OUT A LIST VIEW

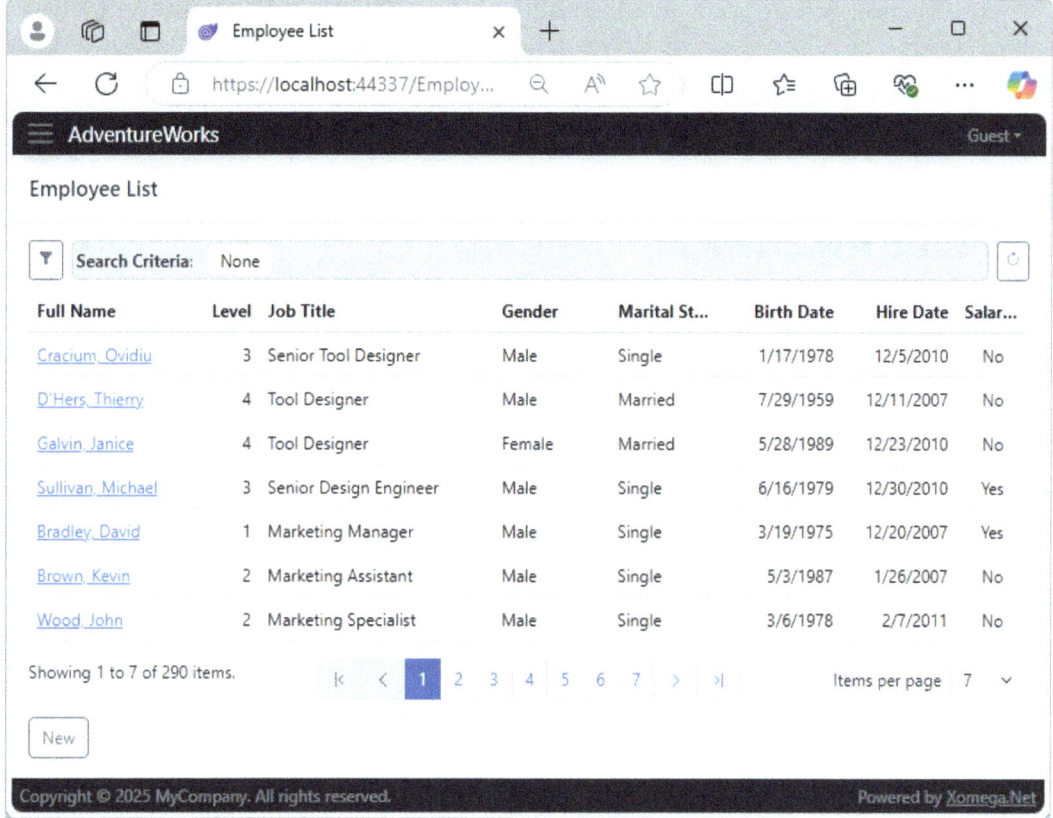

Figure 2-4. Custom field Full Name with a details link.

Note The fact that Full *Name* shows proper results after we built the Model project means that our custom code has been preserved after the services have been regenerated.

Using Child Subobjects

In the previous section, we added a custom field *Full Name* to the Employee List using the first and last name of the Person object that is referenced from the Employee object.

In this section, we are going to add another custom field, but this time around, its source object is not readily accessible from the Employee object. In the process of doing that, you will see how to visualize the Entity Model and learn about Xomega subobjects and how to convert an existing object to a subobject.

City/State Result Field

The AdventureWorks company in our sample database seems to be geographically diverse, as its employees can reside in different cities, states, and even countries. Therefore, it would make sense to display at least the city and state in the Employee List view. To do that, let's add another custom field `city state` to the output parameters of the `read list` operation, as shown in Listing 2-11.

Listing 2-11. Adding city/state custom field to the Employee List

```
<operation name="read list" type="readlist">
  <input>
    <struct name="criteria">[...]
  </input>
  <output list="true">
    <param name="business entity id"/>
    <param name="full name" type="string"/>
    <param name="organization level"/>
    <param name="job title"/>
+   <param name="city state" type="string"/>
    <param name="gender"/>
    <param name="marital status"/>
    <param name="birth date"/>
    <param name="hire date"/>
    <param name="salaried flag" type="yesno" required="true"/>
    <config>[...]
  </output>
</operation>
```

We will also configure a custom label for the `city state` field in the `EmployeeList` data object, as shown in Listing 2-12.

Listing 2-12. Configuring the label for the city/state custom field

```
<xfk:data-object class="EmployeeList" list="true">
  <ui:display>
    <ui:fields>
      <ui:field param="business entity id" hidden="true"/>
+     <ui:field param="city state" label="City/State"/>
      <ui:field param="organization level" label="Level"/>
      <ui:field param="salaried flag" label="Salaried"/>
    </ui:fields>
  </ui:display>
</xfk:data-object>
```

When it comes to implementing custom logic to populate our custom field, we first need to determine the source object(s) for this data and how to access it from the Employee object.

Normally, the city and state information are stored on the Address object in the AdventureWorks database. However, to figure out how it relates to the Employee object, it would be helpful to visualize our entity model.

Entity Model Diagrams

If you remember when we were initially creating the solution for our application using the Xomega Solution wizard, we also selected a project for the Model Diagrams. Its sole purpose is to generate the legacy Entity Data Model file `EntityModel.edmx`, which will help you to build diagrams that depict your entities and their relationships, as shown in Figure 2-5.

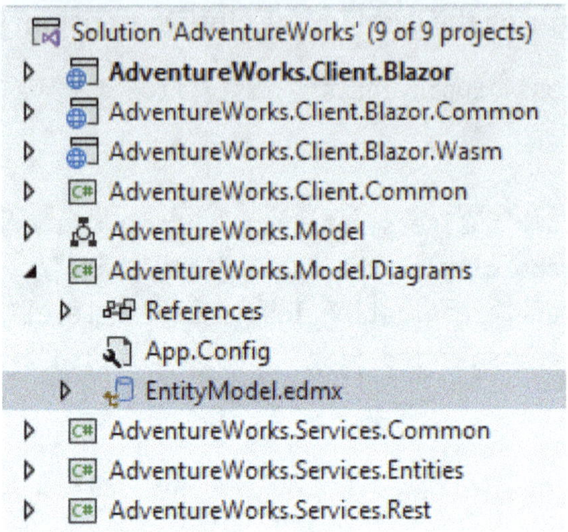

CHAPTER 2   BUILDING OUT A LIST VIEW

Figure 2-5. Entity model diagrams

If you open this file, you will be able to create a number of diagrams where you can add some entities, and it will automatically draw the relationships between them. For example, I have created the following diagram to depict the Employee object, and all the related objects that provide the association with the target Address object (see Figure 2-6).

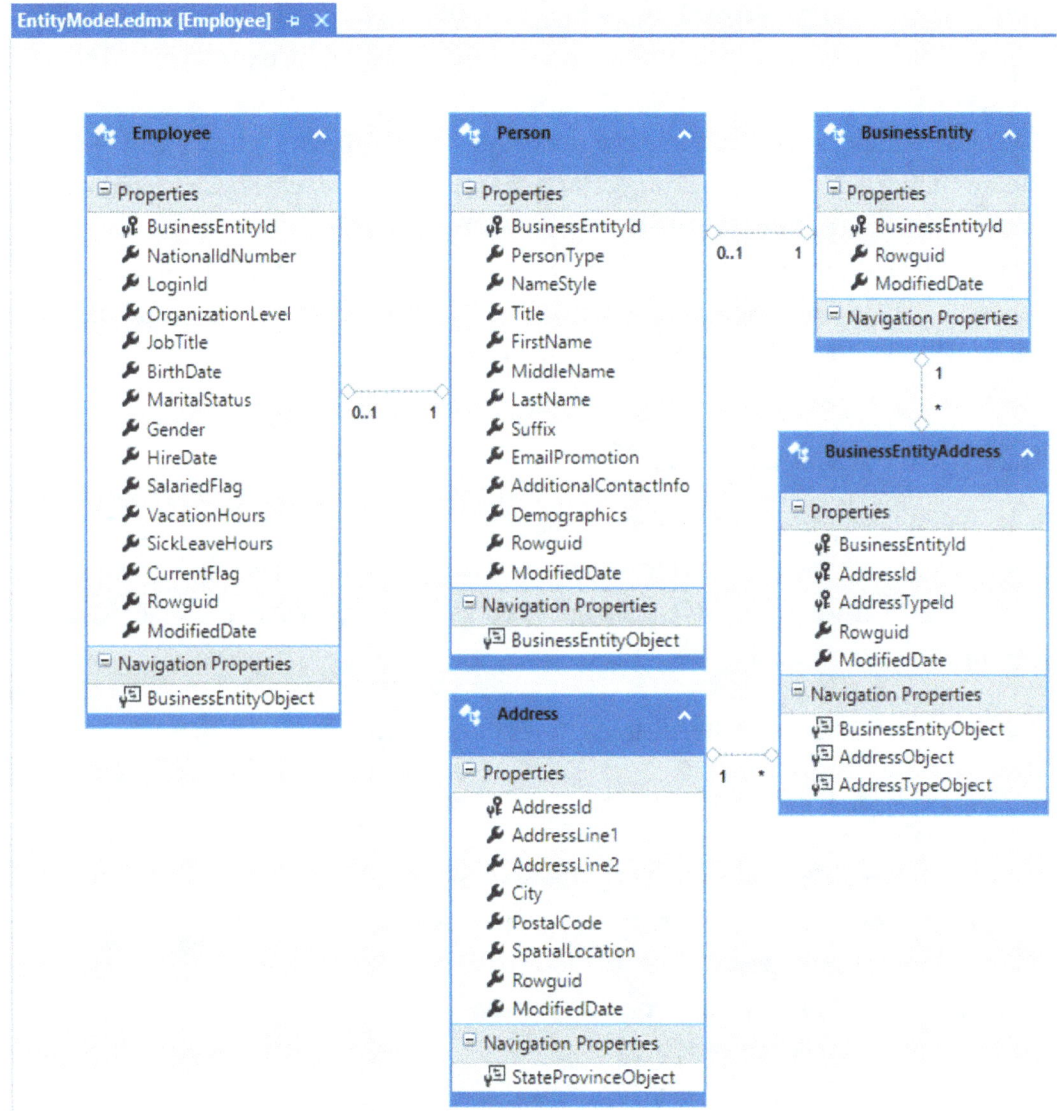

***Figure 2-6.** Employee entity diagram*

As you can see, there is a one-to-many relationship between the `BusinessEntity` and the `BusinessEntityAddress` objects, which allows associating multiple addresses of different types with the same business entity. For employees we want to display the city and state of their Home address.

However, if you look at the `BusinessEntity` object, you will notice that it does not have a navigation property to the list of associated `BusinessEntityAddress` objects, so you cannot access the `Address` object without explicit table joins.

With one-to-many relationships, Xomega generates a navigation property to a child list only if that list is declared as a subobject of the corresponding parent object in the Xomega model.

When we imported our model from the database, the `BusinessEntityAddress` table was imported as a separate object `business entity address`, because there is no cascade delete on the foreign key to the `BusinessEntity` table.

However, within the Xomega model, the `business entity address` object really lends itself to being defined as a subobject of the `business entity` object. So, let's see what it takes to convert it to a subobject in the model.

Subobject As a Child List

If you open the definition of the imported `business entity address` object in the `business_entity_address.xom` file, you will see that it defines a fieldset with the same name for its key fields, which reference the `business entity`, `address`, and `address type` objects, as shown in Listing 2-13.

Listing 2-13. BusinessEntityAddress object definition

business_entity_address.xom
```
<fieldsets>
  <fieldset name="business entity address">
    <field name="business entity id" type="business entity"
           required="true">[...]
    <field name="address id" type="address"
           required="true">[...]
    <field name="address type id" type="address type"
           required="true">[...]
  </fieldset>
</fieldsets>
<objects>
  <object name="business entity address">
    <fields>
      <fieldset ref="business entity address" key="supplied"
                required="true"/>
      <field name="rowguid" type="guid" required="true">[...]
```

```
      <field name="modified date" type="date time"
             required="true">[...]
    </fields>
    <config>[...]
    <doc>[...]
  </object>
</objects>
```

To convert it to a subobject of the business entity object, you need to move the fieldset definition to the business_entity.xom file and move the business entity address object to the subobjects element of the business entity object. There are a couple of caveats though.

First, you need to remove the business entity id field from the fieldset, since subobjects automatically include the parent object's key, which is that field.

Second, you need to change the name of the subobject to address, since Xomega automatically fully qualifies the names of subobjects with the parent object name when generating the entities.

Listing 2-14 shows the updated business_entity.xom file with the business entity address object converted to a subobject of the business entity object.

Listing 2-14. BusinessEntityAddress as a subobject of BusinessEntity

business_entity.xom
```
<fieldsets>
+ <fieldset name="business entity address">
+   <field name="address id" type="address"
+          required="true">[...]
+   <field name="address type id" type="address type"
+          required="true">[...]
  </fieldset>
</fieldsets>
<objects>
  <object name="business entity">
    <fields>
      <field name="business entity id" type="business entity"
             key="serial" required="true">[...]
      <field name="rowguid" type="guid" required="true">[...]
```

```
          <field name="modified date" type="date time"
                 required="true">[...]
      </fields>
      <config>[...]
      <doc>[...]
+     <subobjects>
+       <object name="address">
+         <fields>
+           <fieldset ref="business entity address"
                      key="supplied" required="true"/>
+           <field name="rowguid" type="guid"
                  required="true">[...]
+           <field name="modified date" type="date time"
                  required="true">[...]
+         </fields>
+         <config>[...]
+         <doc>[...]
+       </object>
+     </subobjects>
    </object>
</objects>
```

Note If the `business entity address` key fieldset for the original object had only two fields, without the `address type id`, you would have removed it altogether when converting it to a subobject and used the other `address id` field as the key on the subobject, with the `business entity id` key field being automatically included from the parent object.

If you build the Model project to regenerate all the artifacts and open the Employee diagram again, you will see that the `BusinessEntity` object now contains a navigation property `AddressObjectList` for the `BusinessEntityAddress` object, as shown in Figure 2-7.

CHAPTER 2 BUILDING OUT A LIST VIEW

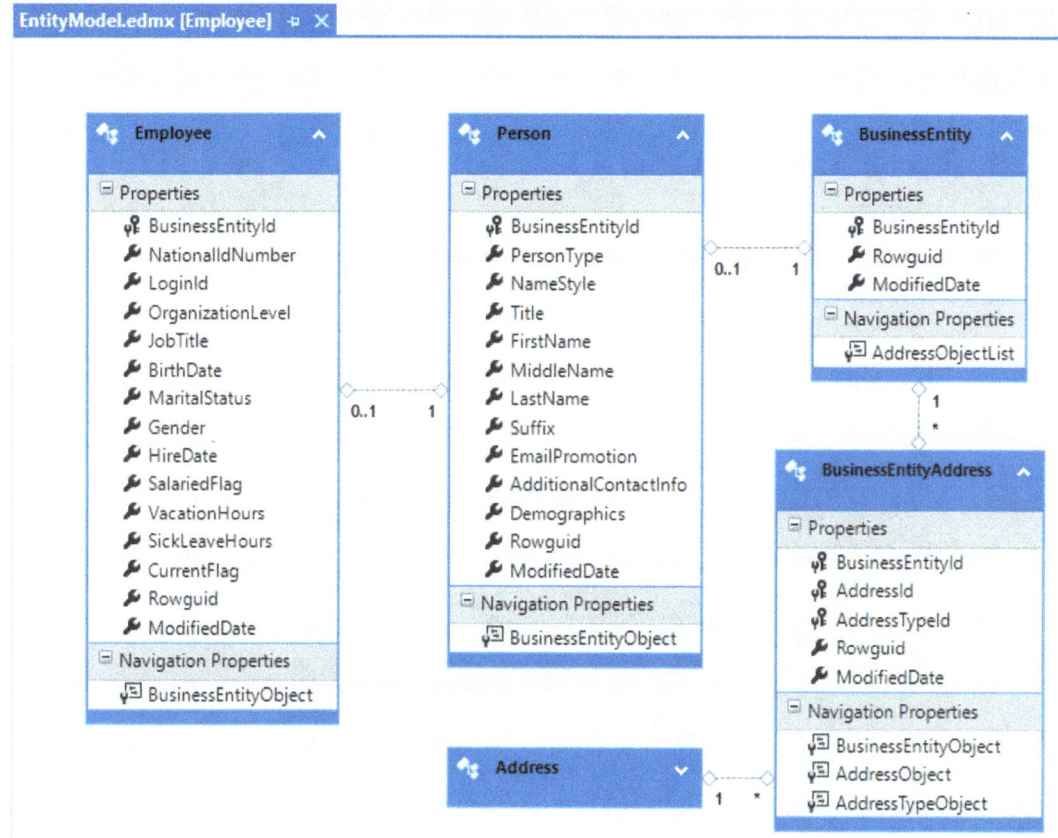

Figure 2-7. *BusinessEntity.AddressObjectList navigation property*

Tip To make entity model diagrams less busy, you can collapse irrelevant entities or property groups there, such as the Address entity on the diagram above.

Reading Subobject Fields

Now that we have added the `AddressObjectList` navigation property to the `BusinessEntity` object, we can access the `Address` object from the `Employee` object and populate the city/state from the `Address` object, as shown in Listing 2-15.

Listing 2-15. Custom logic for the city/state field

EmployeeService.cs
```
public virtual async
  Task<Output<ICollection<Employee_ReadListOutput>>>
  ReadListAsync(
    Employee_ReadListInput_Criteria _criteria,
    CancellationToken token = default)
{
...
    var qry = from obj in src
        select new Employee_ReadListOutput() {
            BusinessEntityId = obj.BusinessEntityId,
            // CUSTOM_CODE_START: set the FullName output parameter of
            ReadList operation below
            FullName = obj.BusinessEntityObject.LastName
              + ", " + obj.BusinessEntityObject.FirstName,
            // CUSTOM_CODE_END
            OrganizationLevel = obj.OrganizationLevel,
            JobTitle = obj.JobTitle,
            // CUSTOM_CODE_START: set the CityState output parameter of
            ReadList operation below
+           CityState = obj.BusinessEntityObject
+             .BusinessEntityObject.AddressObjectList
+             .Where(a => a.AddressTypeObject.Name == "Home")
+             .Select(a => a.AddressObject.City + ", " +
+                         a.AddressObject.StateProvinceObject
+                           .StateProvinceCode)
+             .First(), // CUSTOM_CODE_END
            Gender = obj.Gender,
            MaritalStatus = obj.MaritalStatus,
            BirthDate = obj.BirthDate,
```

CHAPTER 2   BUILDING OUT A LIST VIEW

```
        HireDate = obj.HireDate,
        SalariedFlag = obj.SalariedFlag,
    };
...
}
```

As you see, we pick an address record with the address type "Home" and concatenate the city and state fields to populate the `CityState` output parameter.

Review the Result

That's all you need to do, so let's run the application and review our changes on the Employee List screen. After you open the screen and run the search, you should be able to see the City/State column populated with the proper values for the home address of each employee, as shown in Figure 2-8.

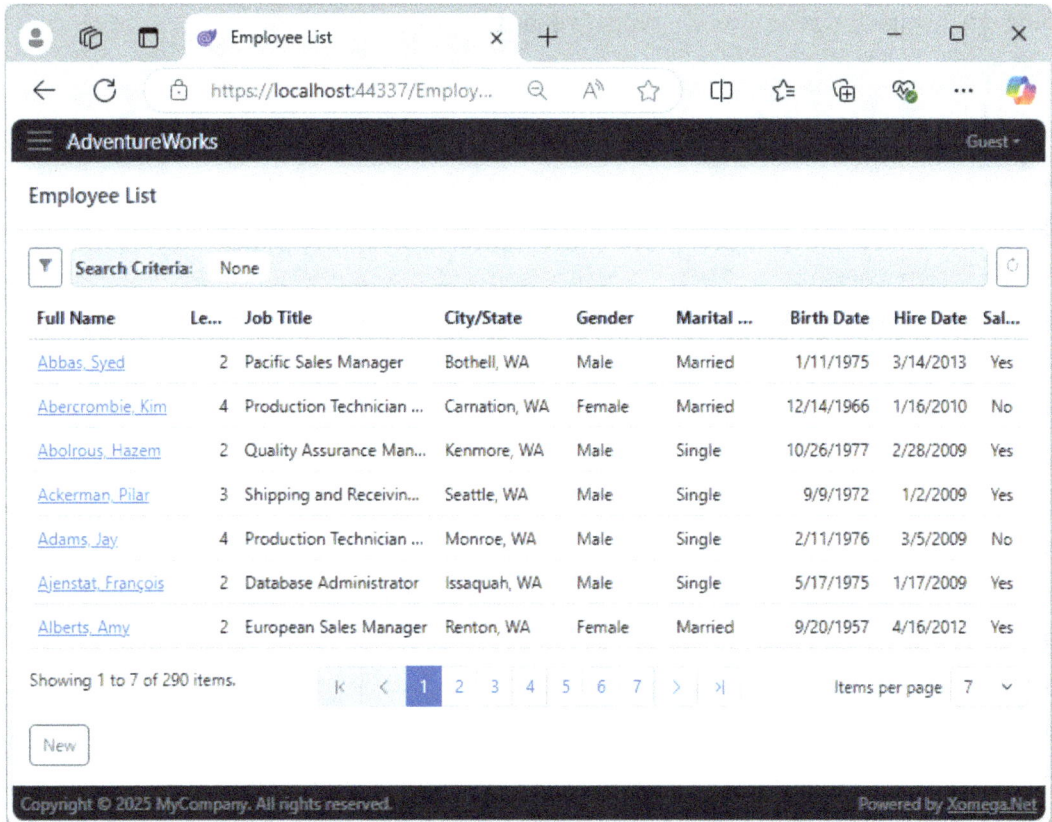

Figure 2-8. *City/State column on the Employee List view*

CHAPTER 2   BUILDING OUT A LIST VIEW

Extend Generated Entities

In the previous section, we added a custom result field, for which we had to define a subobject to get to its source from the Employee object.

In this section, we will add another custom result field, where we cannot define a subobject to get to its source, so we will use a different technique by extending the generated entity.

In the AdventureWorks database, an employee can also be a salesperson, and the data related to their sales is stored in a separate table `SalesPerson` in the `Sales` schema. For the search results on the Employee List screen, it may be useful to just show a Boolean column indicating whether an employee is a salesperson or not.

So, let's add a new `sales` output parameter to the `read list` operation and set the type to `yesno` to display it as Yes/No values on the screen, as shown in Listing 2-16.

Listing 2-16. Adding a sales indicator

```
<operation name="read list" type="readlist">
  <input>[...]
  <output list="true">
    <param name="business entity id"/>
    <param name="full name" type="string"/>
    <param name="organization level"/>
    <param name="job title"/>
+   <param name="sales" type="yesno"/>
    <param name="city state" type="string"/>
    <param name="gender"/>
    <param name="marital status"/>
    <param name="birth date"/>
    <param name="hire date"/>
    <param name="salaried flag" type="yesno" required="true"/>
    <config>[...]
  </output>
</operation>
```

To figure out how to populate this value, let's first review the structure of the `SalesPerson` object.

Why Not a Subobject

If we create an entity model diagram for the `SalesPerson` object, you will see that it has an optional one-to-one association with the `Employee` object, as illustrated in Figure 2-9. However, there is no navigation property from the generated `Employee` entity to the `SalesPerson` entity, since the latter is not a subobject of the `Employee` object.

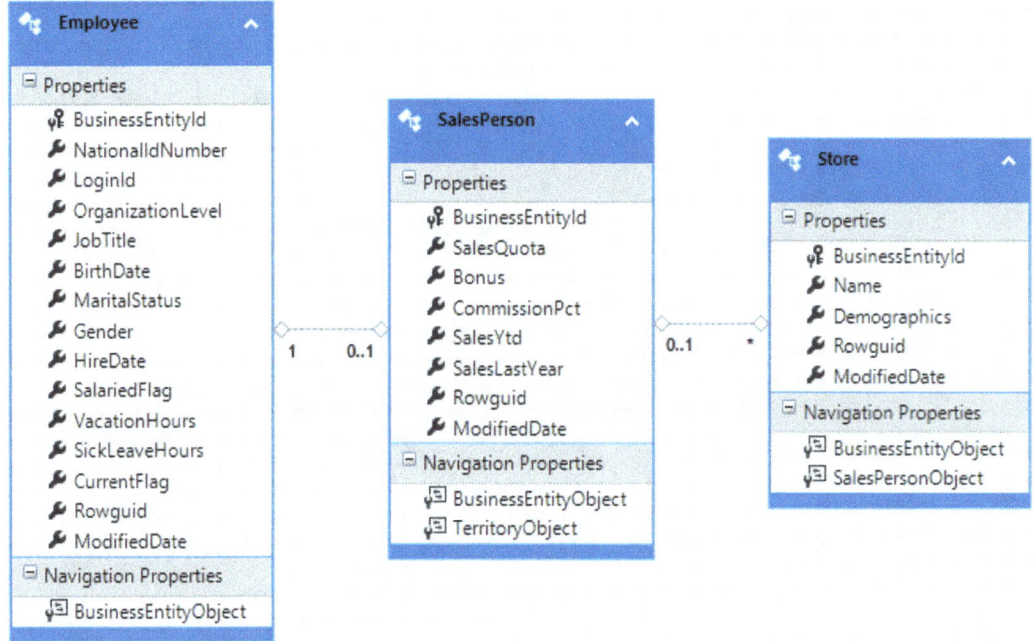

Figure 2-9. *Sales person diagram*

Xomega model does allow you to define a subobject with an optional one-to-one association by not setting a key field on the subobject, which will just inherit the key from the parent object. However, there are a couple of reasons why the `sales person` object cannot be and should not be a subobject of the `employee` object.

First, a subobject in the Xomega model would be automatically declared in the same module as the parent object. However, the `sales person` object was imported in the `sales` module based on the database schema of the corresponding table, while the `employee` object is in the `human resources` module, and it would make sense to keep them in their respective modules.

CHAPTER 2   BUILDING OUT A LIST VIEW

But more importantly, subobjects in the Domain Driven Design should not be referenced independently outside of the parent aggregate object. As you can see from Figure 2-9, the SalesPerson object is referenced directly by the Store object, for example.

In fact, if you open the sales_person.xom file, right-click on the sales person type, and select the *Find All References* context menu, as shown in Figure 2-10, you will be able to see all the references to the sales person object in the model.

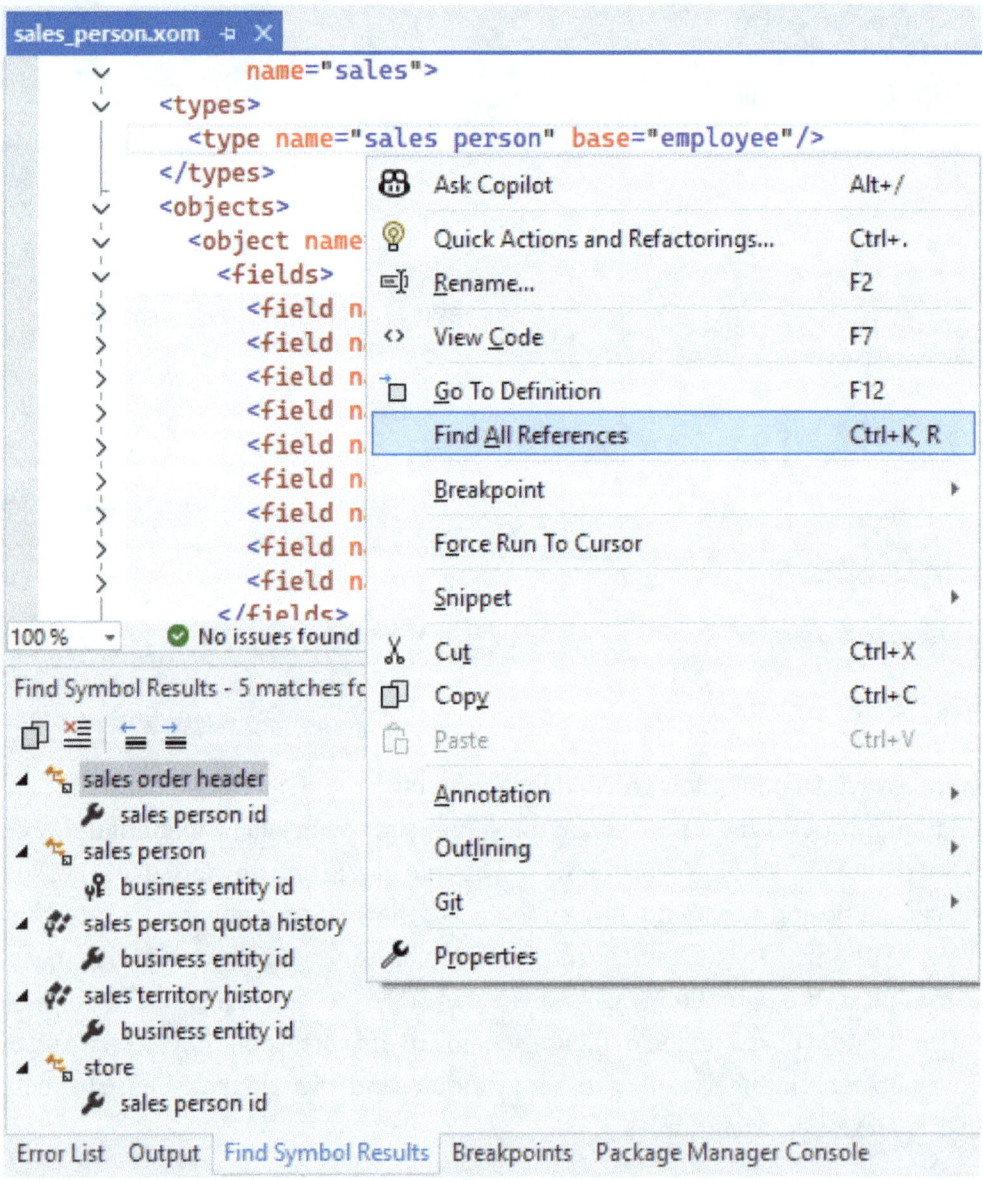

Figure 2-10. *Finding all references to a logical type*

So, if we cannot make it a subobject to get that navigation property from the Employee object generated, let's see how we can add that property manually by extending the generated entities.

Customize Generated Entities

The generated Employee entity is a partial class, which you can easily extend by creating a new file with the same class name and adding your custom properties and methods to it.

You can also have such a class generated for you by Xomega, by adding an edm:customize element to the object's config element in the model, and setting the attribute extend="true", as shown in Listing 2-17.

Listing 2-17. Extending the Employee entity

```
<object name="employee">
  <fields>[...]
  <operations>[...]
  <config>
    <sql:table name="HumanResources.Employee">
      <sql:trigger name="dEmployee"/>
    </sql:table>
+    <edm:customize extend="true"/>
  </config>
  <doc>[...]
</object>
```

Once you build the model to regenerate the code, you will see a new file EmployeeExtended.cs nested under the generated Employee.cs file in the AdventureWorks.Services.Entities project, as shown in Figure 2-11.

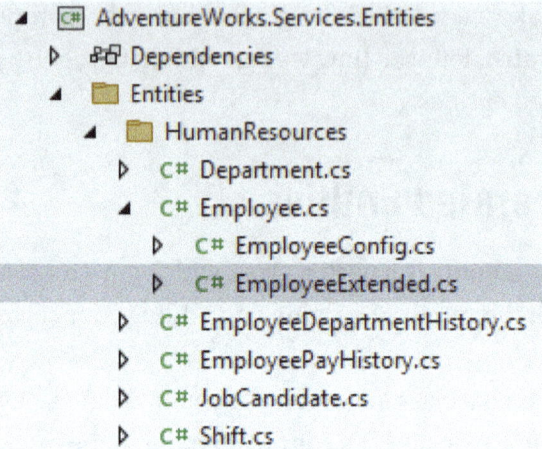

Figure 2-11. *Generated EmployeeExtended entity*

In the generated file for the extended `Employee` entity, you can add a new navigation property to the `SalesPerson` entity, as shown in Listing 2-18.

Listing 2-18. Adding navigation property in the extended entity

EmployeeExtended.cs
```
namespace AdventureWorks.Services.Entities;

public partial class Employee
{
    // add custom methods and properties here
+   public virtual SalesPerson SalesPersonObject { get; set; }
}
```

However, for Entity Framework Core to recognize this new navigation property, you also need to update the Entity Model configuration, accordingly, so let's see how to do it.

Note The `EmployeeExtended.cs` file is generated only once, if it does not exist, so you can safely add your custom code to it without worrying about it being overwritten whenever you regenerate the entities.

Customize Entity Configuration

To customize the EF Core configuration of our entity model, we need to create a subclass of the generated DbContext class, which is called AdventureWorksEntities. So, let's create a new class called AdventureWorksEntitiesCustomized, which will make it nested under the generated AdventureWorksEntities.cs file, as shown in Figure 2-12.

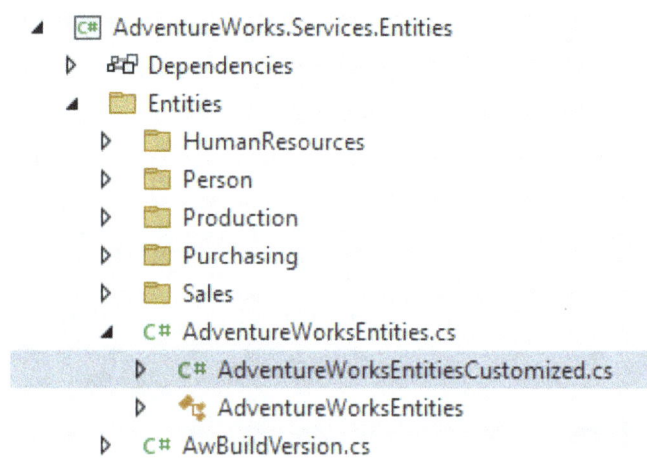

Figure 2-12. *Customized DbContext*

In the new file, we will extend our class from the generated AdventureWorksEntities class and override the OnModelCreating method, where we will fluently configure the SalesPerson entity using a WithOne method that takes our new navigation property, as shown in Listing 2-19.

Listing 2-19. Customizing entity model configuration

AdventureWorksEntitiesCustomized.cs
```
using Microsoft.EntityFrameworkCore;

namespace AdventureWorks.Services.Entities;

public class AdventureWorksEntitiesCustomized
  (DbContextOptions<AdventureWorksEntitiesCustomized> options)
    : AdventureWorksEntities(options)
{
    protected override void OnModelCreating(
```

```
        ModelBuilder modelBuilder)
{
    base.OnModelCreating(modelBuilder);

    modelBuilder.Entity<SalesPerson>()
        .HasOne(e => e.BusinessEntityObject)
        .WithOne(e => e.SalesPersonObject)
        .HasForeignKey<SalesPerson>(e => e.BusinessEntityId)
        .OnDelete(DeleteBehavior.NoAction);
    }
}
```

To make our application actually use the customized class, we need to update the Program class in the AdventureWorks.Client.Blazor project to use our new class AdventureWorksEntitiesCustomized as the concrete implementation for the DbContext, as shown in Listing 2-20.

Listing 2-20. Using the customized DbContext

Program.cs
```
services.AddDbContext<AdventureWorksEntities,
    AdventureWorksEntitiesCustomized>(
        o => o.UseLazyLoadingProxies()
            .UseSqlServer(connStr));
```

Note You still need to use the generated AdventureWorksEntities class as the generic type for the AddDbContext method, since that's the class that is injected into all the generated services.

Caution The UseLazyLoadingProxies() call enables lazy loading in EF, but you should carefully consider its use to avoid performance issues such as the N+1 problem.

Use Enhanced Entity

Now that we have enhanced the Employee entity with a custom navigation property SalesPersonObject, we can use it in the service implementation to set the new Sales output parameter in the ReadListAsync method by checking if that property is not null, as shown in Listing 2-21.

Listing 2-21. Using enhanced entity in the service implementation

EmployeeService.cs
```
public virtual async
  Task<Output<ICollection<Employee_ReadListOutput>>>
  ReadListAsync(
    Employee_ReadListInput_Criteria _criteria,
    CancellationToken token = default)
{
...
    var qry = from obj in src
        select new Employee_ReadListOutput() {
            BusinessEntityId = obj.BusinessEntityId,
            // CUSTOM_CODE_START: set the FullName output parameter of
            ReadList operation below
            FullName = obj.BusinessEntityObject.LastName
              + ", " + obj.BusinessEntityObject.FirstName,
            // CUSTOM_CODE_END
            OrganizationLevel = obj.OrganizationLevel,
            JobTitle = obj.JobTitle,
            // CUSTOM_CODE_START: set the Sales output parameter of
            ReadList operation below
+           Sales = obj.SalesPersonObject != null,
            // CUSTOM_CODE_END
            // CUSTOM_CODE_START: set the CityState output parameter of
            ReadList operation below
            CityState = obj.BusinessEntityObject
              .BusinessEntityObject.AddressObjectList
              .Where(a => a.AddressTypeObject.Name == "Home")
```

```
                    .Select(a => a.AddressObject.City + ", " +
                                a.AddressObject.StateProvinceObject
                                .StateProvinceCode)
                    .First(), // CUSTOM_CODE_END
            Gender = obj.Gender,
            MaritalStatus = obj.MaritalStatus,
            BirthDate = obj.BirthDate,
            HireDate = obj.HireDate,
            SalariedFlag = obj.SalariedFlag,
        };
...
}
```

> **Note** The entire body of this generated method will be surrounded by the try/catch blocks to handle any exceptions and report them to the calling client as errors that are part of the `Output`.
>
> However, the LINQ query in the listing will be converted to a SQL query, so you don't have to worry about getting a `NullReferenceException` when accessing related objects and properties.

Review the Results

To check the results, let's run our application again and open the Employee List view. Once you run the search, you will see that our new *Sales* column is populated with Yes/No values to indicate whether the current employee is a salesperson, as shown in Figure 2-13.

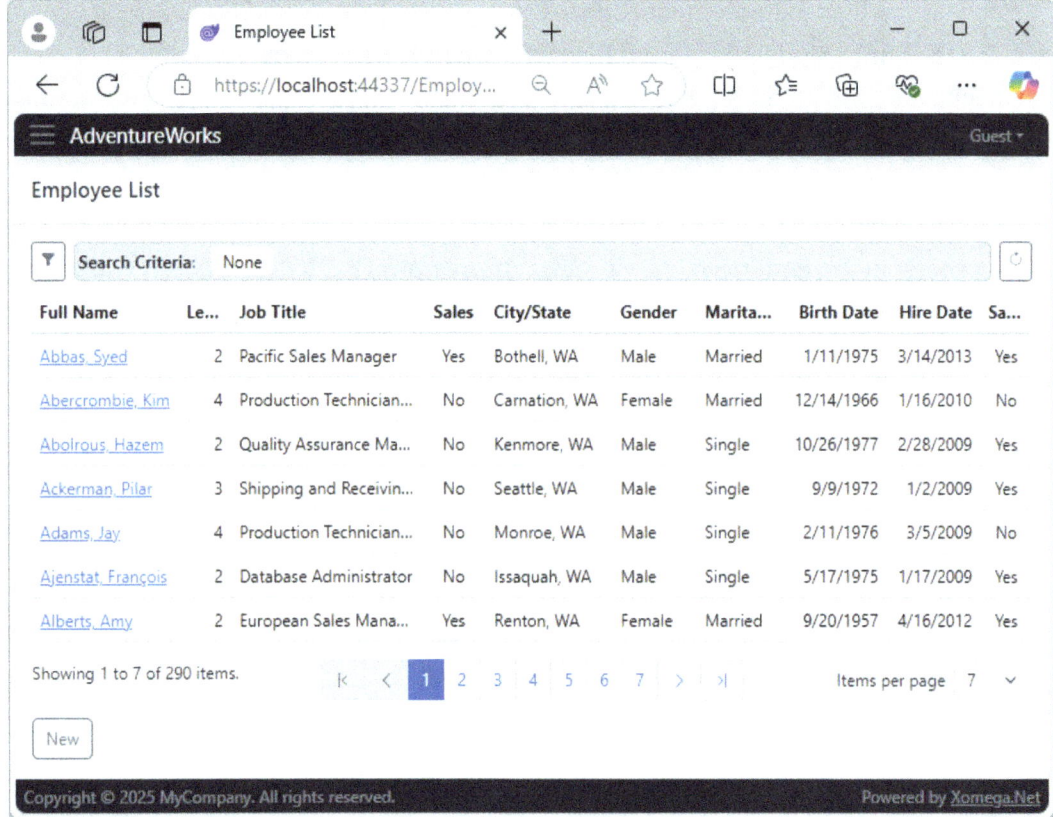

Figure 2-13. Sales column on EmployeeListView

Note You may have noticed that sales employees also have the word "Sales" in their job title, which is a good indicator that our logic is working correctly.

Summary

In this chapter, you saw how to update the search results grid on the Employee List view to make it display more relevant information and how easy it is with Xomega.

Along the way, you learned some useful Xomega concepts and development techniques, such as how to define static enumerations to allow displaying short internal codes as user-friendly names and selecting those values from a drop-down list.

You learned how to implement code for custom result fields and the different ways to enhance the Entity Model that would help you to write such custom code.

Specifically, you learned about subobjects in the Xomega model, when using them is appropriate, and how to extend the generated entities with custom navigation properties when you cannot use subobjects.

In the next chapter, you will learn how to use Xomega criteria framework to make the search criteria in the Employee List view even more powerful. In the process, you will get familiar with more advanced Xomega concepts and techniques that we'll also keep building on in subsequent chapters.

CHAPTER 3

Configuring Search Criteria

In the previous chapters, we created a Blazor application using the Xomega Solution wizard, imported the model from the sample AdventureWorks database, and generated standard search and details views for the Employee object. Then we customized the employee search results grid to display more relevant information.

In this chapter, we will learn how to customize the search criteria in the Employee List view using flexible Xomega criteria framework. In addition to adding and implementing custom criteria, you will learn how to configure the operators for each criteria field or simplify the criteria selection by hiding the operators or displaying criteria fields statically.

You will also learn how to set up a dynamic enumeration for a field, where the list of possible values is sourced from the database rather than defined statically. Finally, you will see how to set up cascading selection, where the possible values of one field depend on the value(s) of another field.

Add or Remove Criteria

As with the search results grid, the generated Employee List view was configured to have every Employee object field as criteria by default.

While all of them are tucked away in a drop-down list for selecting a criteria field, you still want to clean up that list and remove any criteria that are useless, and then add other, more helpful criteria.

CHAPTER 3 CONFIGURING SEARCH CRITERIA

Removing Useless Criteria

Employee List search criteria are based on the parameters in the "criteria" structure under the input of the `employee` object's `read list` operation, so we can go ahead and remove the criteria that we think the users will barely, if ever, use, as shown in Listing 3-1.

Listing 3-1. Removing criteria fields

```
employee.xom
<object name="employee">
  <operations>
    <operation name="read list" type="readlist">
      <input>
        <struct name="criteria">
-         <param name="business entity id"/>
          <param name="national id number"/>
          <param name="login id"/>
          <param name="organization level"/>
          <param name="job title"/>
          <param name="birth date"/>
          <param name="marital status"/>
          <param name="gender"/>
          <param name="hire date"/>
          <param name="salaried flag" type="yesno"/>
-         <param name="vacation hours"/>
-         <param name="sick leave hours"/>
          <param name="current flag" type="yesno"/>
-         <param name="rowguid"/>
          <param name="modified date"/>
          <config>[...]
        </struct>
      </input>
      <output list="true">[...]
    </operation>
  </operations>
</object>
```

> **Note** Given how easy it is to add them back, if needed, you don't have to feel bad about removing some useful functionality here.

Adding Non-field Criteria

If you have a custom result field that is not a field on the underlying object, then you can also easily add that field to the criteria under the same name, and Xomega will automatically generate the code to implement it, without you having to write any custom code.

For example, in the previous chapter, we added a custom field *Full Name* to the Employee List view. To allow filtering by that field, we can just add a parameter with the same name and type to the `criteria` input structure, as shown in Listing 3-2.

Listing 3-2. Adding non-field criteria

```
<operation name="read list" type="readlist">
  <input>
    <struct name="criteria">
+     <param name="full name" type="string"/>
      <param name="national id number"/>
      <param name="login id"/>
      <param name="organization level"/>
      <param name="job title"/>
      <param name="birth date"/>
      <param name="marital status"/>
      <param name="gender"/>
      <param name="hire date"/>
      <param name="salaried flag" type="yesno"/>
      <param name="current flag" type="yesno"/>
      <param name="modified date"/>
      <config>[...]
    </struct>
  </input>
  <output list="true">[...]
</operation>
```

Review the Results

If you build the model project to regenerate all the code now, run the application, and open the Employee List screen, you will see that the list of available criteria will be updated to reflect the changes you made. Figure 3-1 illustrates how filtering by *Full Name* works out of the box.

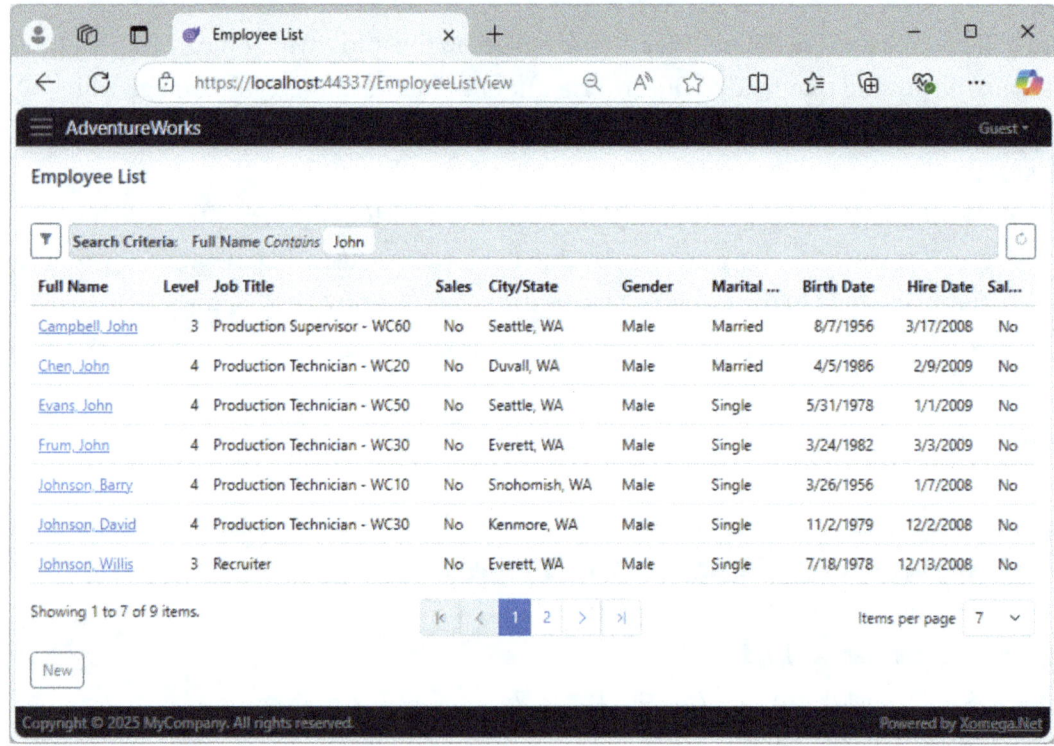

Figure 3-1. *Non-field result criteria*

Configuring Operators

If you remember from the first chapter, when selecting a criteria field, you also needed to select an operator, such as *Is Equal To*, *Is Greater Than*, etc.

The default list of operators is defined in the `operators.xom` file as part of the `operators` enumeration, which extends from the `base operators` enumeration, as illustrated in Listing 3-3.

Listing 3-3. Default operators

operators.xom
```
<enum name="base operators" abstract="true">
  <properties>[...]
  <item name="Is Null" value="NL">[...]
  <item name="Is Not Null" value="NNL">[...]
</enum>
<enum name="operators" base="base operators">
  <item name="Is Equal To" value="EQ">[...]
  <item name="Is Not Equal To" value="NEQ">[...]
  <item name="Is One Of" value="In">[...]
  <item name="Is None Of" value="NIn">[...]
  ...
</enum>
```

The base operators enumeration defines some properties that you can specify for each operator, such as the number of additional values that the operator requires or the types of criteria fields that it applies to. This allows Xomega Framework to display only the appropriate operators for each field and then, if required, display one or two additional fields to collect the criteria values, when you select a specific operator.

You can also customize this default operators enumeration as needed to add or remove operators, or to change their names.

> **Note** For all the items in static enumerations, Xomega generates resource files, which are used to display the localized names of these items on the UI. So, if you need to show the operator names in a different language, you can just provide the translations for those resource files.

Configure Default Operator

While selecting an operator provides you with great flexibility when specifying filter criteria by any field, having to select an operator every time can be a bit cumbersome and slow.

For some criteria fields, you may want to pick an operator that is used most often and set it up as the default operator for that field. This way, that operator will be pre-populated when the user selects the field, so they don't have to manually select it every time.

For example, for many text fields, it makes sense to use the *Contains* operator (see Listing 3-4) as the default, so that you could search for any substring in the text.

Listing 3-4. Contains operator

operators.xom
```
<enum name="operators" base="base operators">
  ...
  <item name="Contains" value="CN">[...]
  <item name="Does Not Contain" value="NCN">[...]
  <item name="Starts With" value="SW">[...]
  <item name="Does Not Start With" value="NSW">[...]
  ...
</enum>
```

Let's configure the operator *Contains* as the default operator for the *Job Title* employee criteria. In the Xomega model, you can do it on the `ui:field` element of the `EmployeeCriteria` data object definition, similar to how we were configuring the result fields for the `EmployeeList` data object earlier.

All you need to do is to set the value of that operator (CN) in the `op-default` attribute for the job title parameter, as shown in Listing 3-5.

Listing 3-5. Configuring a default operator

```
employee.xom
<xfk:data-object class="EmployeeCriteria">
  <ui:display>
    <ui:fields>
+     <ui:field param="job title" op-default="CN"/>
    </ui:fields>
  </ui:display>
</xfk:data-object>
```

CHAPTER 3   CONFIGURING SEARCH CRITERIA

If you build the Model project and then run the application, you will notice that the *Contains* operator is pre-selected when you select the *Job Title* criteria field (see Figure 3-2).

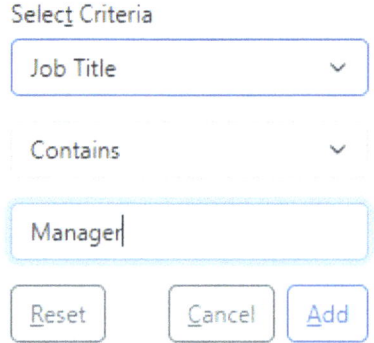

Figure 3-2. Default operator Contains

Remove Criteria Operators

Some fields are simple enough, so that they don't need any criteria operator. For example, if the gender field contains only two values, and it's required on the employee object, which means that the *Is Null* operator is not applicable, then you can remove the operator selection for that field altogether by setting the op-none="true" attribute on that parameter, as shown in Listing 3-6.

Listing 3-6. Removing criteria operator

```
employee.xom
<xfk:data-object class="EmployeeCriteria">
  <ui:display>
    <ui:fields>
      <ui:field param="job title" op-default="CN"/>
+     <ui:field param="gender" op-none="true"/>
    </ui:fields>
  </ui:display>
</xfk:data-object>
```

111

CHAPTER 3   CONFIGURING SEARCH CRITERIA

If you build the model and run the application, you will see that, after selecting the *Gender* criteria, you get to select the value directly, without any operator, as shown in Figure 3-3. The selected and applied criteria for *Gender* will also be displayed without any operator.

Figure 3-3. *Criteria without operator*

Under the hood, criteria fields with no operator will use either *Is Equal To* or *Is One Of* operators by default, depending on whether or not the criteria field is multi-valued. However, you can still change that by setting a different default operator in the `op-default` attribute, as needed.

There is also an easy way to remove operators for all fields at once on your criteria object. For that, you can just set the `op-none="true"` attribute on the `ui:fields` element, as shown in Listing 3-7.

Listing 3-7. Removing all criteria operators

employee.xom
```
<xfk:data-object class="EmployeeCriteria">
  <ui:display>
    <ui:fields op-none="true">
      <ui:field param="job title" op-default="CN"/>
    </ui:fields>
  </ui:display>
</xfk:data-object>
```

Note If you want to remove operators for all criteria fields but one, you can also set the op-none="true" attribute on the ui:fields element, and then override it with op-none="false" on the ui:field element for that field.

Custom Range Operators

If you remember from the previous chapters (see Figure 1-19), the default list of operators for date/time fields includes some predefined ranges, such as *Today*, *This Week*, *Last 30 Days*, etc.

These ranges are defined in the operators enumeration and use special format for the value, which can specify a relative or an absolute date range. For example, the *Last 30 Days* operator has a value [bod-30d,ct], which is interpreted as "from the beginning of the current day (bod) minus 30 days (30d) to the current time (ct), inclusive on both ends of the range ([,])", as illustrated in Listing 3-8.

Listing 3-8. Default range operators

operators.xom
```
<enum name="operators" base="base operators">
  ...
  <item name="Today" value="[bod,eod)">[...]
  <item name="This Week" value="[bow,eow)">[...]
  <item name="This Month" value="[boM,eoM)">[...]
  <item name="This Year" value="[boy,eoy)">[...]
  <item name="Last 30 Days" value="[bod-30d,ct]">[...]
  ...
</enum>
```

While these operators can be useful for searching date/time fields that contain relatively current time, such as the *Modified Date*, they may not be as useful for other date fields, such as employee's *Birth Date*. Let's see how we can define a custom set of operators for the *Birth Date* field, which would allow filtering by specific generations.

For that, we will define a new enumeration generation operator in the employee.xom file, which extends from the base operators enumeration and lists different generations with their respective birth date ranges as values, as shown in Listing 3-9.

To still provide flexibility for filtering by a custom date range, we will also add the standard *Is Between* operator, for which we also need to set the value of the property addl props to 2, to indicate that it requires two additional values.

Listing 3-9. Custom range operators

employee.xom
```
<enum name="generation operator" base="base operators">
  <item name="Baby Boomers" value="[1946-01-01,1965-01-01)"/>
  <item name="Generation X" value="[1965-01-01,1981-01-01)"/>
  <item name="Millennials" value="[1981-01-01,1997-01-01)"/>
  <item name="Generation Z" value="[1997-01-01,2013-01-01)"/>
  <item name="Generation Alpha" value="[2010-01-01,ct]"/>
  <item name="Is Between" value="BW">
    <prop ref="addl props" value="2"/>
  </item>
</enum>
```

Next, we need to add a new type generation operator that extends from the operator type and references the generation operator enumeration, as shown in Listing 3-10.

Listing 3-10. Custom operator type

```
<types>
  <type name="employee" base="person"/>
  <type name="gender" base="enumeration" size="1">[...]
  <type name="marital status" base="enumeration"
        size="1">[...]
+ <type name="generation operator" base="operator">
+   <enum ref="generation operator"/>
+ </type>
</types>
```

Finally, we need to add the birth date field to the EmployeeCriteria data object and set the op-type attribute to generation operator, as shown in Listing 3-11.

CHAPTER 3 CONFIGURING SEARCH CRITERIA

Listing 3-11. Using a custom operator type

```
<xfk:data-object class="EmployeeCriteria">
  <ui:display>
    <ui:fields>
      <ui:field param="job title" op-default="CN"/>
      <ui:field param="gender" op-none="true"/>
+     <ui:field param="birth date"
+               op-type="generation operator"/>
    </ui:fields>
  </ui:display>
</xfk:data-object>
```

If you build the model and run the application, you will see that the list of operators for the *Birth Date* criteria field allows you to pick a specific generation or select a custom range using the *Is Between* operator, as shown in Figure 3-4.

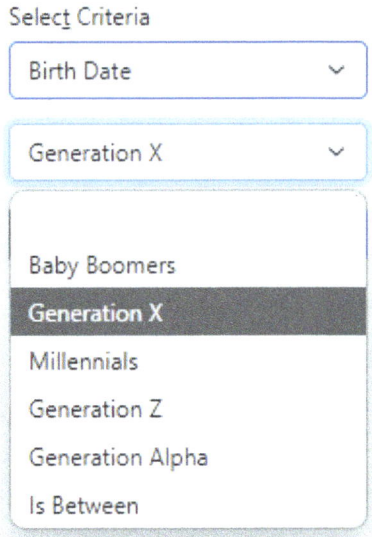

Figure 3-4. *Custom operator selection*

Figure 3-5 illustrates how the Employee List view looks like when filtered for the Generation X employees.

115

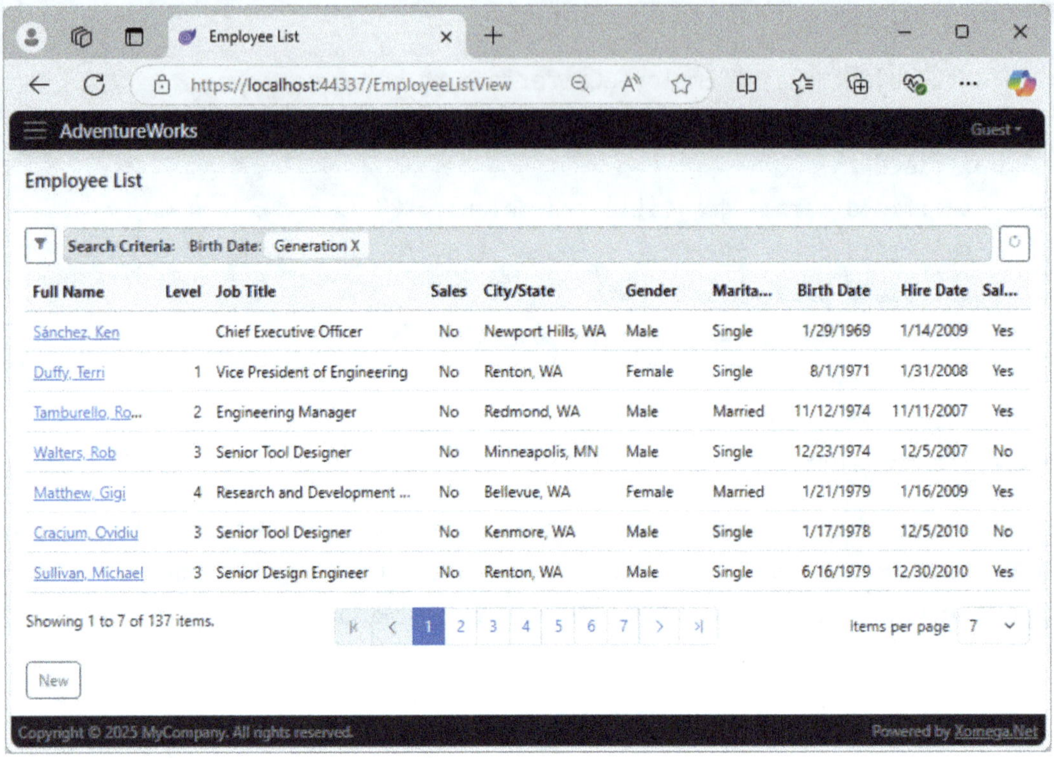

CHAPTER 3   CONFIGURING SEARCH CRITERIA

Figure 3-5. Custom operator display

As you can see, we were able to implement custom filtering for the *Birth Date* field with no extra coding whatsoever.

Custom Operator Logic

Now let's consider a more advanced example, where you can implement operators with custom logic.

If you look at Figure 3-5 above, you will notice that the organization level is populated in the sample AdventureWorks database for all but one employee, the Chief Executive Officer. Presumably, the CEO is at the top of the organization hierarchy, which means that the `null` value has a higher ranking than any other value in that column.

However, if you set the *Organization Level* criteria to *Is Less Than* 2, for instance, you will see employees with level 1, but not the CEO in the result list, since comparing NULL to any value in the database always returns `false`. The only operator that will allow returning the CEO in the result list is the *Is Null* operator, but it's not that useful, as it will always return a single record.

Adding a Custom Operator

Given that the smaller number in that column indicates a higher organization level, let's define a custom set of operators for the *Organization Level*, which will consist of the following operators: *Above*, *Below*, *Equal*, and *Between*.

The *Above* operator will return all employees with a level less than the specified value, **including the null** value, so we'll use a special value LT_NL for it. The *Below* operator will act as the *Is Greater Than* operator with the value GT, while the *Equal* and *Between* operators will use the standard values EQ and BW, respectively.

So, let's define a custom enum org level operator, which extends from the base operators enumeration, and add these custom operators with their respective values. Also, given that the *Is Null* and *Is Not Null* operators from the base operators enum are basically useless, we'll want to remove them by including these items with the overrideAction="delete" attribute, as shown in Listing 3-12.

Listing 3-12. Enum with a custom operator

employee.xom
```xml
<enum name="org level operator" base="base operators">
  <item name="Is Null" value="NL" overrideAction="delete"/>
  <item name="Is Not Null" value="NNL"
        overrideAction="delete"/>
  <item name="Above" value="LT_NL">
    <prop ref="addl props" value="1"/>
  </item>
  <item name="Below" value="GT">
    <prop ref="addl props" value="1"/>
  </item>
  <item name="Equal" value="EQ">
    <prop ref="addl props" value="1"/>
  </item>
  <item name="Between" value="BW">
    <prop ref="addl props" value="2"/>
  </item>
</enum>
```

CHAPTER 3 CONFIGURING SEARCH CRITERIA

Next, we need to add a new type org level operator that extends from the operator type and references the org level operator enumeration, as shown in Listing 3-13.

Listing 3-13. Org level operator type

```
<type name="org level operator" base="operator">
  <enum ref="org level operator"/>
</type>
```

Finally, we'll set the new org level operator type for the organization level field in the EmployeeCriteria data object, as well as a custom label *Org Level* to shorten the field name, as shown in Listing 3-14.

Listing 3-14. Configuring org level operator and label

```
<xfk:data-object class="EmployeeCriteria">
  <ui:display>
    <ui:fields>
      <ui:field param="job title" op-default="CN"/>
      <ui:field param="gender" op-none="true"/>
      <ui:field param="birth date"
                op-type="generation operator"/>
+     <ui:field param="organization level" label="Org Level"
+               op-type="org level operator"/>
    </ui:fields>
  </ui:display>
</xfk:data-object>
```

After you build the model and run the application, you will see these custom operators for the *Org Level* criteria field, as shown in Figure 3-6.

CHAPTER 3   CONFIGURING SEARCH CRITERIA

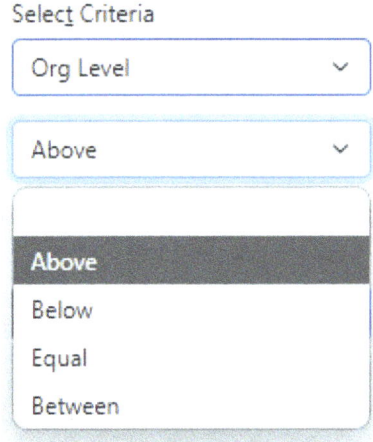

Figure 3-6. Operators with custom logic

However, if you select the *Above* operator and run the search, you'll see an error, saying that the LT_NL operator is not supported, as shown in Figure 3-7, since it's not one of the standard operators that Xomega Framework provides out of the box.

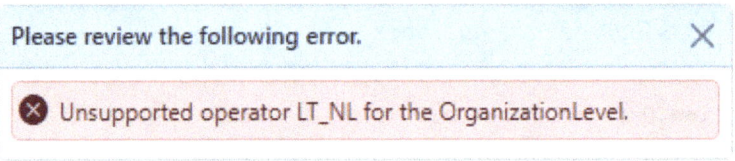

Figure 3-7. Unsupported operator error

Luckily, implementing such an operator is very simple in Xomega Framework, as you will see in a moment.

Implement Operator Logic

To implement operator's logic, let's add a new class LessThanOrNullOperator to the AdventureWorks.Services.Entities project, which extends from the existing LessThanOperator class.

In the new class, we'll override the GetNames method to return our custom operator's name LT_NL, and the BuildExpression method to return an expression that combines LessThan and Is Null expressions using the Or operator, as shown in Listing 3-15.

Listing 3-15. Custom operator implementation

LessThanOrNullOperator.cs

```csharp
using System;
using System.Linq.Expressions;
using Xomega.Framework.Operators;

namespace AdventureWorks.Services.Entities;

public class LessThanOrNullOperator : LessThanOperator
{
    public override string[] GetNames() => ["LT_NL"];

    protected override Expression
      BuildExpression<TElement, TValue>(
          Expression<Func<TElement, TValue>> prop,
          params Expression<Func<TValue>>[] vals
    ) => prop.Body.Type.IsValueType &&
          Nullable.GetUnderlyingType(prop.Body.Type) == null ?
      // use LessThan if non-nullable
      base.BuildExpression(prop, vals) :
      Expression.Or(
        Expression.LessThan(prop.Body, vals[0].Body),
        Expression.Equal(prop.Body, Expression.Constant(null))
      );

    protected override bool Match(
      object value, params object[] criteria)
        => criteria[0] == null || base.Match(value, criteria);
}
```

Note We also override the `Match` method to return `true` if the value is `null` or less than the specified value. This method is needed when the operator is used for in-memory filtering, rather than for building a LINQ expression.

Finally, we need to register the custom operator in the `OperatorRegistry` service in the main `Program` file for the Blazor app, as shown in Listing 3-16.

CHAPTER 3   CONFIGURING SEARCH CRITERIA

Listing 3-16. Registering the custom operator

Program.cs

```
...
  var app = builder.Build();

+ app.Services.GetRequiredService<OperatorRegistry>()
              .Register(new LessThanOrNullOperator());
...
```

After you run the application and select the *Above* 2 criteria for the *Org Level* field, you will see the CEO in the result list, in addition to all employees of level 1, as shown in Figure 3-8.

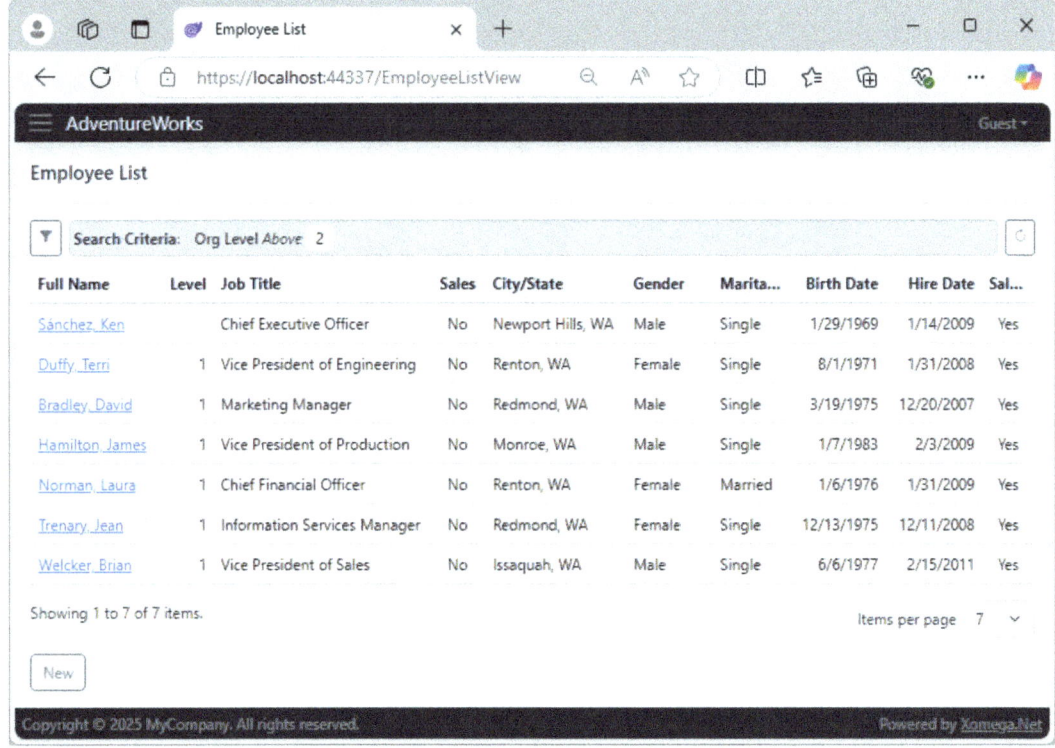

Figure 3-8. *Applying operators with custom logic*

Multi-value Criteria

By default, the search criteria allow you to select only one single value, or two if you specify a range for the *Is Between* operators. Oftentimes though, you need to be able to select multiple values to filter by, which would use the IN operator for the SQL query.

Luckily, the Xomega model makes turning a single-value criteria into multi-value extremely easy. All you need to do is to set the `list="true"` attribute on the criteria input parameter. Since we added some extra values to the `marital status` enumeration, let's turn it into multi-value criteria, as shown in Listing 3-17.

Listing 3-17. Configuring multi-value criteria

```
<operation name="read list" type="readlist">
  <input>
    <struct name="criteria">
      <param name="full name" type="string"/>
      <param name="national id number"/>
      <param name="login id"/>
      <param name="organization level"/>
      <param name="job title"/>
      <param name="birth date"/>
      <param name="marital status" list="true"/>
      <param name="gender"/>
      <param name="hire date"/>
      <param name="salaried flag" type="yesno"/>
      <param name="current flag" type="yesno"/>
      <param name="modified date"/>
      <config>[...]
    </struct>
  </input>
  <output list="true">[...]
</operation>
```

You don't have to write any custom code for it, just build the model to regenerate the code. If you run the application, you will see that the *Marital Status* criteria field has a different set of operators now: *Is One Of* and the inverse *Is None Of*. The value selection control will be a multi-select list now, instead of a drop-down list, as shown in Figure 3-9.

CHAPTER 3   CONFIGURING SEARCH CRITERIA

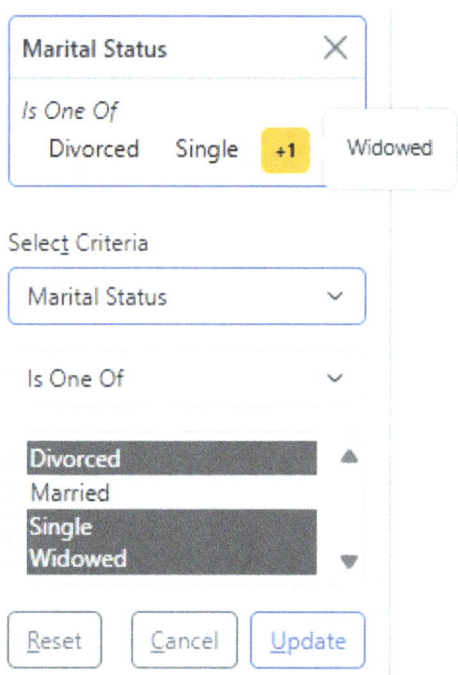

Figure 3-9. Multi-select criteria

If you select multiple values, the selected criteria will show you the first two values, plus the number of additional values selected, which you can also view by clicking on that number, as shown in Figure 3-9 above. This should be still useful in most cases without bloating the criteria display panel.

Configure Multi-value Control

Given that the `marital status` contains only four values, we can do a couple of things to improve the user experience for selecting values. First, it doesn't make sense to have the operator field for them, since all it offers is the additional *Is None Of* operator, which you don't need for such a small list of values.

Therefore, let's go ahead and set the `op-none="true"` attribute on the `marital status` field to remove the operator, as shown in Listing 3-18.

123

Listing 3-18. Removing operator on multi-value criteria

```
<xfk:data-object class="EmployeeCriteria">
  <ui:display>
    <ui:fields>
      <ui:field param="job title" op-default="CN"/>
      <ui:field param="gender" op-none="true"/>
+     <ui:field param="marital status" op-none="true"/>
      <ui:field param="birth date"
                op-type="generation operator"/>
      <ui:field param="organization level" label="Org Level"
                op-type="org level operator"/>
    </ui:fields>
  </ui:display>
</xfk:data-object>
```

Next, for a list of four values, it may be better to use a set of check box items, instead of the default multi-select list box. To configure a custom Blazor control for editing fields of a specific type, you need to just add it under the `config` element of the corresponding logical type in the model.

In our case, we want to use the `XOptions` Blazor control for selecting multiple marital statuses. So let's add it under the `ui:blazor-control` config element with the attribute `multi-value="true"`, as shown in Listing 3-19.

Listing 3-19. Configuring control for multi-value criteria

```
  <type name="marital status" base="enumeration" size="1">
+   <config>
+     <ui:blazor-control multi-value="true">
+       <XOptions />
+     </ui:blazor-control>
+   </config>
    <enum ref="marital status"/>
  </type>
```

CHAPTER 3 CONFIGURING SEARCH CRITERIA

Note As you might have guessed, that's how you can configure a custom control for editing any field, and not just the criteria. To specify a control for editing single-value fields, you just need to add another `ui:blazor-control` without the `multi-value` attribute.

Once you build the model and run the application, you will see that the *Marital Status* criteria field no longer has an operator and presents a set of checkbox values, instead of the multi-select list box, as shown in Figure 3-10.

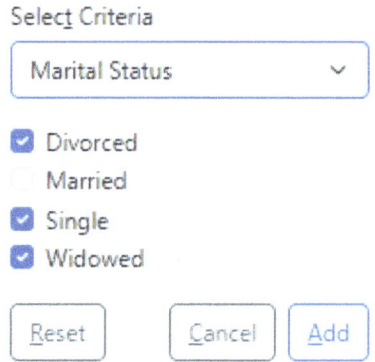

Figure 3-10. *Checkbox options criteria*

If you run the search, you'll see that the summary of the applied criteria also shows no operator, and just the first two selected marital statuses, while the rest of them can be viewed by clicking on the number of the additional values next to it, as shown in Figure 3-11.

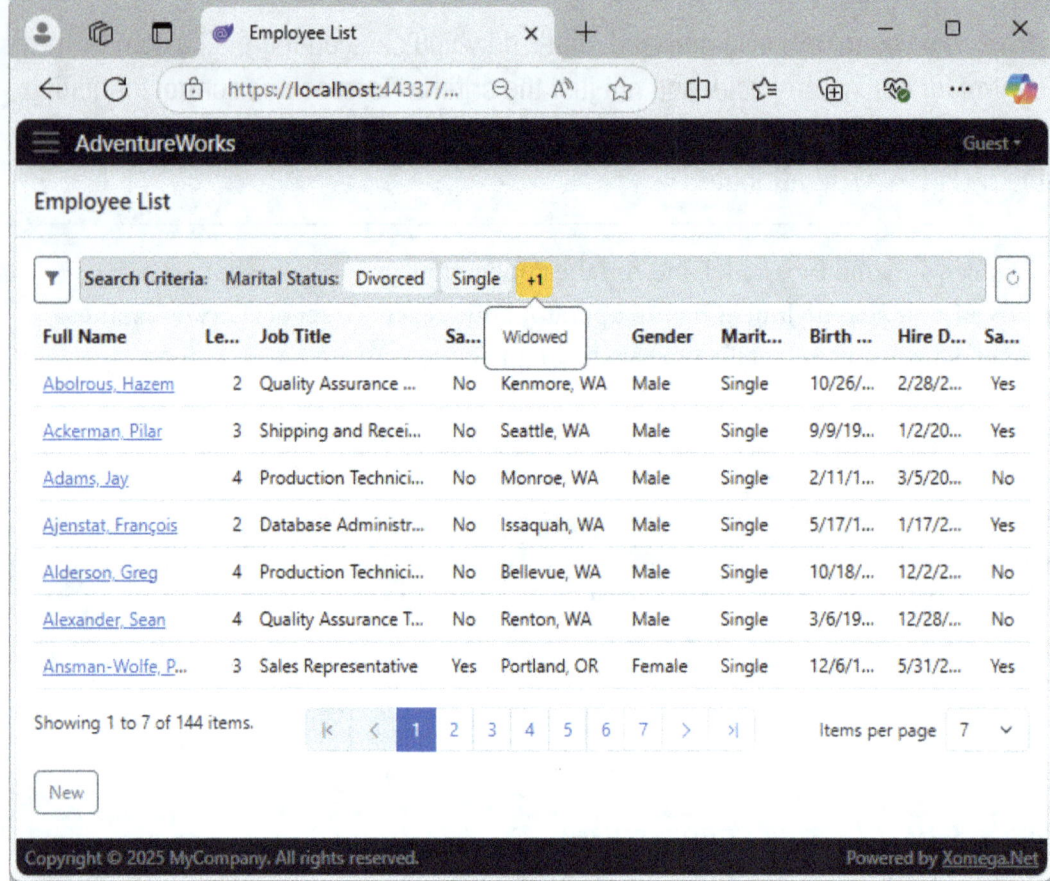

Figure 3-11. Applied multi-value criteria

Dynamic Enumeration

In the previous chapter, you learned how to define static enumerations in the Xomega model and how to use them to select values in the UI and to display user-friendly names instead of internal codes. However, this only covers the case where this list can be defined statically in the model and does not change from one release of the application to another.

In another common use case, the list of possible values is stored in the database and may change occasionally. If this data is changed infrequently and is not too large, then we can read it as a dynamic enumeration, cache on the UI layer, and then use it for value selection and for decoding internal values on the UI, just like a static enumeration.

An example of such data could be a list of states or countries that are stored in the database, since those lists are relatively small and don't change often. Even the very list of employees that we are building here can be used as a dynamic enumeration to allow selecting an employee on other screens.

Configure Dynamic Enumeration

To learn how to define and work with dynamic enumerations in Xomega, we are going to add a criteria field to our Employee List, which allows you to filter employees by one or more of their states or provinces.

First, we need to define an operation to read a list of states from the database and cache it in the UI. Xomega makes it quite easy by providing a Model Enhancement generator, like the one that we use to generate the CRUD operations.

All you need to do is to navigate to the `state_province.xom` model file under the `Person` module, right-click it, and select the context menu to generate the *Read Enum Operation*, as shown in Figure 3-12.

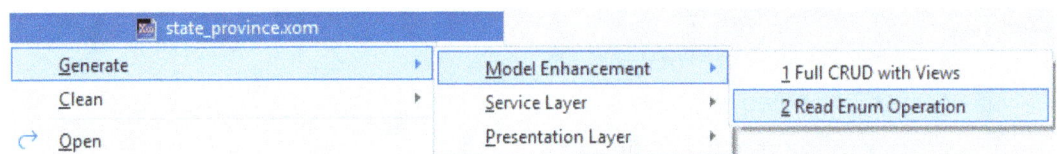

Figure 3-12. *Generating Read Enum operation*

This will add a `read enum` operation to the `state province` object, which returns all fields of this object by default. It also adds a special configuration `xfk:enum-cache` to that operation, which configures the dynamic enumeration name, as well as which output parameter returns an internal ID and which one returns a user-friendly description for the states.

Just like static enumerations, dynamic enumerations are cached on the client side, so that they can be used in the UI without having to read them from the server every time. This caching is intended for data that is not too large, and does not change often, so there is no automatic invalidation of the cache. However, you can always manually clear the cache for any specific enumeration whenever its data is changed in the database.

CHAPTER 3 CONFIGURING SEARCH CRITERIA

Let's go ahead and delete any output parameters that we don't need. In our case, we will keep the state province id as the internal ID, the name as the user-friendly description, as well as the state province code and country region code, which will be stored as additional attributes, as illustrated in Listing 3-20.

Listing 3-20. Configuring read enum operation

state_province.xom
```
<object name="state province">
  <fields>[...]
  <operations>
    <operation name="read enum">
      <output list="true">
        <param name="state province id"/>
        <param name="state province code"/>
        <param name="country region code"/>
-       <param name="is only state province flag"/>
        <param name="name"/>
-       <param name="territory id"/>
-       <param name="rowguid"/>
-       <param name="modified date"/>
      </output>
      <config>
        <rest:method verb="GET"
                     uri-template="state-province/enum"/>
        <xfk:enum-cache enum-name="state province"
                        id-param="state province id"
                        desc-param="name"/>
      </config>
      <doc>[...]
    </operation>
  </operations>
</object>
```

128

In addition to adding and configuring the read enum operation, you will notice that the generator has updated the key state province type to make it extend from the integer enumeration base type and reference the new state province dynamic enumeration that was configured in the xfk:enum-cache element, as illustrated in Listing 3-21.

Listing 3-21. Enum type changes

```
<type name="state province" base="integer enumeration">
  <enum ref="state province"/>
</type>
```

Note This will automatically configure this enumeration for any parameter that uses this logical type.

Custom Criteria Implementation

To add employee criteria by state, let's go back to the employee object and add the state parameter with state province type to the criteria input structure, as shown in Listing 3-22.

Listing 3-22. Adding state criteria

employee.xom
```
<operation name="read list" type="readlist">
  <input>
    <struct name="criteria">
+     <param name="state" type="state province"/>
      <param name="full name" type="string"/>
      ...
    </struct>
  </input>
  <output list="true">[...]
</operation>
```

CHAPTER 3 CONFIGURING SEARCH CRITERIA

Once you build the model and regenerate all the code, you will see that the `ReadListAsync` method in the generated `EmployeeService` has a *TODO* comment for you to add custom code to implement these criteria. You can go ahead and implement it by calling the `AddCriteriaClause` method and passing it an expression to get the `StateProvinceId` of the employee, as shown in Listing 3-23.

Listing 3-23. Custom logic for the state criteria

EmployeeService.cs
```
public virtual async
  Task<Output<ICollection<Employee_ReadListOutput>>>
  ReadListAsync(
    Employee_ReadListInput_Criteria _criteria,
    CancellationToken token = default)
{
   ...
   var src = from obj in ctx.Employee select obj;

   // Source filter
   if (_criteria != null)
   {
      // CUSTOM_CODE_START: add code for State criteria of ReadList
         operation below
+     src = AddCriteriaClause(src, "State",
+        o => o.BusinessEntityObject.BusinessEntityObject
+           .AddressObjectList.First()
+           .AddressObject.StateProvinceId,
+        _criteria.State);
      // CUSTOM_CODE_END
      ...
```

If you run the application now and try to add criteria by *State* on the Employee List screen, you will see that it offers you a selection from a drop-down list that displays user-friendly state names, as shown in Figure 3-13.

CHAPTER 3　CONFIGURING SEARCH CRITERIA

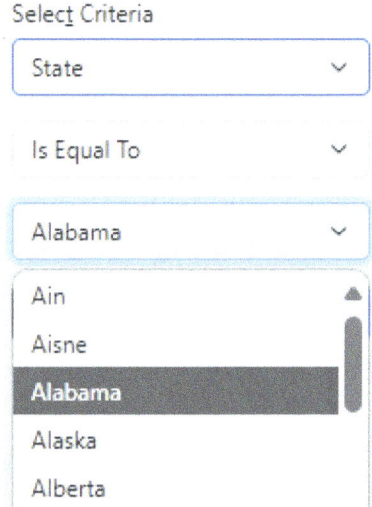

Figure 3-13. *Dynamic enumeration selection*

If you remember, we were going to make the *State* criteria multi-value to allow filtering employees by one or more states. However, the number of available states to select from is large enough to make selection from a list box quite cumbersome. A checkbox list that we used before would not work well here either.

The best user experience for selecting multiple states could be by using a text box with an auto-complete, where the user can start typing the text and then select the value from the list of matching states. So, let's implement it and see how it looks like.

Auto-complete for Multi-value

If you recall from the previous section, turning *State* into multi-value criteria is as simple as adding the `list="true"` attribute, as shown in Listing 3-24.

Listing 3-24. Making state criteria multi-value

employee.xom
```
<operation name="read list" type="readlist">
  <input>
    <struct name="criteria">
      <param name="state" type="state province" list="true"/>
      <param name="full name" type="string"/>
      ...
```

```
    </struct>
  </input>
  <output list="true">[...]
</operation>
```

To configure the auto-complete control for the *State* criteria field, we just need to add the appropriate ui:blazor-control config with the XAutoComplete control to the underlying state province type, as shown in Listing 3-25.

Listing 3-25. Configuring auto-complete control

state_province.xom
```
 <type name="state province" base="integer enumeration">
+  <config>
+    <ui:blazor-control multi-value="true">
+      <XAutoComplete/>
+    </ui:blazor-control>
+  </config>
   <enum ref="state province"/>
 </type>
```

To review the results, you just need to build the model to regenerate the code and run the application. If you add this *State* criteria now, you will see that it offers you a text box to enter comma-separated list of states, allowing you to enter a partial state name and select the state from a matching list, as illustrated in Figure 3-14.

CHAPTER 3 CONFIGURING SEARCH CRITERIA

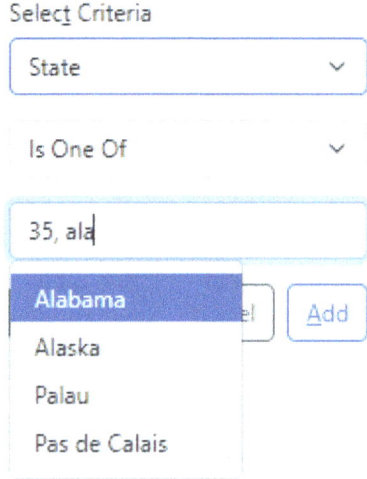

Figure 3-14. *Auto-complete for enumeration*

One problem with this implementation is that selected states are displayed using their internal IDs in the text box, as you can see from the picture above. Before we address it though, let's learn another technique on how to display search criteria statically.

Statically Displayed Criteria

For the demo purposes, let's pretend that the users always work with employees within certain geographical regions and therefore must specify a list of states in almost every search.

To make it easier for them and to save them from having to select the *State* field and then add it to the criteria, we may want to always display the *State* criteria field right on the Search Criteria panel. For even more simplicity, we also want to get rid of the operator selection, which we've done before.

To do both things, you need to configure the `state` criteria field on the `EmployeeCriteria` data object with the `static="true"` and `op-none="true"` attributes, respectively, as demonstrated in Listing 3-26.

133

Listing 3-26. Configuring static display for criteria

```
<xfk:data-object class="EmployeeCriteria">
  <ui:display>
    <ui:fields>
      <ui:field param="state" op-none="true" static="true"/>
      <ui:field param="job title" op-default="CN"/>
      <ui:field param="gender" op-none="true"/>
      <ui:field param="marital status" op-none="true"/>
      <ui:field param="birth date"
                op-type="generation operator"/>
      <ui:field param="organization level" label="Org Level"
                op-type="org level operator"/>
    </ui:fields>
  </ui:display>
</xfk:data-object>
```

If you build the model and run the application now, you'll see that the *State* criteria with an auto-complete field is always visible at the top of the Search Criteria panel, without any operator selection, as shown in Figure 3-15.

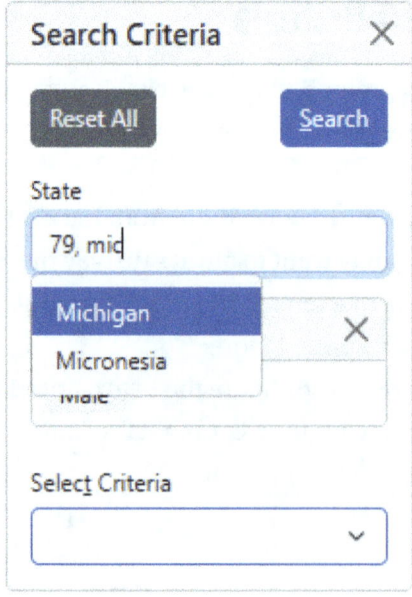

Figure 3-15. *Static display of criteria*

> **Note** If your list view contains only a few criteria and you would like to display them all statically, then you can also set the `static="true"` attribute on the parent `ui:fields` element. You can then further override it for any specific criteria field by setting the `static="false"` attribute to display it dynamically.

Customizing Criteria Object

The `XAutoComplete` Blazor control in Xomega Framework allows you to use different formats for values displayed in the drop-down list versus the values displayed in the text box field. Typically, you can use a longer, user-friendly name for values in the drop-down list to help the users clearly see what they are selecting.

Of course, you can use the same display format for the selected values in the text field, but this may not work well when you select multiple values, as they may not all fit into the small text field. Therefore, it may be useful to display selected values using a shorter format that would be enough to identify each value, such as an internal code.

As I pointed out earlier, when you select one of the matching states from the list in the auto-complete box, it inserts the internal `state providence id` into the text box, but this is not quite what the users would like to see, since they don't know the internal state IDs.

Instead, it would make more sense to display short state codes, such as NJ or NY, which we return in the `state province code` output parameter when reading the `state province` enumeration.

While Xomega model does not specifically provide any configuration elements for this, you can code this behavior in a customized class for the generated `EmployeeCriteria` data object. To have Xomega generate such a customized class for you, you can set the `customize="true"` attribute on the `EmployeeCriteria` object, as shown in Listing 3-27.

Listing 3-27. Customizing data objects

```
<xfk:data-object class="EmployeeCriteria"
                 customize="true">[...]
```

After building the model, nested under the generated `EmployeeCriteria.cs` in the `AdventureWorks.Client.Common` project, you'll find a new file added with the name `EmployeeCriteriaCustomized.cs`, as shown in Figure 3-16.

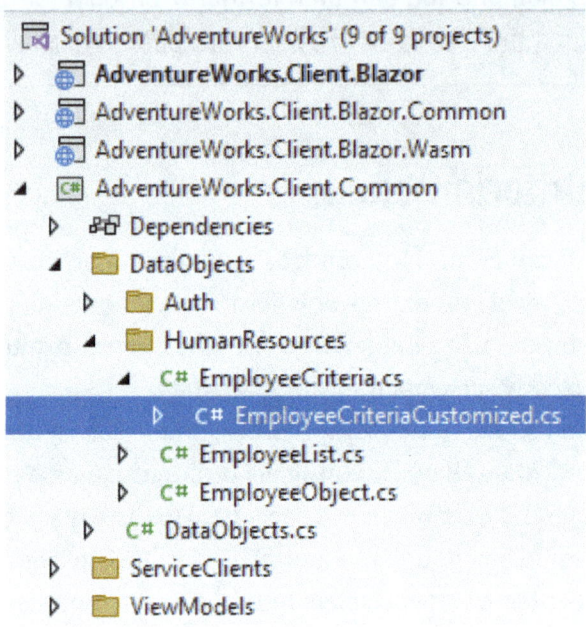

Figure 3-16. *Customized data object*

If you open this file, you will see that it defines a subclass of the generated `EmployeeCriteria` object, where you can override certain methods to add your custom code.

Note The `EmployeeCriteriaCustomized.cs` file is generated only once, if it does not exist, so you can safely add your custom code to it without worrying that it will be overwritten when you regenerate your data objects.

In our case, we want to add custom code to the overridden `OnInitialized` method, where we take the `State` property as an `EnumProperty`, and set its `KeyFormat` such that it takes the value from the `state province code` attribute of the value, as shown in Listing 3-28.

Listing 3-28. Configuring key format on enum properties

EmployeeCriteriaCustomized.cs
```
using AdventureWorks.Services.Common.Enumerations;
using System;
using Xomega.Framework;
using Xomega.Framework.Properties;

namespace AdventureWorks.Client.Common.DataObjects;

public class EmployeeCriteriaCustomized : EmployeeCriteria
{
    ...
    // perform post initialization
    protected override void OnInitialized()
    {
        base.OnInitialized();
        // add custom initialization code here
+       var stateProp = this[State] as EnumProperty;
+       if (stateProp == null) return; // shouldn't happen
+       stateProp.KeyFormat = string.Format(
+           Header.AttrPattern,
+           StateProvince.Attributes.StateProvinceCode);
    }
}
```

Note To avoid hardcoding the name of the additional attribute, we use the constant StateProvince.Attributes.StateProvinceCode, which was also generated for us by Xomega.

If you run the application now, you will see that the auto-complete field for the *State* criteria displays the state code after the selection, rather than the internal state ID, as shown in Figure 3-17.

CHAPTER 3   CONFIGURING SEARCH CRITERIA

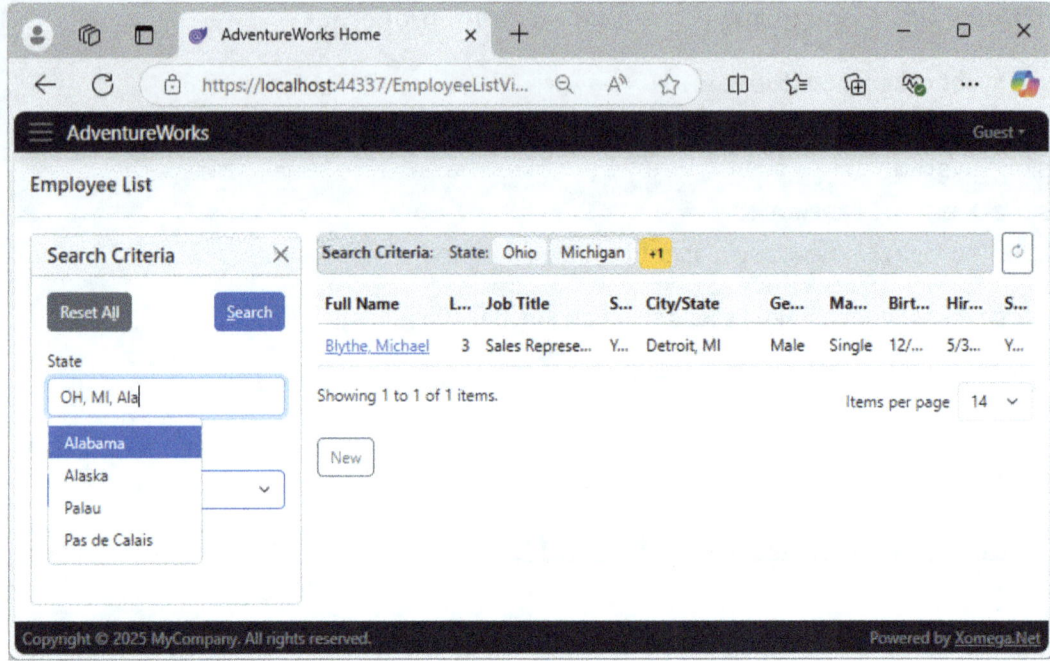

Figure 3-17. Custom edit key format

Note   The summary of applied criteria above the results grid still uses the display format for the value, showing the full state names. The extra space it takes is less of a problem, since it only shows the first two of the selected values.

You just saw how easy it is to add a statically displayed criteria field that allows multiple selection based on a dynamic enumeration, using custom UI logic to configure the value display. We will use all these techniques in the next section, where you will also learn how to set up a cascading selection.

Cascading Selection

If you were paying close attention when reading the previous section, you might have noticed that the *State* selection in our auto-complete field shows matching states from various countries (see, e.g., Figure 3-17).

CHAPTER 3   CONFIGURING SEARCH CRITERIA

Imagine that in addition to filtering employees by their states, the users also want to be able to see employees from a specific country or region. For that, we would add another employee criteria field *Country*, with value selection from a dynamic enumeration based on the country region object.

If the users select a specific country though and then want to further filter by certain states, then, while entering the states, they'd expect the auto-complete field to only show states for the selected country.

The case where a list of values in one field depends on the value of another field is called **cascading selection**, so let's see how to implement it with Xomega by adding the *Country* criteria that we discussed.

Country Dynamic Enumeration

We will start by adding dynamic enumeration for the `country region` object. Just like we did before with the `state province` object, let's right-click the `country_region.xom` file and select *Generate* ▶ *Model Enhancement* ▶ *Read Enum Operation* context menu.

The generator will add a `read enum` operation configured with `xfk:enum-cache` element and the `country region` type converted to an enumeration. All you need to do there is to remove the extraneous output parameter `modified date`, as shown in Listing 3-29.

Listing 3-29. Adding country dynamic enumeration

```
country_region.xom
<types>
  <type name="country region" base="enumeration" size="3">
    <config>[...]
    <enum ref="country region"/>
  </type>
</types>
<objects>
  <object name="country region">
    <fields>[...]
    <operations>
      <operation name="read enum">
        <output list="true">
```

139

```
          <param name="country region code"/>
          <param name="name"/>
-         <param name="modified date"/>
        </output>
        <config>
          <rest:method verb="GET"
                       uri-template="country-region/enum"/>
          <xfk:enum-cache enum-name="country region"
                          id-param="country region code"
                          desc-param="name"/>
        </config>
      </operation>
    </operations>
  </object>
</objects>
```

Adding Country Criteria

Next, we will add the country criteria with type country region to the read list operation on the employee object, as shown in Listing 3-30.

Listing 3-30. Adding employee country criteria

employee.xom
```
<operation name="read list" type="readlist">
  <input>
    <struct name="criteria">
+     <param name="country" type="country region"/>
      <param name="state" type="state province" list="true"/>
      ...
    </struct>
  </input>
  <output list="true">[...]
</operation>
```

We want the country criteria to be displayed before the state, so we listed it first in the input criteria. We also need to make that field statically displayed and without an operator, as shown in Listing 3-31.

Listing 3-31. Making country criteria static

```
<xfk:data-object class="EmployeeCriteria">
  <ui:display>
    <ui:fields>
+     <ui:field param="country" op-none="true" static="true"/>
      <ui:field param="state" op-none="true" static="true"/>
      <ui:field param="job title" op-default="CN"/>
      ...
    </ui:fields>
  </ui:display>
</xfk:data-object>
```

Once you build the model and regenerate all the code, you can open the generated EmployeeService, and add custom code for the *Country* criteria, just like we've done it for the *State* criteria, as shown in Listing 3-32.

Listing 3-32. Implementing country criteria logic

EmployeeService.cs
```
public virtual async
  Task<Output<ICollection<Employee_ReadListOutput>>>
  ReadListAsync(
    Employee_ReadListInput_Criteria _criteria,
    CancellationToken token = default)
{
    ...
    var src = from obj in ctx.Employee select obj;

    // Source filter
    if (_criteria != null)
    {
        // CUSTOM_CODE_START: add code for Country criteria of ReadList
            operation below
```

CHAPTER 3 CONFIGURING SEARCH CRITERIA

```
+       src = AddCriteriaClause(src, "Country",
+           o => o.BusinessEntityObject.BusinessEntityObject
+               .AddressObjectList.First().AddressObject
+               .StateProvinceObject.CountryRegionCode,
+           _criteria.Country);
        // CUSTOM_CODE_END
        // CUSTOM_CODE_START: add code for State criteria of ReadList
            operation below
        src = AddCriteriaClause(src, "State",
            o => o.BusinessEntityObject.BusinessEntityObject
                .AddressObjectList.First().AddressObject
                .StateProvinceId,
            _criteria.State);
        // CUSTOM_CODE_END
        ...
```

Configuring Cascading Selection

Finally, let's go ahead and implement cascading selection, so that available values for the *State* in the employee search criteria could be filtered based on the selected country. We made this filtering possible by including the country region code output parameter in the read enum operation for the state province object (see Listing 3-33).

Listing 3-33. Country region code attribute

state_province.xom
```
<object name="state province">
    <operation name="read enum">
      <output list="true">
        <param name="state province id"/>
        <param name="state province code"/>
        <param name="country region code"/>
        <param name="name"/>
      </output>
    </operation>
</object>
```

Now, just open our customized data object EmployeeCriteriaCustomized and call the method SetCascadingProperty on the State property, passing it the name of that country region code attribute, as well as the Country property, whose value will be used for filtering, as shown in Listing 3-34.

Listing 3-34. Configuring cascading selection

EmployeeCriteriaCustomized.cs
```
public class EmployeeCriteriaCustomized : EmployeeCriteria
{
    ...
    // perform post initialization
    protected override void OnInitialized()
    {
        base.OnInitialized();
        // add custom initialization code here

        var stateProp = this[State] as EnumProperty;
        if (stateProp == null) return; // shouldn't happen
        stateProp.KeyFormat = string.Format(
            Header.AttrPattern,
            StateProvince.Attributes.StateProvinceCode);
+
+       stateProp.SetCascadingProperty(
+           StateProvince.Attributes.CountryRegionCode,
+           this[Country]);
    }
}
```

Note The AdventureWorks.Client.Common project that contains data objects does not have any dependency on any Blazor packages. So, any custom code that we are developing here is UI-agnostic and can be reused with other UI frameworks, such as WPF or MAUI.

If you run the application now, you will see that we have a country selection as the first field in the employee search criteria panel. If you select United States as the country and start entering states to select, you will see that the auto-complete field will offer only the US states, as shown in Figure 3-18.

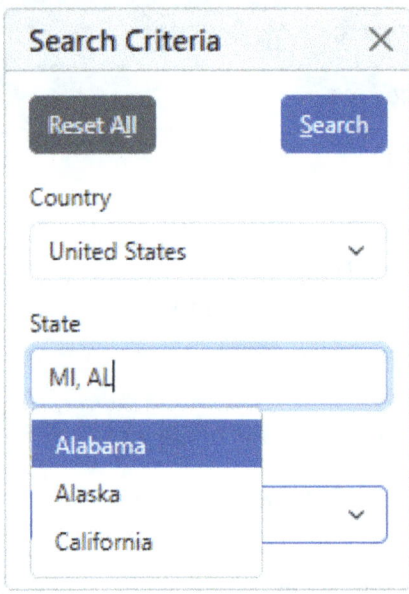

Figure 3-18. Cascading selection

This cascading selection would also work if we had the country as a multi-value field. In that case, the *State* selection would be limited to the states in any of the selected countries.

If you change the selected countries after having entered the states, then the framework will automatically remove any states that don't match the new country selection. In our case of the single selection for the country, it will effectively clear the *State* field when the selected country is changed.

If the `country region code` was not a required field on the `state province` object, you would also be able to configure how to handle `null` values during cascading selection. For example, no country selection can be treated such as to show either states from all countries or just states with no country assigned.

Summary

In this chapter, you have learned how to add or remove criteria to list views, implement custom code for the criteria that don't match any object field or result field, use multi-value criteria, and configure a custom set of operators, including ones, for which you can write custom filtering logic.

You also learned the concept of dynamic enumeration and how to define it in the Xomega model to supply a list of values for a field from a database table. You saw how to customize the generated Blazor control for editing or selecting a single value or multiple values of a certain logical type.

Finally, you saw how to further customize generated UI data objects in the code to configure certain behaviors, such as using a specific value format or setting up cascading selection.

In the next chapter, we will delve into the development of Details screens, where you will be able to use what you've learned so far, as well as get familiar with additional concepts that are specific to this type of screen.

CHAPTER 4

Building Out a Details View

In the first chapter of this book, we created the initial application and generated default Search and Details views for the Employee entity. In subsequent chapters, we built out the Employee List view to display the columns we needed and to use flexible search criteria. In the process, we enriched the model with subobjects, enums, and new logical types, but we haven't done anything for the Details view yet.

In this chapter, we will turn the default Details view for all the Employee fields into a complex, full-fledged Employee Details view with child lists, custom fields from related entities, as well as UI-only computed fields. You will learn how to create or edit related entities in a separate Details view, as well as how to build and use a Lookup View for selecting an existing entity.

In addition to adding new fields and functionality, you will also learn how to configure the layout for the Details view by grouping fields into tabs and panels, as well as how to convert the Details view into a master-detail layout when opening it from the List view.

Displaying Child Lists

In this section, we will review the current Employee Details view that was generated by default, make some basic updates to the CRUD operations, and then add two child lists: *Pay History* and *Department History* by making them subobjects of the employee object.

CHAPTER 4   BUILDING OUT A DETAILS VIEW

Removing Fields and Actions

Let's open the details view for an employee record from our list view. It should look almost exactly like when we reviewed the initially generated screen in the first chapter, displaying all employee fields using appropriate controls, laid out neatly in four columns, as shown in Figure 4-1.

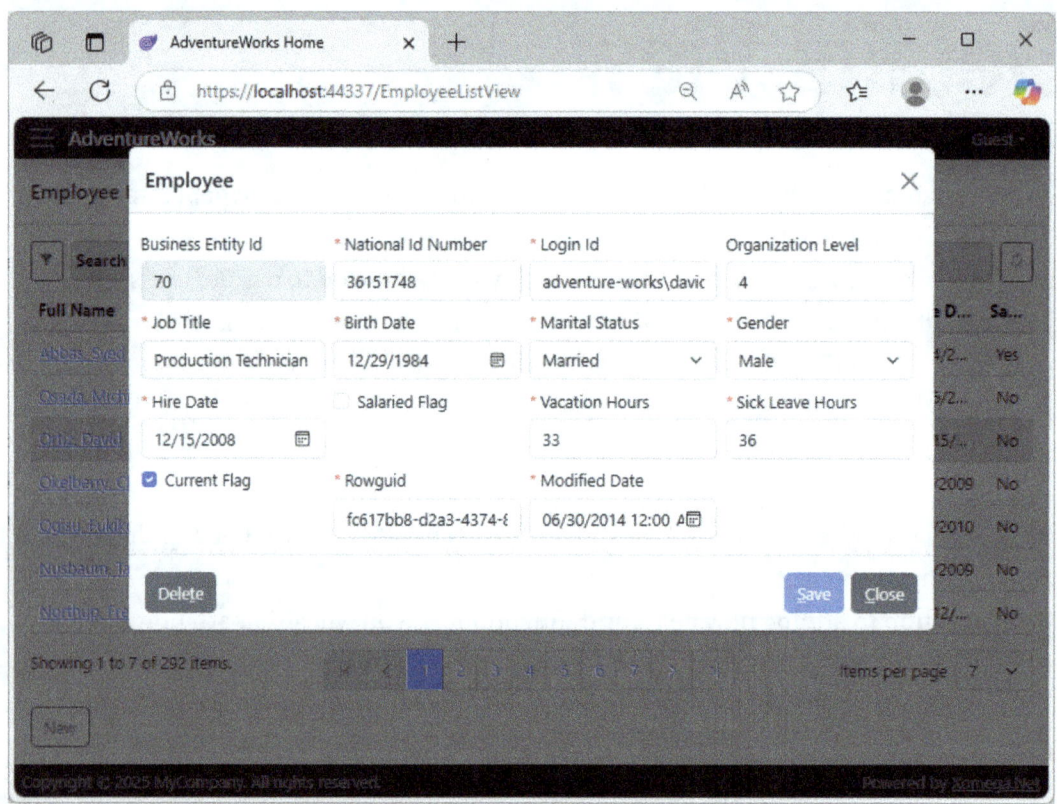

Figure 4-1. Default details view

If you pay close attention, you will notice that the only difference is the display of the *Marital Status* and *Gender* fields, which now use drop-down lists with user-friendly text from the static enumerations we defined, instead of text fields with internal codes.

Some of these fields are not meant to be displayed to end users, such as the internal *Business Entity ID*, *Rowguid*, and even the *Modified Date* audit field. We will remove these fields from the details view, but first, let's take a look at the *Delete* button that was auto-generated for us.

As it turns out, the *Employee* table in the *AdventureWorks* sample database has a trigger on delete, which always raises an error stating that you cannot delete an employee but only make them "not current" instead. Therefore, we also want to remove the *Delete* button from this screen.

Removing the Delete Operation

The *Delete* button was generated solely because of the delete operation on the employee object, which was added as part of the standard CRUD operations. Since you cannot delete an employee, there is no need for this operation either, so we'll remove it from the employee object, as shown in Listing 4-1.

Listing 4-1. Removing the Delete operation

```
<object name="employee">
  <operations>
    ...
-   <operation name="delete" type="delete">[...]
  </operations>
</object>
```

This will automatically remove the *Delete* button from the generated Employee Details view.

Note Marking an entity as inactive instead of deleting it is a standard enterprise data design pattern, which allows you to preserve the history of the data.

Removing from Read Output

If we don't want to show the internal audit fields rowguid and modified date, nor do we need them for anything else on the client side, then we should remove the corresponding parameters from the read operation output, as shown in Listing 4-2.

CHAPTER 4 BUILDING OUT A DETAILS VIEW

Listing 4-2. Removing fields from Read output

```
<operation name="read" type="read">
  <input>[...]
  <output>
    ...
-    <param name="rowguid"/>
-    <param name="modified date"/>
  </output>
</operation>
```

> **Note** Sometimes it might be useful to show the last modified timestamp to the end user, in which case you would keep the `modified date` field in the output. However, it is less useful on the Employee Details view, which will be based on multiple database records from different tables, as it will show only the last update to the *Employee* table, but not to the *Person* table, for example.

Removing from Update Input

We should also remove the `rowguid` and `modified date` parameters from the input of the update operation, as shown in Listing 4-3, since those fields should be managed by the system and not updated by the user.

Listing 4-3. Removing fields from Update input

```
<operation name="update" type="update">
  <input>
    <param name="business entity id"/>
    <struct name="data">
      ...
-      <param name="rowguid"/>
-      <param name="modified date"/>
    </struct>
  </input>
</operation>
```

150

CHAPTER 4　BUILDING OUT A DETAILS VIEW

Tip　If you want to display the `modified date` to the user, or use it on the client side, then you should move this parameter to the output of the `update` operation to read back the updated value.

Restructuring the Create Operation

The situation with the `create` operation is a little more complicated. The default operation was generated based on the assumption that the `business entity id` is provided by the client, since it's marked as a "supplied" key type on the `employee` object, because it references the corresponding `person` entity.

However, when creating a new employee, we want to automatically create the corresponding `person` record, as well as the underlying `business entity` object. This means that in the context of the `create` operation, the `business entity id` should be auto-generated by the service and returned from the operation, instead of being passed in.

Therefore, we'll move the `business entity id` parameter to the output of the operation, which allows us to flatten the input data structure. We will also remove the `rowguid` and `modified date` parameters from the input, as shown in Listing 4-4.

Listing 4-4. Restructuring the Create operation

```
<operation name="create" type="create">
+   <input arg="data">
-   <input>
-       <param name="business entity id"/>
-       <struct name="data">
            <param name="national id number"/>
            ...
-           <param name="rowguid"/>
-           <param name="modified date"/>
-           <config>[...]
-       </struct>
        <config>
          <xfk:add-to-object class="EmployeeObject"/>
        </config>
```

CHAPTER 4 BUILDING OUT A DETAILS VIEW

```
      </input>
+   <output>
+     <param name="business entity id"/>
+     <config>
+       <xfk:add-to-object class="EmployeeObject"/>
+     </config>
+   </output>
    <config>
-     <rest:method verb="POST" uri-template="employee/{business entity id}"/>
+     <rest:method verb="POST" uri-template="employee"/>
    </config>
  </operation>
```

Note You also need to remove the business entity id from the uri-template and make sure that the output parameters are added to the EmployeeObject data object. This will allow the framework to automatically populate this property on the client side with the newly generated business entity id after the create operation is executed.

Hiding the Internal Key Field

Since business entity id is a key field and cannot be removed from the CRUD operations, to hide it on the UI, we can simply mark it as hidden in the EmployeeObject data object, as shown in Listing 4-5.

Listing 4-5. Hiding the business entity id field

```
<xfk:data-object class="EmployeeObject">
  <ui:display>
    <ui:fields>
+     <ui:field param="business entity id" hidden="true"/>
    </ui:fields>
  </ui:display>
</xfk:data-object>
```

CHAPTER 4   BUILDING OUT A DETAILS VIEW

> **Note**   If the `business entity id` key field had been marked as "serial" on the `employee` object, the generator of the default CRUD operations would have automatically marked it as hidden, provided that the *Make Serial Keys Hidden* parameter is set to `True`.

Reviewing the Result

To review our updates, build the model and run the application. If you open the details of an employee, you should see that the *Delete* button is gone, and the *Business Entity ID*, *Rowguid*, and *Modified Date* fields are no longer displayed, as illustrated in Figure 4-2.

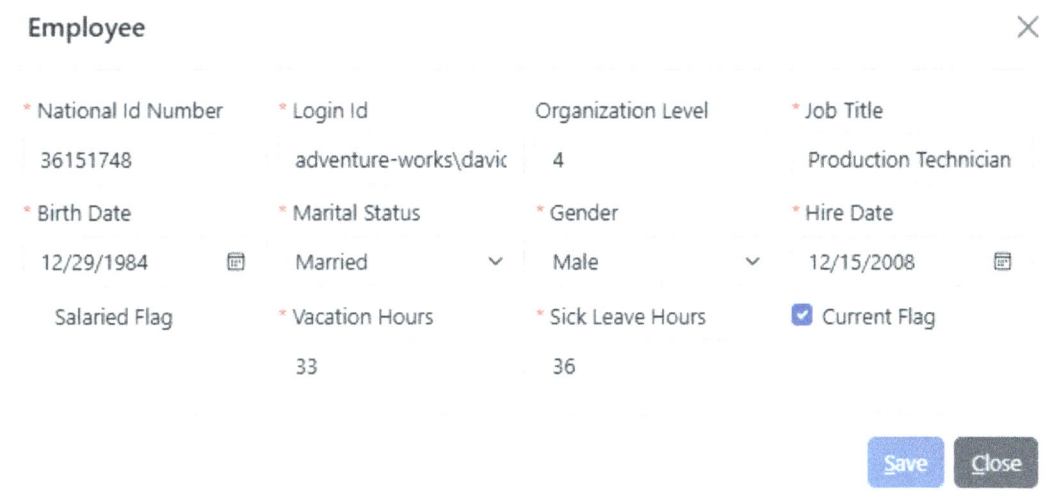

Figure 4-2.   Removed fields and actions

Adding the Pay History Child List

In addition to the regular field controls, more complex details screens may also contain data grids for child lists. Our sample database has a table `EmployeePayHistory`, which stores the current and historical pay rates for each employee. Viewing the pay history of an individual employee may be quite useful, so let's see how we can add it to the Employee Details view.

153

Pay History Subobject

Since its foreign key to the Employee table does not have a cascade delete option (since you cannot delete employees anyway), the EmployeePayHistory table was imported as its own primary object in the model, with a composite key represented by a fieldset consisting of business entity id and rate change date, as shown in Listing 4-6.

Listing 4-6. *Imported employee pay history object*

```
<fieldset name="employee pay history">
  <field name="business entity id" type="employee"
        required="true">[...]
  <field name="rate change date" type="date time"
        required="true">[...]
</fieldset>
...
<object name="employee pay history">
  <fields>
    <fieldset ref="employee pay history" key="supplied"
            required="true"/>
    <field name="rate" type="money" required="true">[...]
    <field name="pay frequency" type="tiny int"
            required="true">
      <config>[...]
      <doc>
        <summary>1 = Salary received monthly,
                2 = Salary received biweekly</summary>
      </doc>
    </field>
    <field name="modified date" type="date time"
            required="true">[...]
  </fields>
</object>
```

If you look at the description of the pay frequency field, you will see that it can assume only one of two tiny int values for a monthly or biweekly pay frequency. As you've already learned, this is best modeled by creating a static enumeration with these values, as well as a logical type referencing that enumeration.

So, let's go ahead and add the pay frequency type and enumeration in the employee.xom file, as shown in Listing 4-7.

Listing 4-7. Adding pay frequency enumeration and type

```
+<type name="pay frequency" base="tiny int enumeration">
+   <enum ref="pay frequency"/>
+</type>
...
+<enum name="pay frequency">
+   <item name="Monthly" value="1"/>
+   <item name="Biweekly" value="2"/>
+</enum>
```

Next, similar to how we did it before, let's turn the employee pay history object into a subobject of the employee by moving it into the subobjects section and then make the following changes, which you can see in Listing 4-8:

- Rename the employee pay history object to pay history, since it will be qualified with the parent object's name.

- Change the type of pay frequency field to our newly created logical type pay frequency.

- Change the key to be the rate change date field, since the business entity id key field of the parent object will be automatically included in the subobject key.

Listing 4-8. Adding pay history subobject

```
<object name="employee">
  <subobjects>
-   <object name="employee pay history">
+   <object name="pay history">
      <fields>
```

```
-           <fieldset ref="employee pay history" key="supplied"
-               required="true"/>
+        <field name="rate change date" key="supplied"
+            type="date time" required="true">[...]
         <field name="rate" type="money" required="true">[...]
-        <field name="pay frequency" type="tiny int"
-            required="true">[...]
+        <field name="pay frequency" type="pay frequency"
+            required="true">[...]
         <field name="modified date" type="date time"
             required="true">[...]
      </fields>
      <config>
        <sql:table name="HumanResources.EmployeePayHistory">
+          <sql:parent-foreign-key delete="no action"/>
        </sql:table>
      </config>
    </object>
  </subobjects>
</object>
```

Tip Optionally, you can also configure the foreign key to the parent object to use no action on delete. This will help you avoid extra diffs if you try to generate a script that updates the database with the model changes.

After that, you can safely delete the employee_pay_history.xom file, as it is no longer needed.

Subobject Read List Operation

Now that we have it as a subobject, you can add a read list operation to it, which should populate a child list object of the EmployeeObject data object. Xomega provides an easy way to generate all this automatically by creating and running a copy of one of the *Model Enhancement* CRUD generators.

CHAPTER 4 BUILDING OUT A DETAILS VIEW

You can just select an existing generator where most of the properties are turned off, such as the Read Enum Operation, press Ctrl+C to clone it, change the name to Subobject Read List Operation, and set the following parameters:

- *Generate Data Objects*: True
- *Generate Read Enum*: False
- *Generate Subobject Read List*: True

Your generator properties should look like what's illustrated in Figure 4-3.

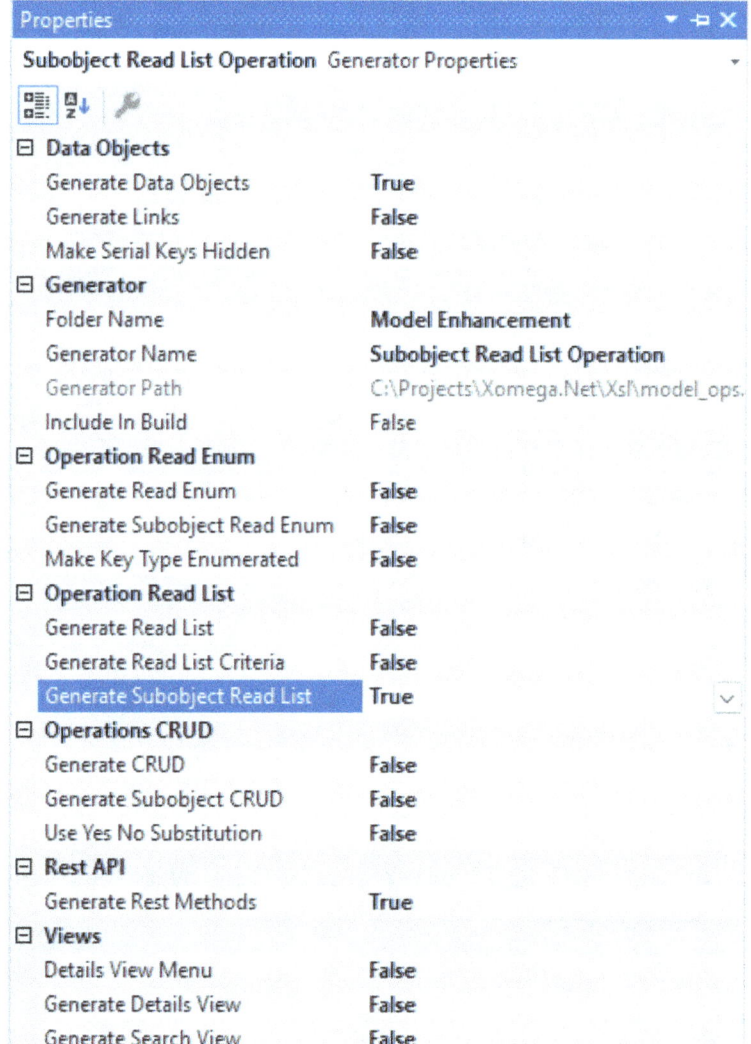

Figure 4-3. *Properties of the Subobject Read List Operation generator*

157

CHAPTER 4 BUILDING OUT A DETAILS VIEW

Next, you can just right-click the employee.xom file and select the *Generate* ▶ *Model Enhancement* ▶ *Subobject Read List Operation* menu. This will generate the read list operation that populates the EmployeePayHistoryList data object, which will be added as a child of the EmployeeObject.

To configure the columns of the child grid, remove the modified date output parameter, move the rate change date parameter to the end, and change its type to date to display it without the time part, as shown in Listing 4-9.

Listing 4-9. Generated Read List operation for Pay History subobject

```
<object name="pay history">
  <operations>
    <operation name="read list" type="readlist">
      <input>
        <param name="business entity id" type="employee"
               required="true"/>
      </input>
      <output list="true">
-       <param name="rate change date"/>
        <param name="rate"/>
        <param name="pay frequency"/>
+       <param name="rate change date" type="date"/>
-       <param name="modified date"/>
        <config>
          <xfk:add-to-object class="EmployeePayHistoryList"/>
        </config>
      </output>
      <config>
-       <xfk:paging mode="client"/>
+       <xfk:paging mode="none"/>
        <rest:method verb="GET" uri-template="employee/{business entity
        id}/pay-history"/>
      </config>
    </operation>
  </operations>
</object>
```

CHAPTER 4 BUILDING OUT A DETAILS VIEW

Since the *Pay History* grid will usually contain just a few records, we can also set the paging mode to none to avoid extra paging controls, making it look cleaner.

Pay History Child Table

If you build the model now, run the application, and open the Employee Details view, you should see a new *Pay History* child table right below the main employee details panel, as shown in Figure 4-4.

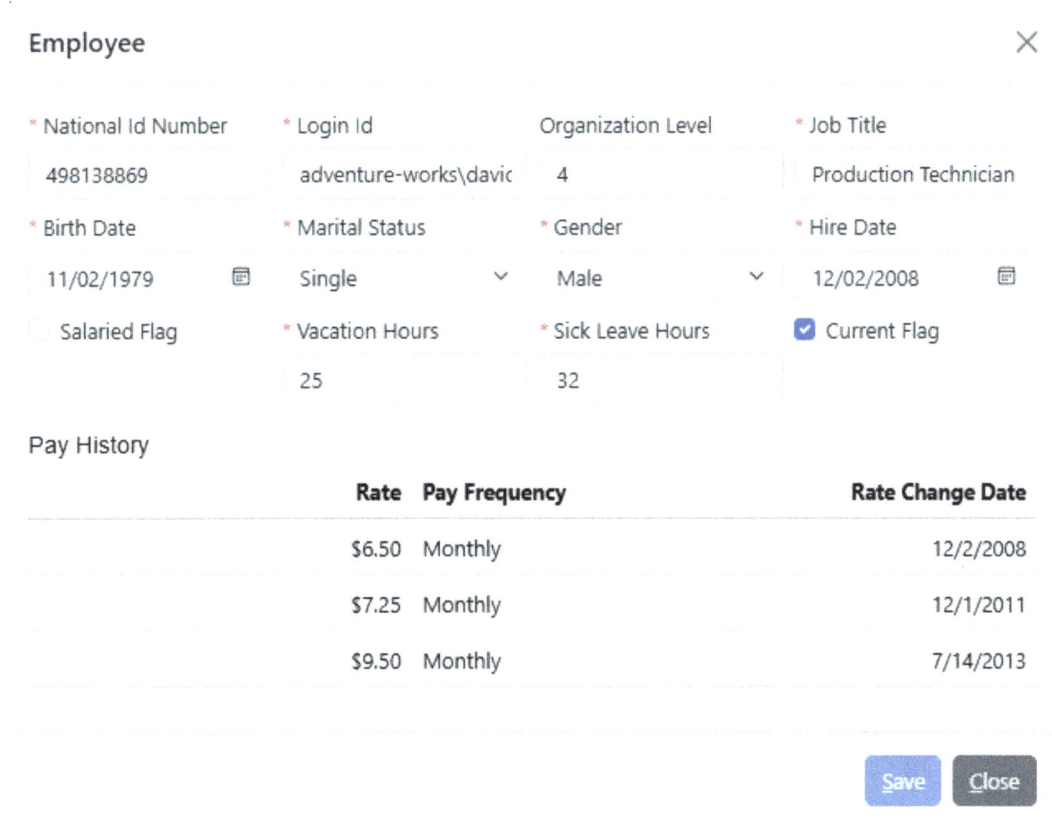

Figure 4-4. *Pay History child table*

As you can see, the *Pay Frequency* shows user-friendly values from the static enumeration we added, and the *Rate Change Date* is displayed as just a date.

CHAPTER 4 BUILDING OUT A DETAILS VIEW

Department History Child List

Like `EmployeePayHistory`, our sample database also has a table `EmployeeDepartmentHistory`, which stores the current and historical department assignments for each employee.

It has a slightly more complex structure, but was also imported as a separate primary object, which lends itself to being a subobject of the employee object. So, let's add the *Department History* as another child grid to the Employee Details view.

Department History Subobject

The primary key of the `employee department history` object consists of four fields, which, in addition to the `business entity id`, include `department id`, `start date`, and `shift id`, so we will not be able to get rid of the corresponding `fieldset`, like we did with the `employee pay history`.

Therefore, we will just copy the `employee department history` fieldset without the `business entity id` field to the `employee.xom` file and then copy the `employee department history` object definition as a subobject of the `employee` object, renaming it to `department history`, as shown in Listing 4-10.

Listing 4-10. Employee Department History subobject

```
<fieldset name="employee department history">
-  <field name="business entity id" type="employee"
-        required="true">[...]
   <field name="department id" type="department"
          required="true">[...]
   <field name="start date" type="date time"
          required="true">[...]
   <field name="shift id" type="shift" required="true">[...]
</fieldset>
<enums>[...]
...
<object name="employee">
   <subobjects>
      <object name="pay history">[...]
-     <object name="employee department history">
```

160

```
+   <object name="department history">
      <fields>
        <fieldset ref="employee department history"
                  key="supplied" required="true"/>
        <field name="end date" type="date">[...]
        <field name="modified date" type="date time"
               required="true">[...]
      </fields>
      <config>
        <sql:table name="HumanResources.EmployeeDepartmentHistory">
+         <sql:parent-foreign-key delete="no action"/>
        </sql:table>
      </config>
    </object>
  </subobjects>
</object>
```

As usual, you can also configure the parent foreign key to use no action on delete and then delete the employee_department_history.xom file, which is no longer needed.

Department History Read List

Since we already configured the *Subobject Read List Operation* generator, you can rerun it on the employee.xom file to add the read list operation and the EmployeeDepartmentHistoryList child data object, which will be used to populate the child grid.

After that, remove the business entity id output parameter, and move the start date parameter right before the end date, as shown in Listing 4-11.

Listing 4-11. Generated Read List operation for Department History subobject

```
<object name="department history">
  <operations>
    <operation name="read list" type="readlist">
      <input>
        <param name="business entity id" type="employee"
               required="true"/>
      </input>
```

CHAPTER 4 BUILDING OUT A DETAILS VIEW

```
      <output list="true">
-       <param name="business entity id" type="employee"
-               required="true"/>
-       <param name="start date" type="date" required="true"/>
        <param name="department id" type="department"
                required="true"/>
        <param name="shift id" type="shift" required="true"/>
+       <param name="start date" type="date" required="true"/>
        <param name="end date"/>
-       <param name="modified date"/>
        <config>
           <xfk:add-to-object class="EmployeeDepartmentHistoryList"/>
        </config>
      </output>
      <config>
-        <xfk:paging mode="client"/>
+        <xfk:paging mode="none"/>
         <rest:method verb="GET" uri-template="employee/{business entity
         id}/department-history"/>
      </config>
    </operation>
  </operations>
</object>
```

Since we don't expect many records in the department history list for each employee, we can also set the paging mode to none to avoid extra paging controls.

Adding Department Enum

To display a user-friendly department name instead of the department id, turn it into a dynamic enumeration, as we did before, by right-clicking the department.xom file and running the *Read Enum Operation* generator from the *Model Enhancement* menu.

Then remove the modified date parameter from the additional attributes of the enumeration, as shown in Listing 4-12.

Listing 4-12. Adding Department dynamic enumeration

```
<object name="department">
  <operation name="read enum">
    <output list="true">
      <param name="department id"/>
      <param name="name"/>
      <param name="group name"/>
-     <param name="modified date"/>
    </output>
    <config>
      <rest:method verb="GET" uri-template="department/enum"/>
      <xfk:enum-cache enum-name="department"
          id-param="department id" desc-param="name"/>
    </config>
  </operation>
</object>
```

Adding Shift Enum

Similarly, to display the shift name instead of the internal `shift id`, create a dynamic enumeration for the `shift` object by right-clicking the `shift.xom` file and running the *Read Enum Operation* generator, then remove the `modified date` parameter from the output, as shown in Listing 4-13.

Listing 4-13. Adding Shift dynamic enumeration

```
<object name="shift">
  <operation name="read enum">
    <output list="true">
      <param name="shift id"/>
      <param name="name"/>
      <param name="start time"/>
      <param name="end time"/>
-     <param name="modified date"/>
    </output>
```

```
    <config>
      <rest:method verb="GET" uri-template="shift/enum"/>
      <xfk:enum-cache enum-name="shift"
                      id-param="shift id" desc-param="name"/>
    </config>
  </operation>
</object>
```

Updating Column Names

Finally, update the `EmployeeDepartmentHistoryList` data object to display user-friendly labels for the `department id` and `shift id` fields, as shown in Listing 4-14.

Listing 4-14. Updating column names in the Department History data object

```
  <xfk:data-object class="EmployeeDepartmentHistoryList"
                   list="true">
+   <ui:display>
+     <ui:fields>
+       <ui:field param="department id" label="Department"/>
+       <ui:field param="shift id" label="Shift"/>
+     </ui:fields>
+   </ui:display>
+ </xfk:data-object>
```

Department History Child Table

If you build the model now, run the application, and open the Employee Details view, you should see a new *Department History* child table below the main employee details panel, as shown in Figure 4-5.

CHAPTER 4   BUILDING OUT A DETAILS VIEW

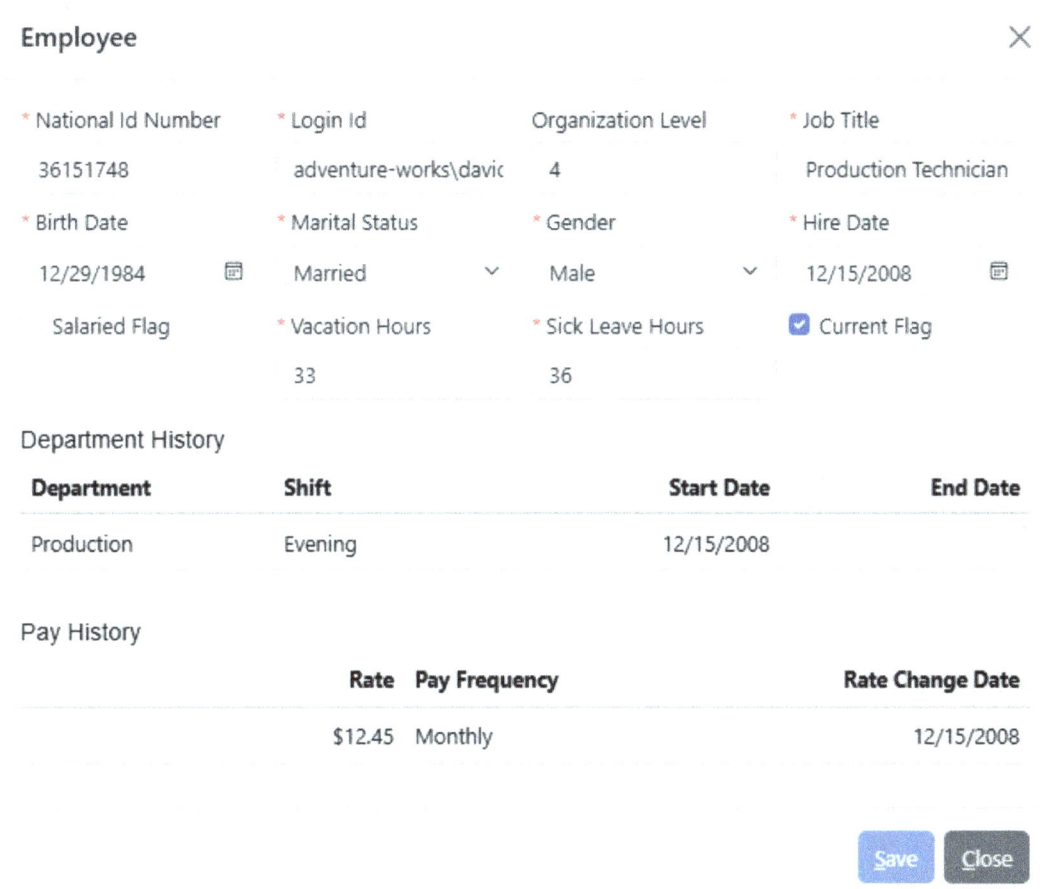

Figure 4-5. Department History child table

Notice that the *Department* and *Shift* columns show user-friendly values from the dynamic enumerations we added.

Summary

In this section, you learned about configuring CRUD operations and saw how easy it is to convert a primary object into a subobject of another object, allowing you to display it as a child list in the details view.

Adding subobjects, child `read list` operations, dynamic enumerations, and other model enhancements is generally a straightforward and mechanical process that can also be delegated to a GenAI agent, such as Copilot, making it even easier.

In the next section, you will learn how to configure the layout of the details view so that the generated screens are more user-friendly and visually appealing.

CHAPTER 4 BUILDING OUT A DETAILS VIEW

Configuring Panel Layout

So far, our Employee Details view displays all employee fields in four columns on the main panel, while the panels for the child lists are stacked below. This default layout is barely useful except for the simplest detail views.

In this section, you will learn how to group fields into panels, organize those panels into tabs, and lay out the fields and panels in a way that makes sense for users.

Grouping Fields into Panels

You can group properties of a data object into logical sets of related fields that can be displayed on the same panel or tab by using multiple `ui:fields` elements with the `group` attribute under the `ui:display` element of the data object.

This also allows you to specify the exact order of the fields in the panel, rather than just the order they appear in the model. The default `ui:fields` element without the `group` attribute will be used for all other fields that are not grouped, using the natural order in which they are defined in the model.

Let's add the following three groups of fields, as shown in Listing 4-15:

- *personal* – fields related to the employee's personal information
- *status* – fields related to employment status
- *benefits* – fields related to the employee's benefits

Listing 4-15. Grouping employee fields into panels

```
<xfk:data-object class="EmployeeObject">
  <xfk:add-child name="department history"
                 class="EmployeeDepartmentHistoryList"/>
  <xfk:add-child name="pay history"
                 class="EmployeePayHistoryList"/>
  <ui:display>
    <ui:fields>
      <ui:field param="business entity id" hidden="true"/>
    </ui:fields>
+   <ui:fields group="personal" title="Personal Info">
+     <ui:field param="birth date"/>
```

```
+      <ui:field param="gender"/>
+      <ui:field param="national id number"/>
+      <ui:field param="marital status"/>
+      <ui:field param="login id"/>
+    </ui:fields>
+    <ui:fields group="status">
+      <ui:field param="current flag" label="Is Current"/>
+      <ui:field param="hire date"/>
+    </ui:fields>
+    <ui:fields group="benefits">
+      <ui:field param="vacation hours"/>
+      <ui:field param="sick leave hours"/>
+    </ui:fields>
  </ui:display>
</xfk:data-object>
```

You can optionally specify the title of each group if you want it to be different from the group name, as well as configure each individual field in the group, just like in the default group.

Organizing Panels with Tabs

Grouping fields into panels helps users easily locate the right fields, but having all the fields in multiple panels on the same screen at once can quickly make it too busy and overwhelming. Therefore, a common UI design pattern is to organize various panels using tabs.

To create a layout for the fields of your data object, add a `ui:panel-layout` element under the `ui:display` element, which will contain a mix of `ui:panel` and `ui:tabs` elements. Each tab can, in turn, contain its own mix of panels and even nested tabs.

For any panel or tab, you can specify the `group` attribute to include all fields from the specified group or the `child` attribute to include all fields from a child data object. You can also set the `title` attribute and other layout parameters, as you will see next.

CHAPTER 4   BUILDING OUT A DETAILS VIEW

For the Employee Details view, we will start by creating the following three tabs, as shown in Listing 4-16:

- *Personal Info* – for the personal group of fields
- *Employment* – for the status and benefits field groups
- *History* – for the department history and pay history child lists

Listing 4-16. Organizing employee panels into tabs

```
<ui:display>
  <ui:fields>[...]
  <ui:fields group="personal" title="Personal Info">[...]
  <ui:fields group="status">[...]
  <ui:fields group="benefits">[...]
+ <ui:panel-layout>
+   <ui:panel/>
+   <ui:tabs>
+     <ui:tab group="personal"/>
+     <ui:tab title="Employment">
+       <ui:panel group="status"/>
+       <ui:panel group="benefits"/>
+     </ui:tab>
+     <ui:tab title="History">
+       <ui:panel child="department history"/>
+       <ui:panel child="pay history"/>
+     </ui:tab>
+   </ui:tabs>
+ </ui:panel-layout>
</ui:display>
```

Note that I also temporarily added an empty `ui:panel` element at the top of the `ui:panel-layout` to show the default panel with all the remaining fields. This will provide visibility into the fields that are not grouped yet while you are still working on the layout.

CHAPTER 4 BUILDING OUT A DETAILS VIEW

Personal Info Tab

Once you build the model, run the application, and open the Employee Details view, you will see our three tabs under the main panel. The first tab, *Personal Info*, will show the fields grouped under the `personal` group, as shown in Figure 4-6.

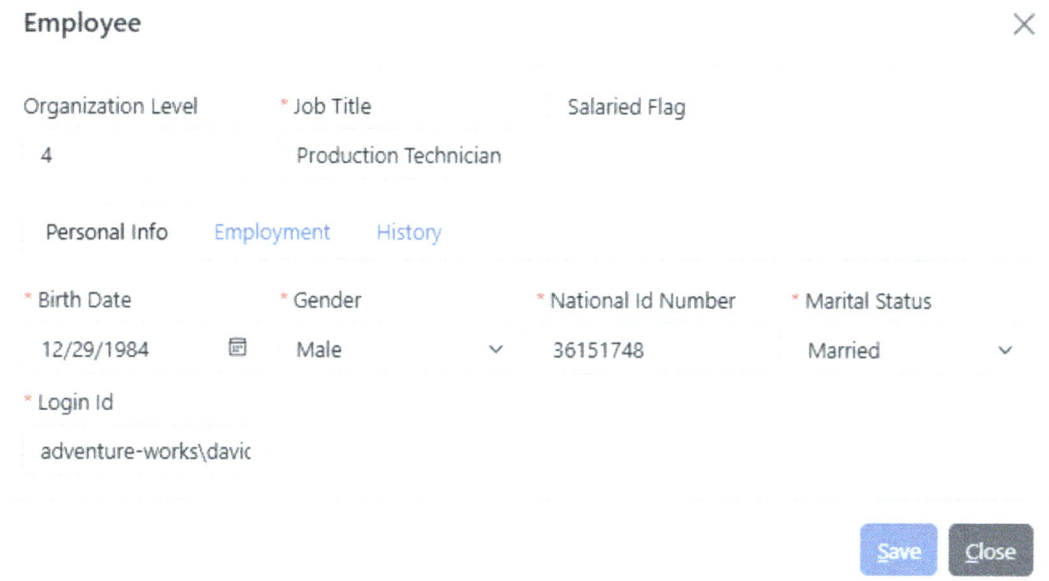

Figure 4-6. *Personal Info tab on the Employee Details view*

History Tab

The tables for the employee's department and pay histories have been placed under the *History* tab, as shown in Figure 4-7.

169

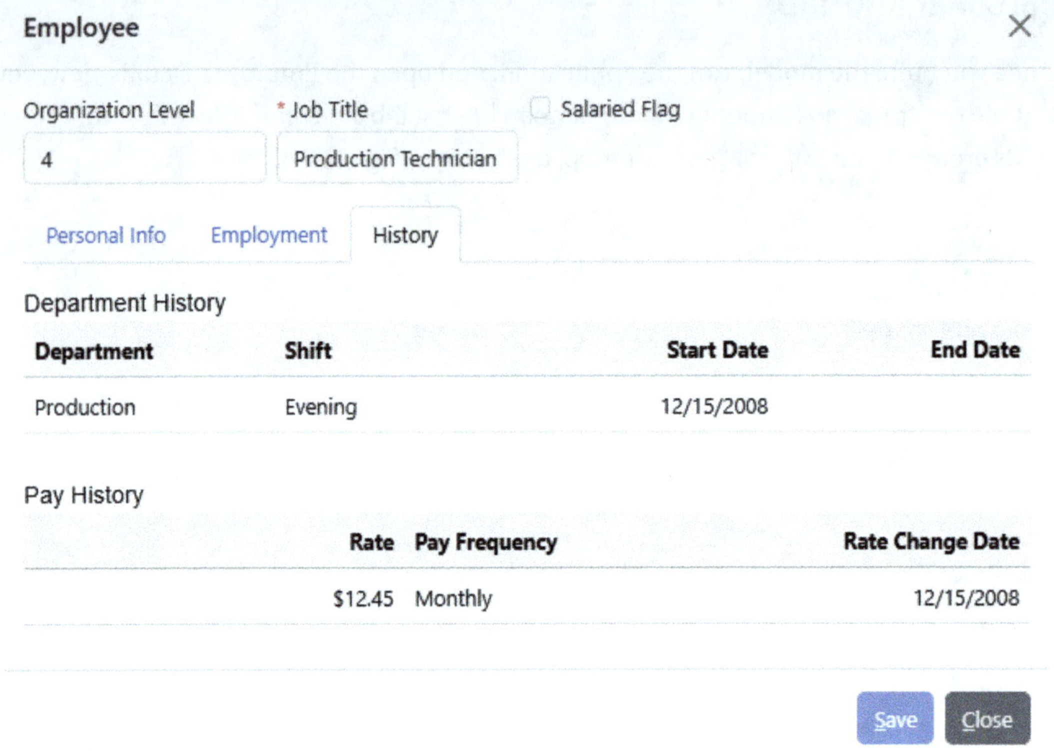

Employee

Organization Level	*Job Title	☐ Salaried Flag
4	Production Technician	

Personal Info | Employment | **History**

Department History

Department	Shift	Start Date	End Date
Production	Evening	12/15/2008	

Pay History

	Rate	Pay Frequency	Rate Change Date
	$12.45	Monthly	12/15/2008

[Save] [Close]

Figure 4-7. History tab on the Employee Details view

Employment Tab

The *Employment* tab in the middle will show two panels for the status and benefits field groups stacked vertically, as shown in Figure 4-8.

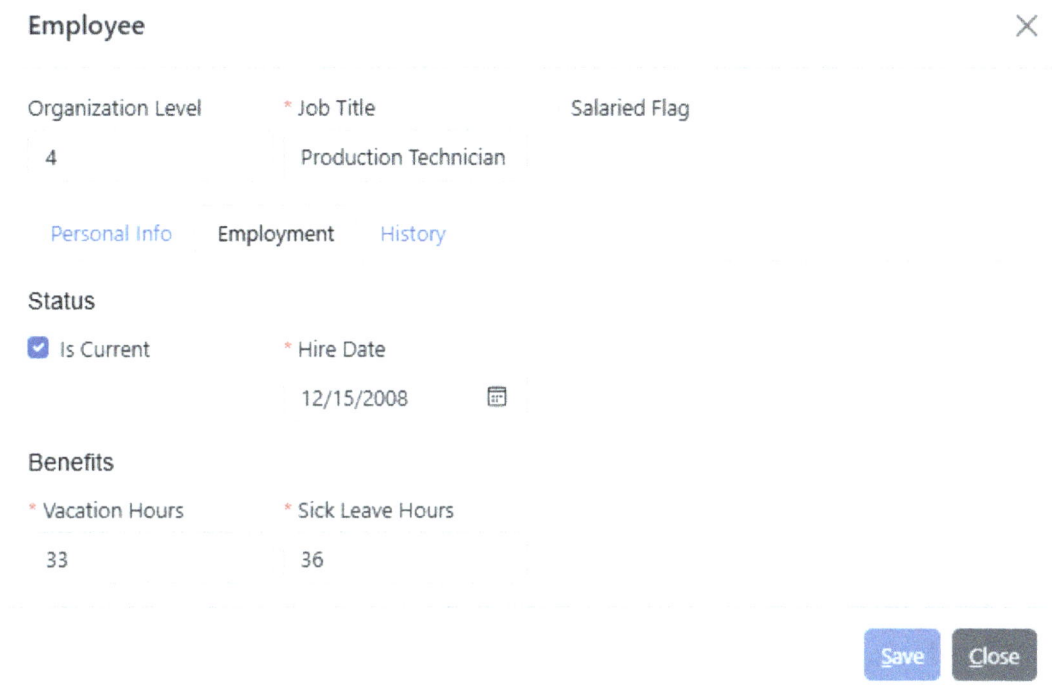

Figure 4-8. Employment tab on the Employee Details view

Laying Out Fields and Panels

Now let's see how we can further lay out panels and fields within those panels to improve the look and feel of the *Employment* tab. Given that the *Status* and *Benefits* panels have only two fields each, it would be better to display them side by side, rather than stack them vertically.

For aesthetic reasons, we may also want to stack the fields in those panels into a single column rather than two columns, if there is enough space on that tab.

Editing Boolean Fields

You might have noticed that Boolean fields, such as *Is Current* and *Salaried Flag*, are displayed as checkboxes with labels on the right side, which doesn't align well with other fields that have labels on top of the control.

CHAPTER 4   BUILDING OUT A DETAILS VIEW

To provide a more consistent look and user experience, we may want to use a drop-down list with two options: *Yes* and *No*, instead of a checkbox. It also works better for showing or setting blank values in Boolean fields. To do this, override the type on these parameters in the CRUD operations to be yesno, as shown in Listing 4-17.

Listing 4-17. Yes/No drop-down for Boolean fields

```
<operation name="read" type="read">
  <input>[...]
  <output>
    ...
-   <param name="salaried flag"/>
+   <param name="salaried flag" type="yesno"/>
    ...
-   <param name="current flag"/>
+   <param name="current flag" type="yesno"/>
  </output>
</operation>
<operation name="create" type="create">
  <input arg="data">
    ...
-   <param name="salaried flag"/>
+   <param name="salaried flag" type="yesno"/>
    ...
-   <param name="current flag"/>
+   <param name="current flag" type="yesno"/>
  </input>
  <output>[...]
</operation>
<operation name="update" type="update">
  <input>
    <param name="business entity id"/>
    <struct name="data">
      ...
-     <param name="salaried flag"/>
+     <param name="salaried flag" type="yesno"/>
```

```
      ...
-     <param name="current flag"/>
+     <param name="current flag" type="yesno"/>
    </struct>
  </input>
</operation>
```

> **Tip** Alternatively, you can set `type="yesno"` on the `field` element of the employee object and remove this override from the corresponding `input` and `output` parameters of the `read list` operation.

Laying Out Employment Tab

To lay out panels into multiple columns within their parent panel, use the `panel-cols` attribute on the `ui:panel` element. The default value for this attribute is 1, which means the panel takes the full width of the parent panel. You can set it to 2 to make it take half the width or to 3 to make it take a third of the width, and so on.

To lay out fields within a panel, use the `field-cols` attribute on the `ui:panel` element. The default value for this attribute is 4, which means the fields are laid out in four columns.

So, to display the *Status* and *Benefits* panels on the *Employment* tab side by side, set the `panel-cols` attribute to 2 on both panels, and to display the fields in a single column, set the `field-cols` attribute to 1, as shown in Listing 4-18.

Listing 4-18. Laying out panels and fields in the Employment tab

```
<ui:tab title="Employment">
  <ui:panel group="status" field-cols="1" panel-cols="2"/>
  <ui:panel group="benefits" field-cols="1" panel-cols="2"/>
</ui:tab>
```

Let's build the model and run the application to review the results. The *Employment* tab will now show the *Status* and *Benefits* panels side by side, with each field stacked in a single column, as shown in Figure 4-9.

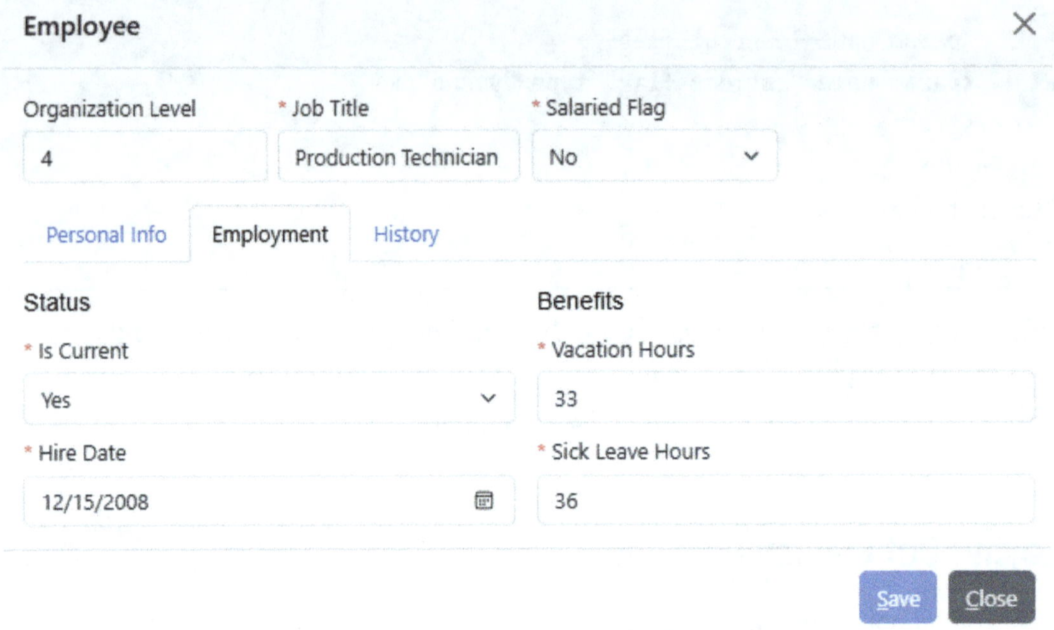

Figure 4-9. Updated layout of the Employment tab

Note Notice how the *Is Current* and *Salaried Flag* fields are now displayed as drop-down lists with *Yes* and *No* options, rather than checkboxes.

Responsive Layout

Note that the generated views use a responsive layout, so the specified number of columns will be used only if there is enough space on the screen. At each Bootstrap breakpoint width, the layout will automatically determine which fields and/or panels need to wrap to the next line and will adjust accordingly.

For example, as you decrease the screen width, fields in the two panels side by side may start wrapping from four columns to three or two columns to fit the available space. However, if the panels themselves get wrapped to be stacked vertically, they will automatically become wider, allowing them to display their fields back in three or four columns, as appropriate.

Custom View Layout

You can use the techniques above to configure the layout of the generated view as you build out your Details view. If you still need to further customize the final layout, add or update elements in the view, or implement other UI-specific features in the view component, you can mark that view as having a custom layout.

To do this, add a `<ui:layout custom="true"/>` element to the `ui:view` element in the model, and the *Blazor Views* generator will stop updating the view component, allowing you to customize it as needed.

Caution This also means that the view will not be updated automatically with any changes you make in the model after that point, so you will need to manually update the view component as needed.

Fields from Related Objects

Except for the simplest cases, detail screens rarely involve viewing and editing just one record from a single database table. Often, you want to view and even edit fields from related entities on the same details screen.

In this chapter, you will learn how to add fields from related objects to the Employee Details screen and organize them into the appropriate tabs and panels.

Fields from the Person Object

If you look at the current Employee Details screen, you will notice that it is missing some basic information about the employee, such as their first and last names. As discussed in previous chapters, this information is stored in the `person` object, which has a one-to-one relationship with the `employee` object.

When adding a new employee, you will need to create the corresponding Person object, so users must be able to specify at least the basic required person fields, such as the employee's names. Let's look at how to add these fields.

175

Defining Logical Types

Before adding fields from the `person` object, let's review the default logical types assigned by the import process and then enhance the model by defining more appropriate logical types for them.

This will help ensure that your fields use consistent physical types, editing controls, and validation rules across the application.

Person Type

If you look at the description of the `person type` field, you'll see that it stores a two-character code for one of the predefined person types, as shown in Listing 4-19.

Listing 4-19. Person type field in the Person object

```
<object name="person">
  ...
    <field name="person type" type="code2" required="true">
      <doc>
        <summary>Primary type of person: SC = Store Contact,
          IN = Individual (retail) customer, SP = Sales person,
          EM = Employee (non-sales), VC = Vendor contact,
          GC = General contact</summary>
      </doc>
    </field>
  ...
</object>
```

As we've already done before, let's create a static enumeration for these values, define a new logical type for this enumeration, and then update the `person type` field of the `person` object to use this logical type, as shown in Listing 4-20.

Listing 4-20. Person type enumeration

```
+<type name="person type" base="enumeration" size="2">
+  <enum ref="person type"/>
+</type>
  ...
```

```
+<enums>
+    <enum name="person type">
+        <item name="Store contact" value="SC"/>
+        <item name="Individual customer" value="IN"/>
+        <item name="Sales person" value="SP"/>
+        <item name="Employee" value="EM"/>
+        <item name="Vendor contact" value="VC"/>
+        <item name="General contact" value="GC"/>
+    </enum>
+</enums>
 ...
<object name="person">
   ...
-   <field name="person type" type="code2" required="true">[...]
+   <field name="person type" type="person type"
+         required="true">[...]
   ...
</object>
```

Name Types

Next, let's look at the logical type for the first, middle, and last name fields. All of them use the `string50` type. However, if you right-click on that type and select *Find All References*, you will see that most fields using it represent some kind of name, as shown in Figure 4-10.

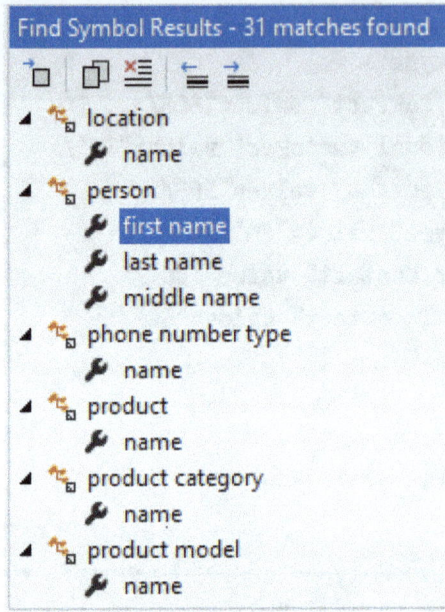

Figure 4-10. *Viewing references to the string50 type*

Therefore, it would be logical to rename this type to name. You can do this by pressing F2 on the type name and entering the new name in the *Rename* dialog, as shown in Figure 4-11.

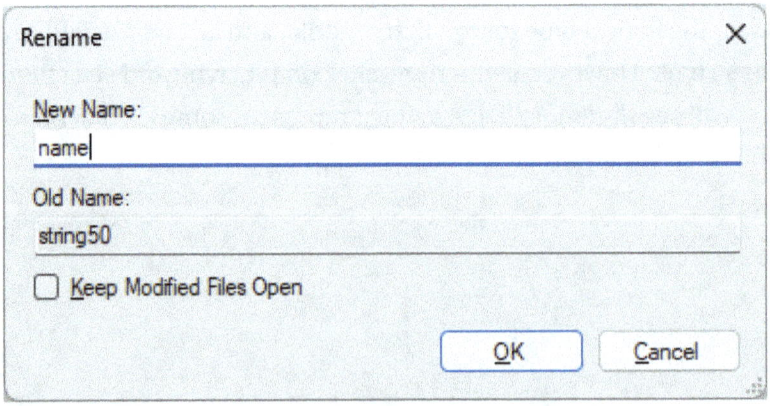

Figure 4-11. *Renaming the string50 type to name*

The types for the person title and suffix, string8 and string10, respectively, are used for various fields, so it doesn't make sense to rename them. Instead, we can define and use specialized logical types person title and person suffix, as shown in Listing 4-21.

CHAPTER 4 BUILDING OUT A DETAILS VIEW

Listing 4-21. Additional types for the Person object

```
+<type name="person title" base="string" size="8"/>
+<type name="person suffix" base="string" size="10"/>
...
<object name="person">
  ...
- <field name="title" type="string8">[...]
+ <field name="title" type="person title">[...]
  <field name="first name" type="name" required="true">[...]
  <field name="middle name" type="name">[...]
  <field name="last name" type="name" required="true">[...]
- <field name="suffix" type="string10">[...]
+ <field name="suffix" type="person suffix">[...]
  ...
</object>
```

Having these logical types defined will make it easier to add fields from the `person` object to the Employee Details screen.

Displaying Name Fields

Now that we have defined the logical types, let's add the employee's name fields from the `person` object to the Employee Details screen.

Adding Read Output Parameters

We'll start by adding the parameters related to the employee's name to the output of the read operation of the `employee` object. Since they come from a different object, we need to specify the `type` attribute for each parameter, as shown in Listing 4-22.

Listing 4-22. Adding name fields to the employee read operation

```
<object name="employee">
  <operation name="read" type="read">
    <output>
+     <param name="title" type="person title"/>
+     <param name="first name" type="name"/>
```

CHAPTER 4　BUILDING OUT A DETAILS VIEW

```
+       <param name="middle name" type="name"/>
+       <param name="last name" type="name"/>
+       <param name="suffix" type="person suffix"/>
        ...
      </output>
    </operation>
</object>
```

Adding Name Field Group

To display the new employee's name fields on the Employee Details screen, we will add them to a new field group called name. We'll place this group in the *Basic Info* tab along with the existing personal info fields. We'll show the two panels side by side, with their fields arranged in one column, as shown in Listing 4-23.

Listing 4-23. Adding name fields to the Employee Details screen

```
<xfk:data-object class="EmployeeObject">
  <ui:display>
    <ui:fields>[...]
+   <ui:fields group="name" title="Employee Name">
+     <ui:field param="title"/>
+     <ui:field param="first name"/>
+     <ui:field param="middle name"/>
+     <ui:field param="last name"/>
+     <ui:field param="suffix"/>
+   </ui:fields>
    <ui:fields group="personal" title="Personal Info">[...]
    <ui:fields group="status">[...]
    <ui:fields group="benefits">[...]
    <ui:panel-layout>
      <ui:panel/>
      <ui:tabs>
-       <ui:tab group="personal"/>
+       <ui:tab title="Basic Info">
+         <ui:panel group="name" field-cols="1"
+                                panel-cols="2"/>
```

180

```
+          <ui:panel group="personal" field-cols="1"
+                                     panel-cols="2"/>
+        </ui:tab>
         <ui:tab title="Employment">[...]
         <ui:tab title="History">[...]
       </ui:tabs>
     </ui:panel-layout>
   </ui:display>
</xfk:data-object>
```

Populating Name Fields

Let's build the model and add custom code to populate the new employee's name fields in the `ReadAsync` method of the `EmployeeService` class. Since we used parameters with the same names as the properties of the `person` object, we can copy the properties from the Person object to the result object, as shown in Listing 4-24.

Listing 4-24. Populating name fields in the employee read operation

```
public virtual async Task<Output<Employee_ReadOutput>>
    ReadAsync(int _businessEntityId,
              CancellationToken token = default)
{
    ...
    Employee obj = await ctx.FindEntityAsync<Employee>(
                   currentErrors, token, _businessEntityId);
    ServiceUtil.CopyProperties(obj, res);
    // CUSTOM_CODE_START: add custom code for Read operation below
+   ServiceUtil.CopyProperties(obj.BusinessEntityObject, res);
    // CUSTOM_CODE_END
    ...
}
```

CHAPTER 4 BUILDING OUT A DETAILS VIEW

Resulting Employee Name Panel

If you run the application now and open the Employee Details view for an existing employee, you will see that the personal info panel is now grouped under the *Basic Info* tab along with the new Employee Name panel. Both panels will show their fields in a single column, side by side, as shown in Figure 4-12.

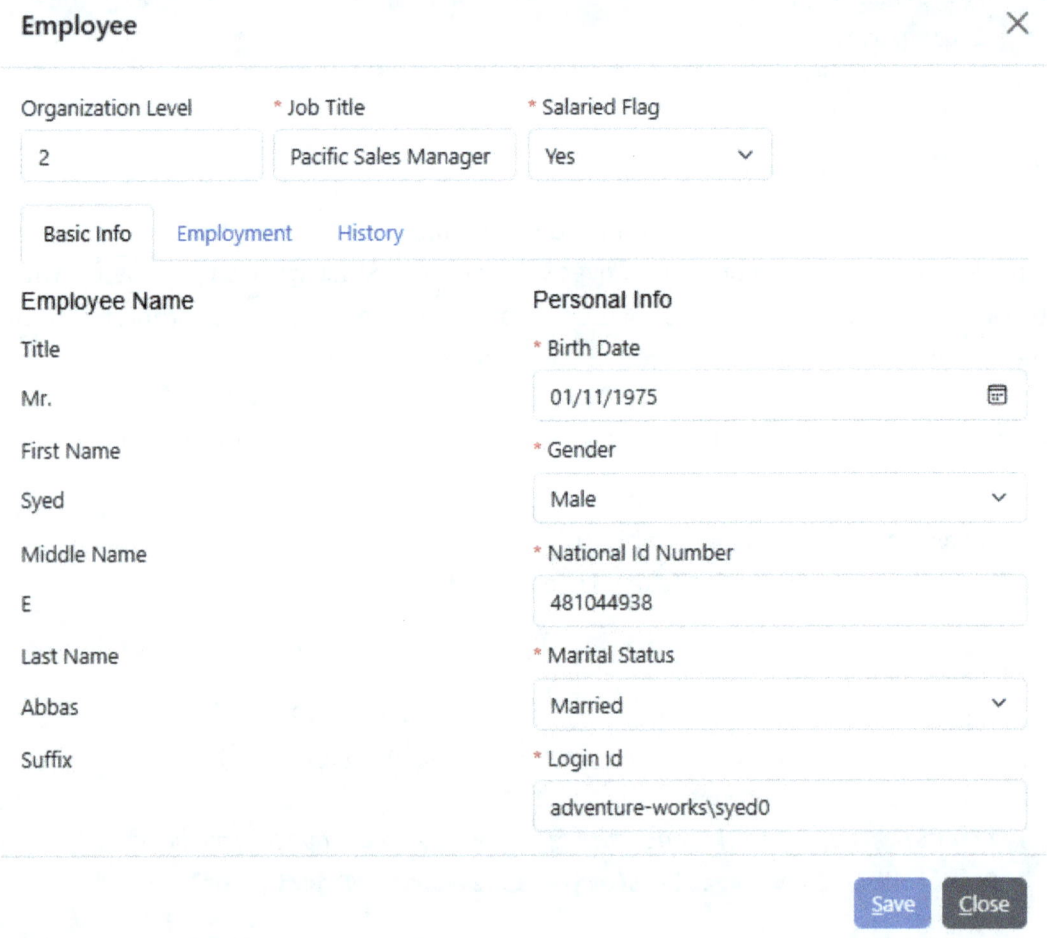

Figure 4-12. Employee Name panel

Since we added employee name parameters only to the output of the `read` operation and not to the input of the `update` or `create` operations, they are considered not editable and use display-only data label controls.

Editing Name Fields

To make employee name fields editable, we need to add them to the input parameters of the `create` and `update` operations of the `employee` object. Then, we must implement the custom code to populate these fields in the corresponding operations in the `EmployeeService` class.

Adding Input Parameters

Normally, you can copy the parameters from the `read` operation to the input structure of the `create` and `update` operations. However, you may need to add the `required` attribute to parameters that are mandatory for creating or updating an employee. In this case, I set the `first name` and `last name` parameters as required, as shown in Listing 4-25.

Listing 4-25. Adding name parameters to the create and update operations

```
<object name="employee">
  <operation name="create" type="create">
    <input arg="data">
+     <param name="title" type="person title"/>
+     <param name="first name" type="name" required="true"/>
+     <param name="middle name" type="name"/>
+     <param name="last name" type="name" required="true"/>
+     <param name="suffix" type="person suffix"/>
      ...
    </input>
    <output>[...]
  </operation>
  <operation name="update" type="update">
    <input>
      <param name="business entity id"/>
      <struct name="data">
+       <param name="title" type="person title"/>
+       <param name="first name" type="name" required="true"/>
+       <param name="middle name" type="name"/>
+       <param name="last name" type="name" required="true"/>
```

```
+            <param name="suffix" type="person suffix"/>
             ...
    </input>
  </operation>
</object>
```

Next, we need to build the model and use these parameters in the custom code for the *Create* and *Update* operations.

Implementing Create Operation

In the custom code of the `CreateAsync` method of the `EmployeeService` class, we will initialize the internal audit fields `Rowguid` and `ModifiedDate`. Then, we will create a new `Person` object with the corresponding `BusinessEntity` object using our name parameters, as well as default values for the other fields, as shown in Listing 4-26.

Listing 4-26. Custom code for Create operation

```
// CUSTOM_CODE_START: add namespaces for custom code below
+using AdventureWorks.Services.Common.Enumerations;
// CUSTOM_CODE_END
...
public virtual async Task<Output<Employee_CreateOutput>>
    CreateAsync(Employee_CreateInput _data,
                CancellationToken token = default)
{
    ...
    EntityState state = EntityState.Added;
    Employee obj = new Employee();
    var entry = ctx.Entry(obj);
    entry.State = state;
    entry.CurrentValues.SetValues(_data);
    // CUSTOM_CODE_START: add custom code for Create operation below
+    obj.Rowguid = Guid.NewGuid();
+    obj.ModifiedDate = DateTime.Now;
+    obj.BusinessEntityObject = new Person
```

```
+   {
+       PersonType = PersonType.Employee,
+       NameStyle = false,
+       Title = _data.Title,
+       FirstName = _data.FirstName,
+       MiddleName = _data.MiddleName,
+       LastName = _data.LastName,
+       Suffix = _data.Suffix,
+       EmailPromotion = 0,
+       AdditionalContactInfo = null,
+       Demographics = null,
+       Rowguid = Guid.NewGuid(),
+       ModifiedDate = DateTime.Now,
+       BusinessEntityObject = new BusinessEntity
+       {
+           Rowguid = Guid.NewGuid(),
+           ModifiedDate = DateTime.Now
+       }
+   };
    // CUSTOM_CODE_END
    ...
}
```

Notice that I set `PersonType` to the constant value `PersonType.Employee`, which is automatically generated from the person type enumeration we defined earlier. To do this, I also had to add a custom namespace at the top of the file to import the enumeration constants.

Implementing Update Operation

The custom code for the *Update* operation will be much simpler. We will just copy the values of the name parameters to the corresponding properties of the *Person* entity and update the `ModifiedDate` field, as shown in Listing 4-27.

Chapter 4 Building Out A Details View

Listing 4-27. Custom code for Update operation

```
public virtual async Task<Output> UpdateAsync(
    int _businessEntityId,
    Employee_UpdateInput_Data _data,
    CancellationToken token = default)
{
    ...
    Employee obj = await ctx.FindEntityAsync<Employee>(
        currentErrors, token, _businessEntityId);
    var entry = ctx.Entry(obj);
    entry.CurrentValues.SetValues(_data);
    // CUSTOM_CODE_START: add custom code for Update operation below
+   obj.ModifiedDate = DateTime.Now;
+   var personEntry = ctx.Entry(obj.BusinessEntityObject);
+   personEntry.CurrentValues.SetValues(_data);
+   obj.BusinessEntityObject.ModifiedDate = DateTime.Now;
    // CUSTOM_CODE_END
    ...
}
```

Note   The generated code uses the `FindEntityAsync` extension method to find the employee. This method will automatically report a validation error if an employee with the specified `businessEntityId` does not exist.

Reviewing Editable Names

If you run the application now and open the Employee Details screen, you will see that the employee's name fields are now editable, as shown in Figure 4-13. With the implemented *Create* and *Update* operations, you can also save the changes.

CHAPTER 4 BUILDING OUT A DETAILS VIEW

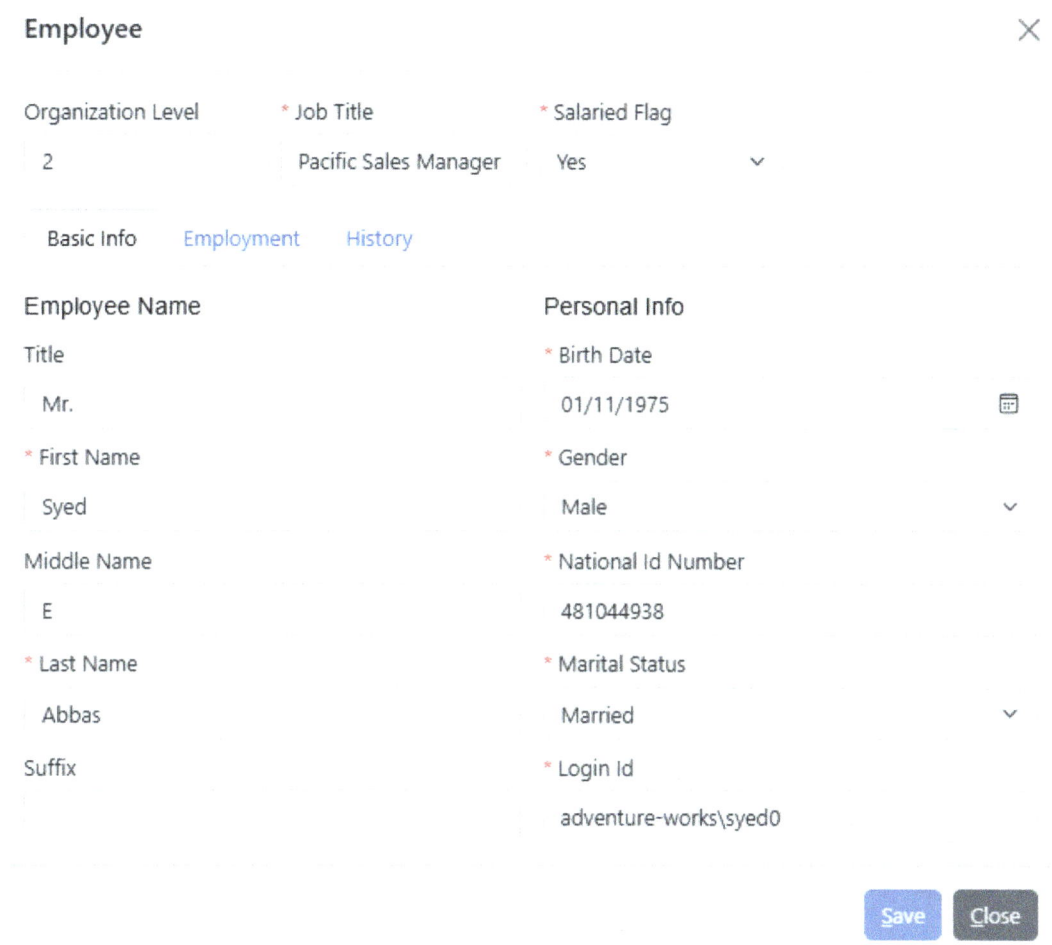

Figure 4-13. Editable employee names

Note The required *First Name* and *Last Name* fields that we added are marked with a red asterisk on the screen.

View and Edit Email Address

Now that we have added the basic employee's name fields from the *Person* object, let's add a field that allows viewing and editing an employee's email address.

CHAPTER 4 BUILDING OUT A DETAILS VIEW

Adding Email Address Parameters

Since the email address field uses the same logical type name that we renamed earlier, we can add the email address parameters to the read, create, and update operations with that type and set the required attribute to true, as shown in Listing 4-28.

Listing 4-28. Adding email address parameters to the Employee CRUD operations

```
<object name="employee">
  <operation name="read" type="read">
    <input>[...]
    <output>
+     <param name="email address" type="name"/>
      ...
    </output>
  </operation>
  <operation name="create" type="create">
    <input arg="data">
+     <param name="email address" type="name"
+             required="true"/>
      ...
    </input>
    <output>[...]
  </operation>
  <operation name="update" type="update">
    <input>
      <param name="business entity id"/>
      <struct name="data">
+       <param name="email address" type="name"
+               required="true"/>
        ...
    </input>
  </operation>
</object>
```

CHAPTER 4 BUILDING OUT A DETAILS VIEW

Adding a Contact Tab

To display the email address on the Employee Details screen, I will add it to a separate field group email phone (to which we'll also add phone number fields later) and then place it in a new *Contact* tab, as shown in Listing 4-29.

Listing 4-29. Adding a Contact tab for the email address

```
<xfk:data-object class="EmployeeObject">
  <ui:display>
    <ui:fields>[...]
    <ui:fields group="name" title="Employee Name">[...]
    <ui:fields group="personal" title="Personal Info">[...]
+   <ui:fields group="email phone" title="Email / Phone">
+     <ui:field param="email address"/>
+   </ui:fields>
    <ui:fields group="status">[...]
    <ui:fields group="benefits">[...]
    <ui:panel-layout>
      <ui:panel/>
      <ui:tabs>
        <ui:tab title="Basic Info">[...]
+       <ui:tab title="Contact">
+         <ui:panel group="email phone"/>
+       </ui:tab>
        <ui:tab title="Employment">[...]
        <ui:tab title="History">[...]
      </ui:tabs>
    </ui:panel-layout>
  </ui:display>
</xfk:data-object>
```

Note If this field group is the only panel in the *Contact* tab, you can set the group attribute directly on the ui:tab element. However, I am planning to add additional panels there, so I am using a nested ui:panel element.

Email Address Service Logic

An employee's email address is stored in a separate `EmailAddress` table, so the logic for updating it will require some custom code. The *Create* operation will also need the same logic, but you don't want to duplicate large chunks of custom code in both operations.

To avoid code duplication and promote code reuse, we will define a separate partial class for `EmployeeService`. In this class, we will add reusable methods with the logic for adding and updating the email address. This way, we can call these methods from both *Create* and *Update* operations.

Extending EmployeeService

You can either manually add a new file with the partial class for `EmployeeService` or have it generated by setting the extend attribute to true in the `svc:customize` element of the employee object's configuration, as shown in Listing 4-30.

Listing 4-30. Generating an extended partial class for EmployeeServiceI

```
<object name="employee">
  <fields>[...]
  <operations>[...]
  <config>
    <sql:table name="HumanResources.Employee">[...]
    <edm:customize extend="true"/>
+   <svc:customize extend="true" preserve-on-clean="true"/>
  </config>
  <subobjects>[...]
</object>
```

If you build the model now, it will generate a new file, `EmployeeServiceExtended.cs`, containing the partial service class. This file will be nested under the `EmployeeService.cs` file in the Solution Explorer.

Note I also set the `preserve-on-clean` attribute to `true` so that the `EmployeeService.cs` file is not deleted when you clean generated files. Otherwise, you would risk losing the custom code you add to this file.

CHAPTER 4 BUILDING OUT A DETAILS VIEW

Email Address Update Methods

In the EmployeeServiceExtended.cs file, we will add two methods: one for adding a new email address and another for updating an existing email address using the first record in the EmailAddress table, as shown in Listing 4-31.

Listing 4-31. Methods for adding and updating email address

```
public partial class EmployeeService
{
+   protected async Task AddEmailAddressAsync(
+       Person person, string email, CancellationToken token)
+   {
+       await ctx.EmailAddress.AddAsync(new EmailAddress
+       {
+           BusinessEntityObject = person,
+           EmailAddress1 = email,
+           Rowguid = Guid.NewGuid(),
+           ModifiedDate = DateTime.Now
+       });
+   }
+
+   protected async Task UpdateEmailAddressAsync(
+       Person person, string email, CancellationToken token)
+   {
+       if (person == null) return;
+       var emailAddress = await ctx.EmailAddress
+           .FirstOrDefaultAsync(e =>
+               e.BusinessEntityId == person.BusinessEntityId,
+               token);
+       if (emailAddress != null)
+           emailAddress.EmailAddress1 = email;
+       else await AddEmailAddressAsync(person, email, token);
+   }
}
```

Reading and Updating Email Address

Now we can add the custom code to ReadAsync, CreateAsync, and UpdateAsync methods of the EmployeeService class to read and update the email address. We will read the first email address for the employee from the EmailAddress table and then use the methods we defined earlier to add or update the email address, as shown in Listing 4-32.

Listing 4-32. Custom code for reading and updating email address

```
public virtual async Task<Output<Employee_ReadOutput>>
    ReadAsync(int _businessEntityId,
            CancellationToken token = default)
{
    // CUSTOM_CODE_START: add custom code for Read operation below
    ServiceUtil.CopyProperties(obj.BusinessEntityObject, res);
+   res.EmailAddress = await ctx.EmailAddress
+       .Where(e => e.BusinessEntityId == _businessEntityId)
+       .Select(e => e.EmailAddress1).FirstOrDefaultAsync();
    // CUSTOM_CODE_END
}
public virtual async Task<Output<Employee_CreateOutput>>
    CreateAsync(Employee_CreateInput _data,
            CancellationToken token = default)
{
    // CUSTOM_CODE_START: add custom code for Create operation below
    ...
+   await AddEmailAddressAsync(obj.BusinessEntityObject,
+                               _data.EmailAddress, token);
    // CUSTOM_CODE_END
}
public virtual async Task<Output> UpdateAsync(
    int _businessEntityId,
    Employee_UpdateInput_Data _data,
    CancellationToken token = default)
```

CHAPTER 4 BUILDING OUT A DETAILS VIEW

```
{
    // CUSTOM_CODE_START: add custom code for Update operation below
    ...
+   await UpdateEmailAddressAsync(obj.BusinessEntityObject,
+                                 _data.EmailAddress, token);
    // CUSTOM_CODE_END
}
```

Contact Tab with Email Address

If you run the application now, you will see that the Employee Details screen has a new *Contact* tab with the required *Email Address* field, as shown in Figure 4-14. You can edit and save this field.

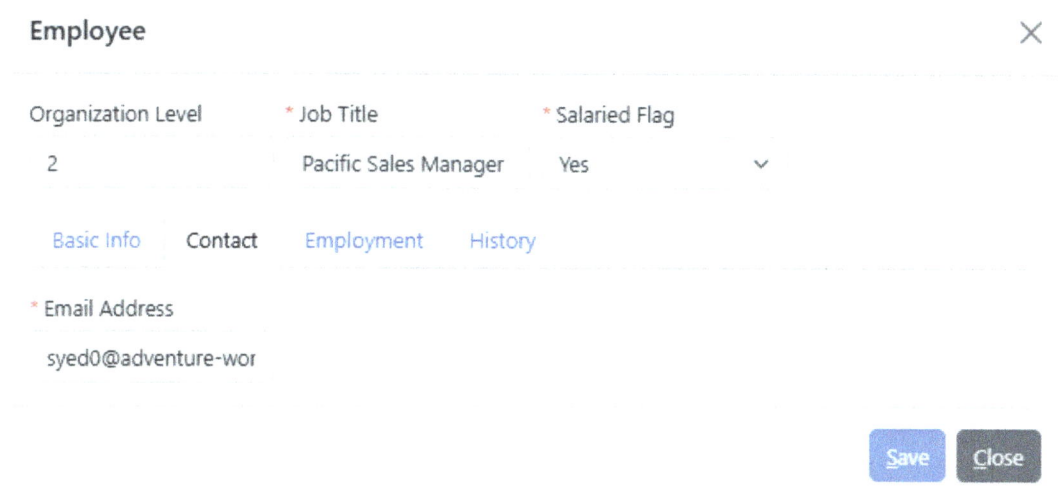

Figure 4-14. Employee Contact tab with email address

Now that we have added the email address field, let's also add employee phone number fields to the *Contact* tab.

View and Edit Phone Number

Phone numbers for any person are stored in the `PersonPhone` table in the AdventureWorks database, which was also imported as a separate object. Using the techniques you've already learned, let's first turn it into a subobject of the `person` object.

193

Person Phone Subobject

In the person.xom file, I will define a new logical type phone number for the phone number field. Then, I will move the person phone key fieldset and object here from person_phone.xom. I will place the object under the subobjects element of the person object and rename it to just phone.

I will also remove the business entity id field from the fieldset, since it is already defined in the person object, and change the type of the phone number field to the new logical type phone number, as shown in Listing 4-33.

Listing 4-33. Converting PersonPhone to a subobject of Person

```
+<type name="phone number" base="string" size="25"/>
...
<fieldsets>
  <fieldset name="person phone">
-    <field name="business entity id" type="person"
-            required="true">[...]
-    <field name="phone number" type="string25"
-            required="true">[...]
+    <field name="phone number" type="phone number"
+            required="true">[...]
    <field name="phone number type id"
            type="phone number type" required="true">[...]
  </fieldset>
</fieldsets>
...
<object name="person">
  <subobjects>
-    <object name="person phone">
+    <object name="phone">
      <fields>
        <fieldset ref="person phone" key="supplied"
                  required="true"/>
        <field name="modified date" type="date time"
                required="true">[...]
      </fields>
```

```
      <config>
        <sql:table name="Person.PersonPhone">
+         <sql:parent-foreign-key delete="no action"/>
        </sql:table>
      </config>
      <doc>[...]
    </object>
  </subobjects>
</object>
```

As before, you can also update the foreign key to the parent person object to use the no action delete rule and then delete the person_phone.xom file, as it is no longer needed.

Phone Number Type Enumeration

If you noticed, part of the primary key of the person phone object was the phone number type id field, which references the phone number type object.

To display the name of the phone number type rather than an internal ID, I will add a dynamic enumeration to it. Right-click the phone_number_type.xom file, and select *Generate* ▶ *Model Enhancement* ▶ *Read Enum Operation*. This will create and configure the read enum operation. All we need to do there is delete the unneeded modified date parameter, as shown in Listing 4-34.

Listing 4-34. Adding phone number type enumeration

```
<object name="phone number type">
  ...
  <operation name="read enum">
    <output list="true">
      <param name="phone number type id"/>
      <param name="name"/>
-     <param name="modified date"/>
    </output>
    <config>
      <rest:method verb="GET"
                   uri-template="phone-number-type/enum"/>
```

```
                <xfk:enum-cache enum-name="phone number type"
                                id-param="phone number type id"
                                desc-param="name"/>
        </config>
    </operation>
</object>
```

Adding Phone Number Parameters

While technically any person can have multiple phone numbers of different types in the database, for simplicity, we will only allow one phone number of a single type for each employee. Therefore, we will add the phone number and phone number type id parameters to the read, create, and update operations of the employee object, as shown in Listing 4-35.

Listing 4-35. Adding phone number parameters to the Employee CRUD operations

```
<object name="employee">
    <operation name="read" type="read">
        <input>[...]
        <output>
            <param name="email address" type="name"/>
+           <param name="phone number" type="phone number"/>
+           <param name="phone number type id"
+                  type="phone number type"/>
            ...
        </output>
    </operation>
    <operation name="create" type="create">
        <input arg="data">
            <param name="email address" type="name"
                   required="true"/>
+           <param name="phone number" type="phone number"/>
+           <param name="phone number type id"
+                  type="phone number type"/>
            ...
```

          </input>
          <output>[...]
        </operation>
        <operation name="update" type="update">
          <input>
            <param name="business entity id"/>
            <struct name="data">
              <param name="email address" type="name"
                     required="true"/>
+   <param name="phone number" type="phone number"/>
+   <param name="phone number type id"
+   type="phone number type"/>
              ...
          </input>
        </operation>
      </object>

> **Note** Notice that I did not make any of these parameters required, to allow for employees without a phone number in the system.

Adding Phone to Contact Tab

Next, we will add the phone number fields to the `email phone` field group we created earlier and configure the proper label for the `phone number type id` field. Since that field group has only three fields, we will add the `field-cols="3"` attribute to display them in three columns rather than four, as shown in Listing 4-36.

Listing 4-36. Adding phone number fields to the Contact tab

```
<xfk:data-object class="EmployeeObject">
  <ui:display>
    <ui:fields>[...]
    <ui:fields group="name" title="Employee Name">[...]
    <ui:fields group="personal" title="Personal Info">[...]
    <ui:fields group="email phone" title="Email / Phone">
```

```
      <ui:field param="email address"/>
+     <ui:field param="phone number"/>
+     <ui:field param="phone number type id"
+             label="Phone Number Type"/>
    </ui:fields>
    <ui:fields group="status">[...]
    <ui:fields group="benefits">[...]
    <ui:panel-layout>
      <ui:panel/>
      <ui:tabs>
        <ui:tab title="Basic Info">[...]
        <ui:tab title="Contact">
-         <ui:panel group="email phone"/>
+         <ui:panel group="email phone" field-cols="3"/>
        </ui:tab>
        <ui:tab title="Employment">[...]
        <ui:tab title="History">[...]
      </ui:tabs>
    </ui:panel-layout>
  </ui:display>
</xfk:data-object>
```

Let's build the model to regenerate all the necessary files so that we can add the custom code to read and update the phone number fields in the `EmployeeService` class.

Phone Number Service Logic

First, in the `EmployeeServiceExtended.cs` file, I will add a new method, `UpdatePhoneNumberAsync`, that will add or update the phone number for the employee, as shown in Listing 4-37.

Listing 4-37. Method for adding or updating phone number

```
public partial class EmployeeService
{
+   protected async Task UpdatePhoneNumberAsync(Person person,
+       string phoneNumber, int? phoneNumberTypeId,
+       CancellationToken token)
```

CHAPTER 4 BUILDING OUT A DETAILS VIEW

```
+   {
+       if (person == null || phoneNumberTypeId == null ||
+           string.IsNullOrEmpty(phoneNumber) ||
+           person.PhoneObjectList.Any(p =>
+               p.PhoneNumber == phoneNumber &&
+               p.PhoneNumberTypeId == phoneNumberTypeId))
+           return;
+
+       var phoneNumberType = await ctx
+           .FindEntityAsync<PhoneNumberType>(currentErrors,
+               token, phoneNumberTypeId.Value);
+       person.PhoneObjectList.Clear();
+       person.PhoneObjectList.Add(new PersonPhone
+       {
+           PersonObject = person,
+           PhoneNumber = phoneNumber,
+           PhoneNumberTypeObject = phoneNumberType,
+           ModifiedDate = DateTime.Now
+       });
+   }
    ...
}
```

Note Generally, you should always check whether the data has changed before updating it to avoid unnecessary database updates if the user has not changed the phone number.

Reading and Updating Phone Number

Now we can add the custom code to ReadAsync, CreateAsync, and UpdateAsync methods of the EmployeeService class to read and update the phone number. We will read the first phone number for the employee from the child PhoneObjectList of the Person entity. Then, we will use the UpdatePhoneNumberAsync method we defined earlier to add or update the phone number, as shown in Listing 4-38.

199

Listing 4-38. Custom code for reading and updating phone number

```
public virtual async Task<Output<Employee_ReadOutput>>
    ReadAsync(int _businessEntityId,
            CancellationToken token = default)
{
    // CUSTOM_CODE_START: add custom code for Read operation below
    ...
+   var phoneNumber = obj.BusinessEntityObject
+                       .PhoneObjectList.FirstOrDefault();
+   res.PhoneNumber = phoneNumber?.PhoneNumber;
+   res.PhoneNumberTypeId = phoneNumber?.PhoneNumberTypeId;
    // CUSTOM_CODE_END
}
public virtual async Task<Output<Employee_CreateOutput>>
    CreateAsync(Employee_CreateInput _data,
            CancellationToken token = default)
{
    // CUSTOM_CODE_START: add custom code for Create operation below
    ...
+   await UpdatePhoneNumberAsync(obj.BusinessEntityObject,
+       _data.PhoneNumber, _data.PhoneNumberTypeId, token);
    // CUSTOM_CODE_END
}
public virtual async Task<Output> UpdateAsync(
    int _businessEntityId,
    Employee_UpdateInput_Data _data,
    CancellationToken token = default)
{
    // CUSTOM_CODE_START: add custom code for Update operation below
    ...
+   await UpdatePhoneNumberAsync(obj.BusinessEntityObject,
+       _data.PhoneNumber, _data.PhoneNumberTypeId, token);
    // CUSTOM_CODE_END
}
```

CHAPTER 4 BUILDING OUT A DETAILS VIEW

> **Note** We cannot use `ServiceUtil.CopyProperties` in the `ReadAsync` method, even though the property names match, because the CLR types of the `PhoneNumberTypeId` property are different in the result and the `PersonPhone` object. The field on the `PersonPhone` entity is required and uses an `int` type, while the result property is nullable and uses `int?`.

Conditionally Required Fields

While we decided not to require employees to have a phone number in the system, we still want to make the `PhoneNumberTypeId` field required if the `PhoneNumber` field is specified, since it's a required field on the `PersonPhone` entity.

We can do that in the customized `EmployeeObject` class. So, let's add a `customize="true"` attribute to the `EmployeeObject` data object, as shown in Listing 4-39.

Listing 4-39. Customizing the EmployeeObject

```
  <xfk:data-object class="EmployeeObject"
+                  customize="true">
```

Once you build the model, you can open the generated `EmployeeObjectCustomized.cs` file and add custom code to set the `PhoneNumberTypeIdProperty` as required based on a LINQ expression that returns `true` if the `PhoneNumber` property is not null, as shown in Listing 4-40.

Listing 4-40. Making a property conditionally required

```
public class EmployeeObjectCustomized : EmployeeObject
{
    protected override void OnInitialized()
    {
        base.OnInitialized();
+       // set PhoneNumberTypeId as required
+       // if PhoneNumber is not null
+       Expression<Func<TextProperty, bool>> expPhNumType =
+           phNum => !phNum.IsNull(null);
```

201

```
+        PhoneNumberTypeIdProperty
+            .SetComputedRequired(expPhNumType,
+                                 PhoneNumberProperty);
     }
 }
```

> **Note** Alternatively, you can add a property change listener to `PhoneNumberProperty` and update the `Required` value of `PhoneNumberTypeIdProperty` whenever the value of `PhoneNumberProperty` changes. However, using `SetComputedRequired` is much easier in this case.

You can also add such conditional validation to the service logic to report a validation error if `PhoneNumberTypeId` is not specified but `PhoneNumber` has a value, instead of just ignoring the phone number.

Contact Tab with Phone Number

If you run the application now, you will see that the *Contact* tab has our new phone number fields next to the *Email Address*, as shown in Figure 4-15.

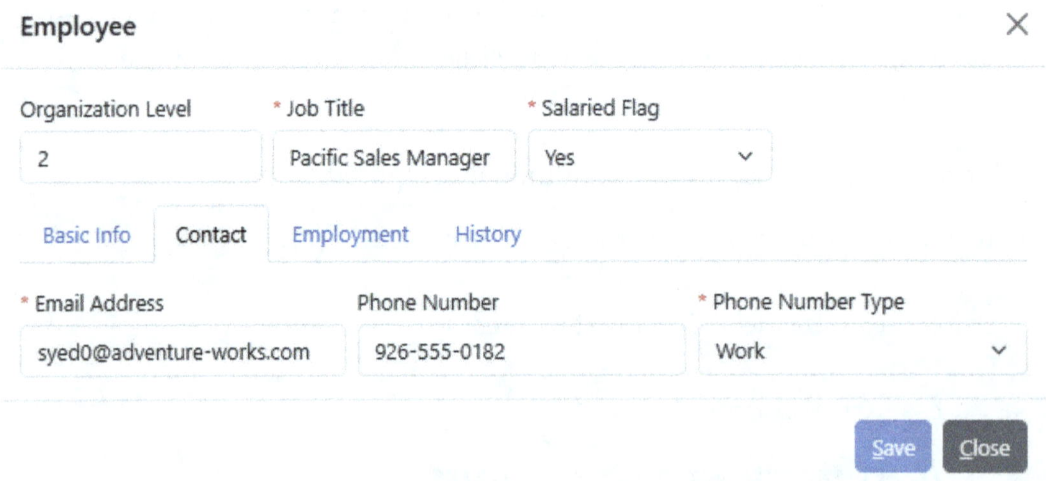

Figure 4-15. Contact tab with phone number

CHAPTER 4 BUILDING OUT A DETAILS VIEW

The *Phone Number Type* field is a drop-down list populated from our dynamic enumeration and is marked as required with a red asterisk whenever the *Phone Number* field has a value.

Master-Detail Layout

Previously, we organized fields on the Employee Details screen into several tabs and panels and added fields from related objects.

This section explains how to display dynamic information in the view title and configure the Employee Details screen to open as a master-detail view instead of a pop-up dialog.

Dynamic View Title

When working with the Employee Details screen, displaying identifying information about the employee in the view title—such as their name—helps users ensure they are editing the correct employee, especially when the *Basic Info* tab containing this information is not active.

Customizing the View Model

You can specify custom logic for the title within the view model. To generate a class for the customized view model, set the `customize="true"` attribute on the `ui:view-model` element in the view definition, as shown in Listing 4-41.

Listing 4-41. Customizing the employee view model

```
<ui:view name="EmployeeView" title="Employee">
  <ui:view-model data-object="EmployeeObject"
+                customize="true"/>
  <ui:main-link name="new employee">[...]
</ui:view>
```

Next, build the model project and navigate to the *ViewModels* ➤ *HumanResources* folder in the `AdventureWorks.Client.Common` project. A new file, `EmployeeViewModelCustomized.cs`, will be nested under the `EmployeeViewModel.cs` file.

Dynamic Employee Title

In the customized view model, you can override the `BaseTitle` property to return a custom title. When creating a new employee, the original localized `BaseTitle` is returned. For existing employees, their last and first names are appended, as demonstrated in Listing 4-42.

Listing 4-42. Customizing the employee view title

```
public class EmployeeViewModelCustomized : EmployeeViewModel
{
    public EmployeeViewModelCustomized(IServiceProvider sp)
        : base(sp) {}
+   public override string BaseTitle =>
+       base.BaseTitle + (MainObj.IsNew ? "" :
+       $" - {MainObj.LastNameProperty.Value}, {MainObj.FirstNameProperty.Value}");
}
```

If you run the application now, the view title will update to include the employee's name when editing an existing employee, as depicted in Figure 4-16.

CHAPTER 4   BUILDING OUT A DETAILS VIEW

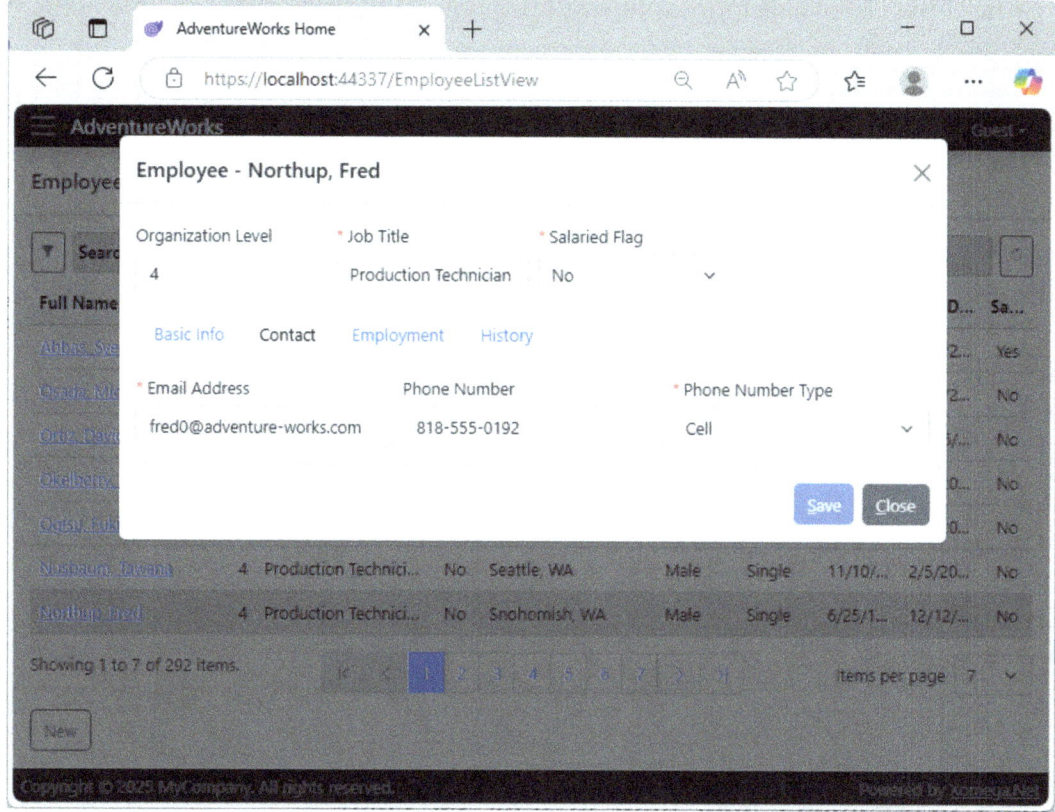

Figure 4-16. Employee name in view title

Note   If you edit the employee's first or last name on the screen, the view title will automatically update to reflect these changes. If this behavior is not desired, you should store the title values after reading the employee's data.

Master-Detail Employee View

As the previous figure illustrates, the Employee Details screen currently opens as a pop-up dialog. To view another employee's details, users must first close the dialog and then select another employee from the list.

205

This design is suitable for viewing or editing one or two employees at a time but becomes less efficient when working with many employees. In such scenarios, opening the Employee Details screen as a master-detail view—where the details view appears on the right side of the Employee List—is preferable.

Switching to a master-detail view is straightforward with Xomega, as outlined below.

Updating Employee Details Links

To implement this, open the `EmployeesList` data object definition. Update the `ui:link` elements for the "details" and "new" links by setting the `mode` attribute to `inline`, as shown in Listing 4-43.

For the "details" link, also update the `ui:display` element so that the details view opens when a row is selected in the employee list, rather than via a hyperlink on the employee's full name.

Listing 4-43. Updating the Employee view to open as a master-detail view

```
<xfk:data-object class="EmployeeList" list="true">
  <ui:display>[...]
  <ui:link name="details" view="EmployeeView" child="true"
+         mode="inline">
    <ui:params>
      <ui:param name="business entity id"
                field="business entity id"/>
    </ui:params>
-   <ui:display on-field="full name"/>
+   <ui:display on-selection="true"/>
  </ui:link>
  <ui:link name="new" view="EmployeeView" child="true"
+         mode="inline">[...]
</xfk:data-object>
```

If you build the model and run the application, the Employee List will no longer display a hyperlink in the *Full Name* column. Instead, clicking an employee row will open the Employee Details view on the right side of the screen, as illustrated in Figure 4-17.

CHAPTER 4   BUILDING OUT A DETAILS VIEW

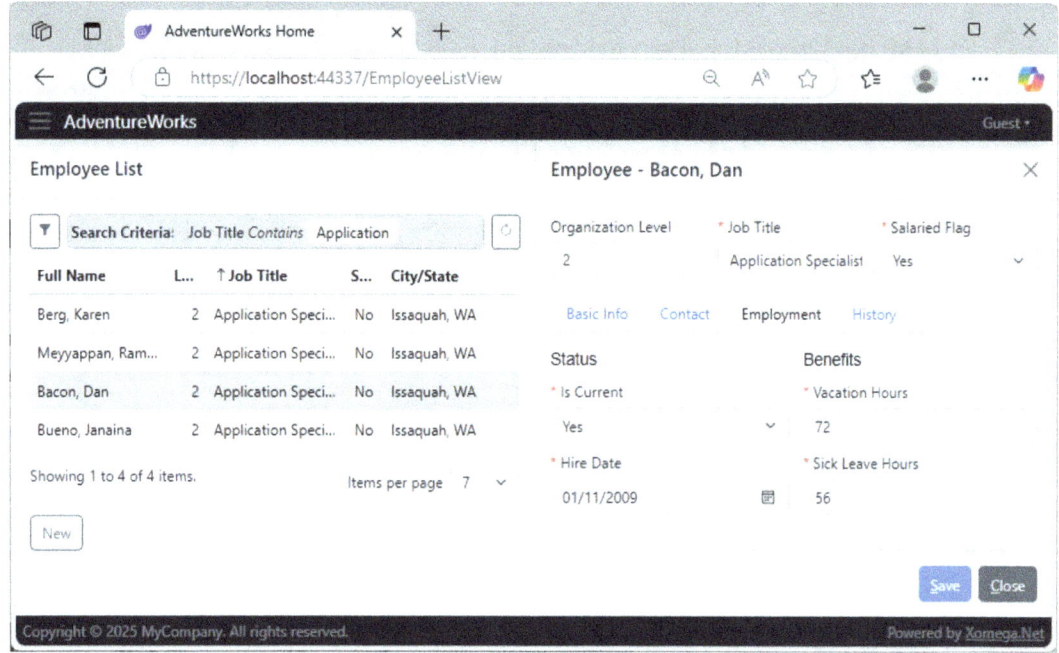

Figure 4-17. Employee List with master-detail view

Users can close the details view, select another row to view a different employee's details, or click the "New" link to create a new employee. This design can significantly improve the user experience for those who frequently view or edit multiple employees, such as HR personnel. However, it also introduces unique challenges.

Employee List Columns

When the Employee Details view opens in a master-detail layout, it occupies the right half of the screen, leaving insufficient space for the Employee List to display all its columns.

You might have noticed that the Employee List automatically hid approximately half of its columns on the right when the Employee Details view opened. Displaying the most important columns on the left ensures users can still see them while interacting with the Employee Details view.

207

> **Tip** You can customize the logic for column visibility in the Employee List view within its customized view model by overriding the `RankedProperties` property or the `UpdateColumnVisibility` method.

Alternatively, the Employee List grid would require a horizontal scroll bar to display all columns.

Unsaved Changes

When using the master-detail view, users can modify employee details and then select another employee without saving. Similar to the pop-up dialog, the Xomega Framework automatically prompts users to confirm whether they want to discard unsaved changes. If the user cancels, the view remains on the current employee, allowing them to save their changes.

Add/Edit Related Objects

In previous sections, you saw how to view and edit fields from related objects directly on the Employee Details screen. Sometimes, however, you may want to display fields from related objects on your screen but edit them in a separate screen designed specifically for that purpose.

For example, if you are adding a new sales order and the customer record does not exist in the system yet, you may want to create that customer in a separate Customer Details screen and then use the ID and other information of the newly created customer in the sales order you are adding.

The AdventureWorks database stores all addresses in a separate `Address` table. In this section, we will show how to display the employee's home address on the Employee Details screen and assume that editing addresses should be done in a separate Address Details screen.

Displaying Home Address

Let's start by displaying the employee's home address on the Employee Details screen in the *Contact* tab. As a learning example, rather than adding the address fields directly to the `EmployeeObject` data object, I will show how to use a separate child data object for that purpose.

Employee Address Data Object

In the employee.xom file, add a new data object, EmployeeAddressObject, and then add it to the EmployeeObject data object as a child named address. Next, add a new panel to the *Contact* tab with the title "Home Address" and set the child="address" attribute, as shown in Listing 4-44.

Listing 4-44. Adding employee address data object

```
<xfk:data-objects>
+ <xfk:data-object class="EmployeeAddressObject"/>
  <xfk:data-object class="EmployeeObject" customize="true">
+   <xfk:add-child name="address"
+                  class="EmployeeAddressObject"/>
    <xfk:add-child name="department history"
                   class="EmployeeDepartmentHistoryList"/>
    <xfk:add-child name="pay history"
                   class="EmployeePayHistoryList"/>
    <ui:display>
      <ui:fields>[...]
      <ui:fields group="name" title="Employee Name">[...]
      <ui:fields group="personal" title="Personal Info">[...]
      <ui:fields group="email phone"
                 title="Email / Phone">[...]
      <ui:fields group="status">[...]
      <ui:fields group="benefits">[...]
      <ui:panel-layout>
        <ui:panel/>
        <ui:tabs>
          <ui:tab title="Basic Info">[...]
          <ui:tab title="Contact">
            <ui:panel group="email phone" field-cols="3"/>
+           <ui:panel child="address" title="Home Address"/>
          </ui:tab>
          <ui:tab title="Employment">[...]
          <ui:tab title="History">[...]
        </ui:tabs>
```

```
      </ui:panel-layout>
    </ui:display>
  </xfk:data-object>
</xfk:data-objects>
```

This structure lets you display the employee address, but you still need to define the fields that the address panel will show and specify how to populate them.

Address Fields

The fields or properties of a data object are defined by parameters added to that data object using the `xfk:add-data-object` configuration in the model.

Reading Address Details

To display the address details, add a new `struct` named `address` to the output of the `read` operation. In that structure, include the internal `address id` for the employee's home address and any other address fields you want to display.

Also, use the `xfk:add-to-object` configuration to add all those fields to the `EmployeeAddressObject` data object, as shown in Listing 4-45.

Listing 4-45. Defining and populating address fields

```
<object name="employee">
  <operations>
    <operation name="read" type="read">
      <input>[...]
      <output>
        ...
+       <struct name="address">
+         <param name="address id" type="address"
+                 required="true"/>
+         <param name="address line1" type="string"/>
+         <param name="address line2" type="string"/>
+         <param name="city" type="string"/>
+         <param name="state province id"
+                 type="state province" required="true"/>
```

CHAPTER 4 BUILDING OUT A DETAILS VIEW

```
+            <param name="postal code" type="string"/>
+            <param name="country" type="country region"/>
+            <config>
+              <xfk:add-to-object class="EmployeeAddressObject"/>
+            </config>
+          </struct>
           <config>[...]
         </output>
       </operation>
       ...
     </operations>
   </object>
```

> **Note** Some integer parameters are set as required to use non-nullable types in the DTO. For some character fields, I used the generic type `string`, but it is better to define appropriate logical types for those fields and use them on these parameters.

Configuring Address Fields

Now that you have defined the fields for the `EmployeeAddressObject` data object, let's configure how the UI will display them. I will hide the `address id` field, set a label for the `state province id` field, and use the `field-cols="2"` attribute to display the fields in two columns, as shown in Listing 4-46.

Listing 4-46. Configuring address fields in EmployeeAddressObject

```
   <xfk:data-objects>
     <xfk:data-object class="EmployeeAddressObject">
+      <ui:display>
+        <ui:fields field-cols="2">
+          <ui:field param="address id" hidden="true"/>
+          <ui:field param="state province id"
+                    label="State/Province"/>
```

211

```
+            </ui:fields>
+        </ui:display>
+    </xfk:data-object>
     ...
   </xfk:data-objects>
```

Now rebuild the model to regenerate all the artifacts, so you can implement custom logic for populating the home address.

Populating Address Fields

To populate the address fields, add custom code to the `ReadAsync` method of the `EmployeeService` class. This constructs the address output structure and populates it with the employee's home address, as shown in Listing 4-47.

Listing 4-47. Custom code for populating address fields

```
public virtual async Task<Output<Employee_ReadOutput>>
    ReadAsync(int _businessEntityId,
            CancellationToken token = default)
{
    // CUSTOM_CODE_START: add custom code for Read operation below
    ...
+   res.Address = new Employee_ReadOutput_Address();
+   var homeAddress = obj.BusinessEntityObject
+       .BusinessEntityObject.AddressObjectList
+       .FirstOrDefault(a =>
+           a.AddressTypeObject.Name == "Home")?
+       .AddressObject;
+   ServiceUtil.CopyProperties(homeAddress, res.Address);
+   res.Address.Country = homeAddress?.StateProvinceObject
+           .CountryRegionCodeObject.CountryRegionCode;
    // CUSTOM_CODE_END
}
```

CHAPTER 4　BUILDING OUT A DETAILS VIEW

Note The `ServiceUtil.CopyProperties` method copies all matching properties from the `AddressObject` to the output structure, but you must set the `Country` property separately, since it is not a direct property of the `AddressObject`.

Contact Tab with Address

If you run the application now and open the *Contact* tab for an existing employee, you will see the employee's home address, as illustrated in Figure 4-18.

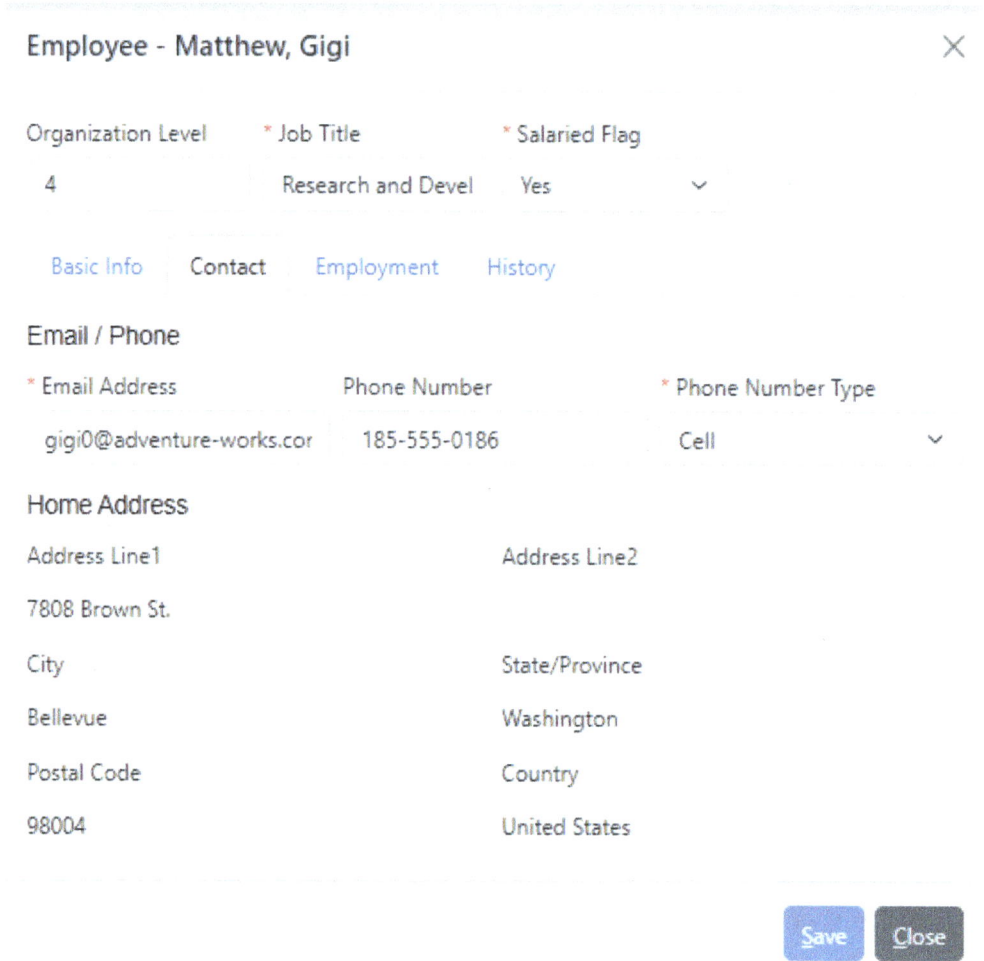

Figure 4-18. Employee contact tab with home address

The UI displays the address fields in two columns and hides the address id field. Both the *State/Province* and *Country* fields show the names of the selected state and country, since we defined a dynamic enumeration for them earlier.

Address Details Screen

Next, create a separate Address Details screen for creating and editing addresses, which you will use to add or edit the employee's home address.

Generating Address Details View

To add CRUD operations, a data object, and a view for the address, run a Model Enhancement generator. Since you only need the Address Details view (without the list or search views generated by the *Full CRUD with Views* generator), clone that generator, rename it to *Details View*, and update its properties as follows:

- *Generate Read List*: False
- *Generate Search View*: False
- *Details View Menu*: False

Next, right-click the address.xom file, and select *Generate* ▶ *Model Enhancement* ▶ *Details View*. This action generates CRUD operations, data object, and a details view for the address object. Remove the internal rowguid and modified date parameters from all CRUD operations, and add the country parameter to the read output, as shown in Listing 4-48.

Listing 4-48. Address CRUD operations updates

```
<object name="address">
  <operations>
    <operation name="read" type="read">
      <input>[...]
      <output>
        <param name="address line1"/>
        <param name="address line2"/>
        <param name="city"/>
+       <param name="postal code"/>
```

CHAPTER 4 BUILDING OUT A DETAILS VIEW

```
            <param name="state province id"/>
+           <param name="country" type="country region"/>
-           <param name="postal code"/>
-           <param name="rowguid"/>
-           <param name="modified date"/>
          </output>
        </operation>
        <operation name="create" type="create">
          <input arg="data">
            ...
-           <param name="rowguid"/>
-           <param name="modified date"/>
          </input>
          <output>[...]
        </operation>
        <operation name="update" type="update">
          <input>
            <param name="address id"/>
            <struct name="data">
              ...
-             <param name="rowguid"/>
-             <param name="modified date"/>
            </struct>
          </input>
        </operation>
      </operations>
    </object>
```

Note I also moved the postal code parameter up in the read output to display it before the state province id field on the UI, since the order of fields is determined by the order of parameters in the first structure in the model by default.

215

CHAPTER 4   BUILDING OUT A DETAILS VIEW

Custom Code for AddressService

Let's build the model to generate all the necessary artifacts, and then we can implement the custom code for the `AddressService` class to populate the `Country` field in the `ReadAsync` method and set the `ModifiedDate` and `Rowguid` fields in the `CreateAsync` and `UpdateAsync` methods, as shown in Listing 4-49.

Listing 4-49. Custom code for AddressService

```
public virtual async Task<Output<Address_ReadOutput>>
    ReadAsync(int _addressId,
              CancellationToken token = default)
{
    ...
    // CUSTOM_CODE_START: add custom code for Read operation below
+   res.Country = obj.StateProvinceObject.CountryRegionCode;
    // CUSTOM_CODE_END
    ...
}

public virtual async Task<Output<Address_CreateOutput>>
    CreateAsync(Address_CreateInput _data,
                CancellationToken token = default)
{
    ...
    // CUSTOM_CODE_START: add custom code for Create operation below
+   obj.ModifiedDate = DateTime.UtcNow;
+   obj.Rowguid = Guid.NewGuid();
    // CUSTOM_CODE_END
    ...
}

public virtual async Task<Output> UpdateAsync(
    int _addressId,
    Address_UpdateInput_Data _data,
    CancellationToken token = default)
{
```

```
    ...
    // CUSTOM_CODE_START: add custom code for Update operation below
+   obj.ModifiedDate = DateTime.UtcNow;
    // CUSTOM_CODE_END
    ...
}
```

Since you added the country only as the out parameter of the read operation, the UI displays it as read-only by default, and only for existing address records.

However, making the country editable is more useful, so the user can select a country when creating a new address, which limits the state selection to that country. You can do this by customizing the AddressObject data object.

Customizing AddressObject

To customize the AddressObject data object, we need to set the customize="true" attribute on it. This lets you implement custom logic for the state and country selection. Also, make the country field editable, set the label for the state province id field, and configure the fields to display in two columns, as shown in Listing 4-50.

Listing 4-50. Customizing AddressObject data object

```
<xfk:data-object class="AddressObject"
+                customize="true">
  <ui:display>
-   <ui:fields>
+   <ui:fields field-cols="2">
      <ui:field param="address id" hidden="true"/>
+     <ui:field param="state province id"
+               label="State/Province"/>
+     <ui:field param="country" editable="true"/>
    </ui:fields>
  </ui:display>
</xfk:data-object>
```

Let's build the model again and open the generated AddressObjectCustomized.cs file. Similar to how we did it for employee criteria, we will set up cascading selection for the StateProvinceIdProperty field based on the selected country.

CHAPTER 4　BUILDING OUT A DETAILS VIEW

However, if the user selects a state first when creating a new address, we want to auto-populate the country based on that state selection. We can do that by subscribing to the property change event of the StateProvinceIdProperty and setting the country based on the selected state, as shown in Listing 4-51.

Listing 4-51. Custom UI logic for AddressObject

```
protected override void OnInitialized()
{
    base.OnInitialized();
+   // filter state selection list to the selected country
+   StateProvinceIdProperty.SetCascadingProperty(
+       StateProvince.Attributes.CountryRegionCode,
+       CountryProperty);
+
+   // auto-populate country based on state selection
+   StateProvinceIdProperty.AsyncChange +=
+   async (sender, e, token) =>
+   {
+       if (e.Change.IncludesValue() &&
+           StateProvinceIdProperty.Editing &&
+           CountryProperty.IsNull())
+       {
+           await CountryProperty.SetValueAsync(
+               StateProvinceIdProperty
+                   .Value[StateProvince.Attributes
+                       .CountryRegionCode],
+               e.Row, token);
+       }
+   };
}
```

Take note of the conditions we use before setting the country value. You should always check if the change includes a value change, since the property change event can be triggered by changes in other attributes of the data property, such as Visible, Editable, or Required.

CHAPTER 4   BUILDING OUT A DETAILS VIEW

This listener also triggers when the state value is set while reading the address. You don't want to change the country in that case, since the read operation also populates it, which would mark the object as modified. Therefore, check if the state property is being edited by the user by checking the Editing attribute.

Address Details View

Let's run the application to review the Address Details view. The generator did not create a menu item for the Address Details view, since you set the Details View Menu property to False. However, you can still open it by navigating directly to its URL, e.g., https://localhost:44337/AddressView?AddressId=25.

This URL opens the Address Details view for an existing address with ID 25, as shown in Figure 4-19.

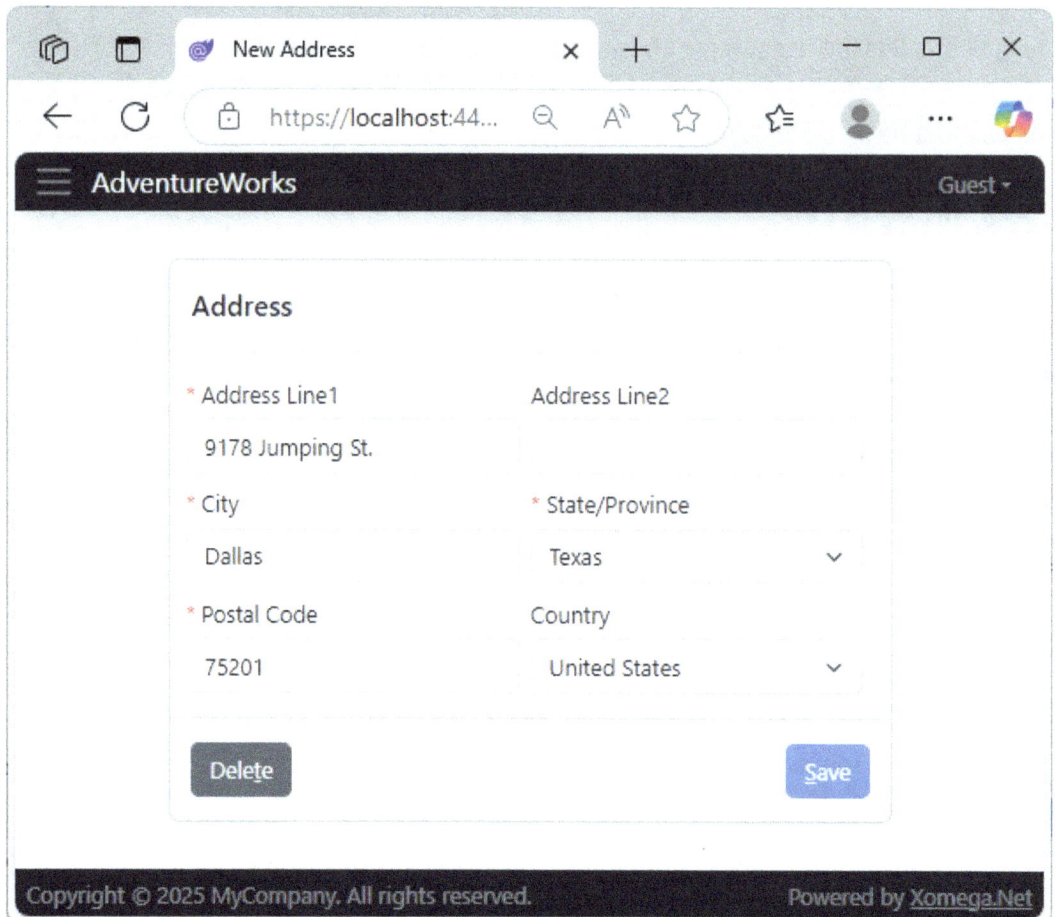

Figure 4-19. *Address details view*

You can see that the `AddressId` field is hidden, while the `Country` field is editable and populated. If you create a new address by navigating to https://localhost:44337/ AddressView?_action=create, you can either select a country first, which limits the state selection to that country, or select a state first, which auto-populates the country field.

Add and Edit Employee Address

Now that you have the Address Details view ready, you can use it to create and edit the employee's home address from the Employee Details screen. To do this, add two links to the Home Address panel as follows.

Links to Address Details

The first link lets the user create and save a new address using the Address Details view and populate the internal address id field with the ID of the newly created address, as well as other address fields displayed on the Employee Details screen.

Create Address Link

Add a new `ui:link` element named "create address" to the `EmployeeAddressObject` data object. This link opens the `AddressView` as a child in popup mode. Set the `_action` parameter to `create` to open the target view in creation mode.

Also, add result parameters for the properties of the `AddressObject` in the `AddressView`, and map them to the corresponding fields in the `EmployeeAddressObject`, as shown in Listing 4-52.

Listing 4-52. Adding Create Address link

```
  <xfk:data-object class="EmployeeAddressObject">
    <ui:display>[...]
+   <ui:link name="create address" view="AddressView"
+           child="true">
+     <ui:params>
+       <ui:param name="_action" value="create"/>
+     </ui:params>
+     <ui:result>
```

CHAPTER 4 ■ BUILDING OUT A DETAILS VIEW

```
+        <ui:param name="address id" field="address id"/>
+        <ui:param name="address line1" field="address line1"/>
+        <ui:param name="address line2" field="address line2"/>
+        <ui:param name="city" field="city"/>
+        <ui:param name="postal code" field="postal code"/>
+        <ui:param name="state province id"
+               field="state province id"/>
+        <ui:param name="country" field="country"/>
+    </ui:result>
+  </ui:link>
</xfk:data-object>
```

This link lets the user create a new address. When the user saves the address, the `AddressView` sets the values of the address fields to the `EmployeeAddressObject`, which then displays them on the Employee Details screen.

Edit Address Link

The second link lets the user edit the current employee's home address in the Address Details view. Similar to the "create address" link, add a new `ui:link` element named "edit address" to the `EmployeeAddressObject` data object.

This link also opens the child `AddressView` in popup mode, but it passes the `address id` of the current employee's home address to the target view. It also updates the employee address fields with the values from the `AddressView` when the user saves the address, as shown in Listing 4-53.

Listing 4-53. *Adding Edit Address link*

```
<xfk:data-object class="EmployeeAddressObject">
  <ui:display>[...]
  <ui:link name="create address" view="AddressView"
          child="true">[...]
+ <ui:link name="edit address" view="AddressView"
+         child="true">
+    <ui:params>
+      <ui:param name="address id" field="address id"/>
+    </ui:params>
```

```
+    <ui:result>
+      <ui:param name="address line1" field="address line1"/>
+      <ui:param name="address line2" field="address line2"/>
+      <ui:param name="city" field="city"/>
+      <ui:param name="postal code" field="postal code"/>
+      <ui:param name="state province id"
+                field="state province id"/>
+      <ui:param name="country" field="country"/>
+    </ui:result>
+  </ui:link>
</xfk:data-object>
```

> **Note** Technically, the user can also delete the existing address on the Address Details view, but this use case is not covered here, since the employee's home address will be required.

Disabling Edit Link Conditionally

Since the Edit Address link requires an `address id` to be passed to the `AddressView`, it should be disabled when the employee's home address is not set yet, i.e., when creating a new employee. We can disable it in the customized `EmployeeAddressObject` data object, so let's add the `customize="true"` attribute to it, as shown in Listing 4-54.

Listing 4-54. Customizing EmployeeAddressObject

```
  <xfk:data-object class="EmployeeAddressObject"
+                  customize="true">
```

After you build the model, open the generated `EmployeeAddressObjectCustomized.cs` file, and add custom logic to the `OnInitialized` method. Make the Enabled attribute of the `EditAddressAction` computed based on a LINQ expression that checks if the `AddressIdProperty` is not null, as shown in Listing 4-55.

Listing 4-55. Disabling Edit Address link for new employee

```
public class EmployeeAddressObjectCustomized : EmployeeAddressObject
{
    protected override void OnInitialized()
    {
        base.OnInitialized();
+       Expression<Func<DataProperty, bool>> expEditAddr =
+           addrId => !addrId.IsNull(null);
+       EditAddressAction.SetComputedEnabled(
+           expEditAddr, AddressIdProperty);
    }
}
```

Note This approach is similar to how you set the conditional Required attribute for the *Phone Number Type* field earlier.

Saving Employee Address

The links you added let you create a new address for an employee and store it in the AddressIdProperty of the EmployeeAddressObject on the UI. However, the application will not save the address if you try to save the employee, since you have not included the address in the employee's create and update operations yet.

Adding Address Input Structures

When you added the address fields to the read operation, you used a nested structure for the address parameters and added it to the child EmployeeAddressObject data object. Therefore, add a similar structure with a single parameter address id to the input of the create and update operations.

Also, add the xfk:add-to-object configuration for the EmployeeAddressObject data object so the framework can handle this parameter automatically, as shown in Listing 4-56.

Listing 4-56. *Adding address input structures to employee operations*

```
<object name="employee">
  <operation name="create" type="create">
    <input arg="data">
+     <struct name="address">
+       <param name="address id" type="address"
+               required="true"/>
+       <config>
+         <xfk:add-to-object class="EmployeeAddressObject"/>
+       </config>
+     </struct>
    </input>
  </operation>
  <operation name="update" type="update">
    <input>
      <param name="business entity id"/>
      <struct name="data">
+       <struct name="address">
+         <param name="address id" type="address"
+                 required="true"/>
+         <config>
+           <xfk:add-to-object class="EmployeeAddressObject"/>
+         </config>
+       </struct>
      </struct>
    </input>
  </operation>
</object>
```

An input structure with a single field may seem unnecessary, but you need it to make that parameter part of the child `EmployeeAddressObject` data object for the framework to work out of the box. If you had more address fields to update on the Employee Details screen, this structure would make more sense.

CHAPTER 4 BUILDING OUT A DETAILS VIEW

Tip Alternatively, you can add the address fields along with other parameters directly to the `EmployeeObject` data object in all CRUD operations. This way, you do not need a separate child data object, and you can create a field group for the address fields in the Employee Details view. However, this example demonstrates how to use a child data object and what it involves.

Service Logic for Saving Employee Address

Build the model to generate the updated operations, then implement custom logic for saving the employee's home address in the `EmployeeService` class.

First, add a new method `UpdateHomeAddressAsync` in the `EmployeeServiceExtended.cs` file. This method takes the base business entity and the address ID as parameters and updates or adds the home address for that business entity, as shown in Listing 4-57.

Listing 4-57. Method for saving a home address

```
public partial class EmployeeService
{
+   protected async Task UpdateHomeAddressAsync(
+       BusinessEntity be, int addressId,
+       CancellationToken token)
+   {
+       if (be == null) return;
+       var addressType = await ctx.AddressType
+           .FirstOrDefaultAsync(at =>
+               at.Name == "Home", token);
+       Address address = await ctx.FindEntityAsync<Address>(
+           currentErrors, token, addressId);
+
+       var beAddress = be.AddressObjectList.FirstOrDefault(
+           a => a.AddressTypeId == addressType.AddressTypeId);
+       if (beAddress != null)
+           beAddress.AddressObject = address;
```

225

CHAPTER 4 BUILDING OUT A DETAILS VIEW

```
+            else be.AddressObjectList.Add(
+                new BusinessEntityAddress
+                {
+                    AddressObject = address,
+                    AddressTypeObject = addressType,
+                    Rowguid = Guid.NewGuid(),
+                    ModifiedDate = DateTime.Now
+                });
+        }
         ...
    }
```

> **Note** `currentErrors` is injected into the base service and allows you to add errors, warnings, or messages to return from the current operation.

Next, call this method from the `CreateAsync` and `UpdateAsync` methods of the `EmployeeService` class, as shown in Listing 4-58.

Listing 4-58. Custom code for saving employee address

```
public virtual async Task<Output<Employee_CreateOutput>>
    CreateAsync(Employee_CreateInput _data
            CancellationToken token = default)
{
    // CUSTOM_CODE_START: add custom code for Create operation below
    ...
+   await UpdateHomeAddressAsync(
+       obj.BusinessEntityObject.BusinessEntityObject,
+       _data.Address.AddressId, token);
    // CUSTOM_CODE_END
}
```

```
public virtual async Task<Output> UpdateAsync(
    int _businessEntityId,
    Employee_UpdateInput_Data _data,
    CancellationToken token = default)
{
    // CUSTOM_CODE_START: add custom code for Update operation below
    ...
+   await UpdateHomeAddressAsync(
+       obj.BusinessEntityObject.BusinessEntityObject,
+       _data.Address.AddressId, token);
    // CUSTOM_CODE_END
}
```

Review Employee Address

If you run the application now and create a new employee from the Employee List screen, you will see that the Home Address has a "Create Address" link and a disabled "Edit Address" link.

When you click the "Create Address" link, the application opens the Address Details view in a popup dialog, where you can enter the address details, as shown in Figure 4-20.

CHAPTER 4   BUILDING OUT A DETAILS VIEW

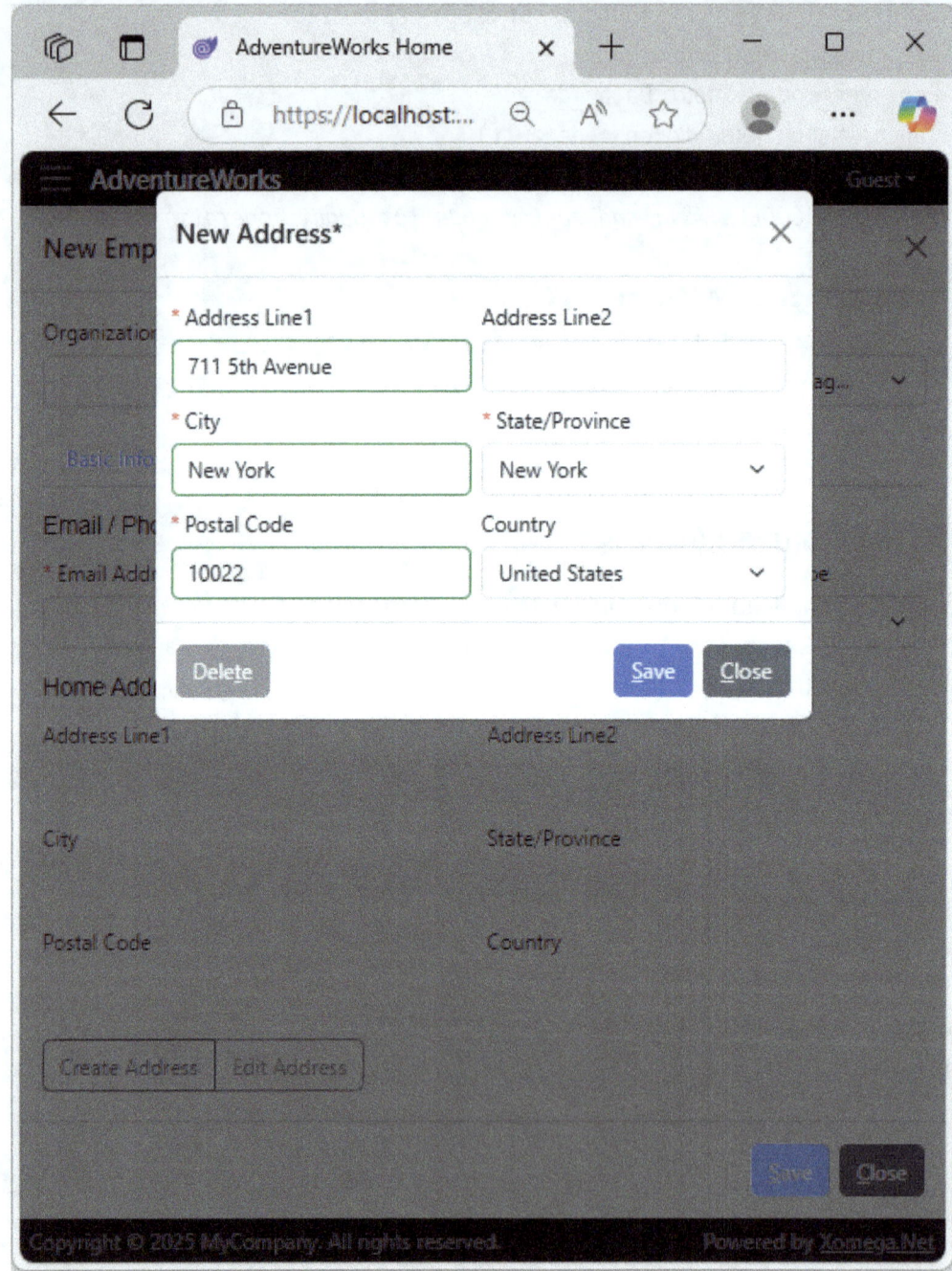

Figure 4-20. *Creating an address for a new employee*

After you save the address, the Home Address panel displays the address details, and the "Edit Address" link becomes enabled.

Lookup Selection Form

In the previous section, we allowed users to create or edit a related object for the employee's home address. In many cases, when objects are managed independently, you only need to select one of the already created objects. For example, when adding a new sales order for an existing customer, you need to select the customer from a list.

When that list is relatively small and static, you can use a simple drop-down list or an autocomplete field, as we did for selecting a country or a state. However, the list may be too large to cache for the drop-down, or you may need to search for the object by multiple criteria and view several of its fields to ensure you select the correct object. In this case, you can use a separate lookup view that allows you to search for the object by multiple criteria and select it from the list of results.

In this section, we will assume that the list of all addresses may have already been imported into the system, and we will create a lookup view for selecting an address for the employee's home address.

Generating a Lookup View

Earlier, we generated an address details view and CRUD operations for it using a separate *Details View* generator that we configured. Similarly, you can configure a generator to add just a Read List operation and a Search View without links to a details view. To do this, clone the *Full CRUD with Views* generator, rename it to *Lookup View*, and set the following parameters:

- *Generate Links*: False
- *Generate CRUD*: False
- *Generate Details View*: False
- *Search View Menu*: False

After that, you can right-click the `address.xom` file and select *Generate* ➤ *Model Enhancements* ➤ *Lookup View* to add the `read list` operation and a search view for the `address` object.

Configuring Lookup Criteria

Next, let's expand the criteria input structure of the read list operation and remove unnecessary parameters, as shown in Listing 4-59.

Listing 4-59. Configuring address criteria parameters

```
<object name="address">
  <operation name="read list" type="readlist">
    <input>
      <struct name="criteria">
-       <param name="address id"/>
        <param name="address line1"/>
-       <param name="address line2"/>
        <param name="city"/>
        <param name="state province id"/>
        <param name="postal code"/>
-       <param name="rowguid"/>
-       <param name="modified date"/>
        <config>[...]
      </struct>
    </input>
    <output list="true">[...]
  </operation>
</object>
```

With only four criteria left, we can configure them to be displayed statically with no operator selection, making it easier for users to specify them. You can do this by adding static="true" and op-none="true" to the ui:fields element of the AddressCriteria data object, as shown in Listing 4-60.

Listing 4-60. Configuring address criteria display

```
<xfk:data-object class="AddressCriteria">
  <ui:display>
-   <ui:fields/>
+   <ui:fields static="true" op-none="true">
+     <ui:field param="state province id"
```

```
+                label="State/Province"/>
+      <ui:field param="address line1" op-default="CN"
+                label="Street Address"/>
+      <ui:field param="city" op-default="CN"/>
+    </ui:fields>
    </ui:display>
</xfk:data-object>
```

I also specified better labels for the *Street Address* and *State/Province* criteria and set the default operator for *Street Address* and *City* to Contains to allow users to search for addresses by partial street or city names.

Lookup Result Fields

We need the results grid on the address list view to include at least all the fields shown on the Employee Details view for the home address, so that we can populate the home address after selecting an address from the grid.

Therefore, we will remove the internal fields rowguid and modified date from the output structure, but add a country output parameter, as shown in Listing 4-61.

Listing 4-61. Configuring address result columns

```
<object name="address">
  <operation name="read list" type="readlist">
    <input>[...]
    <output list="true">
      <param name="address id"/>
      <param name="address line1"/>
      <param name="address line2"/>
      <param name="city"/>
      <param name="state province id"/>
      <param name="postal code"/>
+     <param name="country" type="country region"/>
-     <param name="rowguid"/>
-     <param name="modified date"/>
      <config>[...]
    </output>
  </operation>
```

```
</object>
...
<xfk:data-object class="AddressList" list="true">
  <ui:display>
    <ui:fields>
      <ui:field param="address id" hidden="true"/>
+     <ui:field param="state province id"
+                label="State/Province"/>
    </ui:fields>
  </ui:display>
</xfk:data-object>
```

> **Note** I also updated the label for the *State/Province* column in the AddressList data object.

Changing View Title

To better communicate the purpose of the screen, I will also change the title for the AddressListView to *Address Lookup*, as shown in Listing 4-62.

Listing 4-62. Changing view title for the Address List view

```
- <ui:view name="AddressListView" title="Address List">
+ <ui:view name="AddressListView" title="Address Lookup">
    <ui:view-model data-object="AddressList"/>
  </ui:view>
```

Let's build the model to regenerate the code, so we can add the necessary custom code for the lookup view.

Custom Address Service Code

The only custom output parameter we added for the address lookup is `country`, so you can set it in the `ReadListAsync` method of the `AddressService` class, as shown in Listing 4-63.

Listing 4-63. Adding custom code for the Address Read List operation

```
public virtual async
    Task<Output<ICollection<Address_ReadListOutput>>>
    ReadListAsync(Address_ReadListInput_Criteria _criteria,
                CancellationToken token = default)
{
    ...
    select new Address_ReadListOutput() {
        AddressId = obj.AddressId,
        AddressLine1 = obj.AddressLine1,
        AddressLine2 = obj.AddressLine2,
        City = obj.City,
        StateProvinceId = obj.StateProvinceId,
        PostalCode = obj.PostalCode,
        // CUSTOM_CODE_START: set the Country output parameter of ReadList
            operation below
-       // TODO: Country = obj.???, // CUSTOM_CODE_END
+       Country = obj.StateProvinceObject.CountryRegionCode
+       // CUSTOM_CODE_END
    };
    ...
}
```

Now that we have the address lookup view ready, we can add a link to it from the Employee Details view, so users can select an address for the employee's home address.

Employee Address Lookup Link

Adding an address lookup link to the employee details view is similar to adding links for creating an address. You just need to add a new link named "lookup address" to the `EmployeeAddressObject` data object with `AddressListView` as the target view, set the `_action` parameter to `select`, and add a `_selection` parameter with the value `single`, as shown in Listing 4-64.

Listing 4-64. *Adding address lookup link to Employee Details view*

```
<xfk:data-object class="EmployeeAddressObject"
                 customize="true">
  <ui:display>[...]
  <ui:link name="create address" view="AddressView"
           child="true">[...]
  <ui:link name="edit address" view="AddressView"
           child="true">[...]
+ <ui:link name="lookup address" view="AddressListView"
+          child="true">
+   <ui:params>
+     <ui:param name="_action" value="select"/>
+     <ui:param name="_selection" value="single"/>
+   </ui:params>
+   <ui:result>
+     <ui:param name="address id" field="address id"/>
+     <ui:param name="address line1" field="address line1"/>
+     <ui:param name="address line2" field="address line2"/>
+     <ui:param name="city" field="city"/>
+     <ui:param name="postal code" field="postal code"/>
+     <ui:param name="state province id"
+               field="state province id"/>
+     <ui:param name="country" field="country"/>
+   </ui:result>
+ </ui:link>
</xfk:data-object>
```

This will enable single-row selection in the address lookup view and add a *Select* button, which will return the selected address to the Employee Details view.

Reviewing Address Lookup View

Let's build the model and run the application to see how the address lookup view looks. After you open the *Contact* tab of the Employee Details view, you will see a new *Lookup Address* link next to the *Edit Address* link. Clicking it will pop up the Address Lookup view, where you can search for an address by the criteria we configured earlier, and then select it from the list of results, as shown in Figure 4-21.

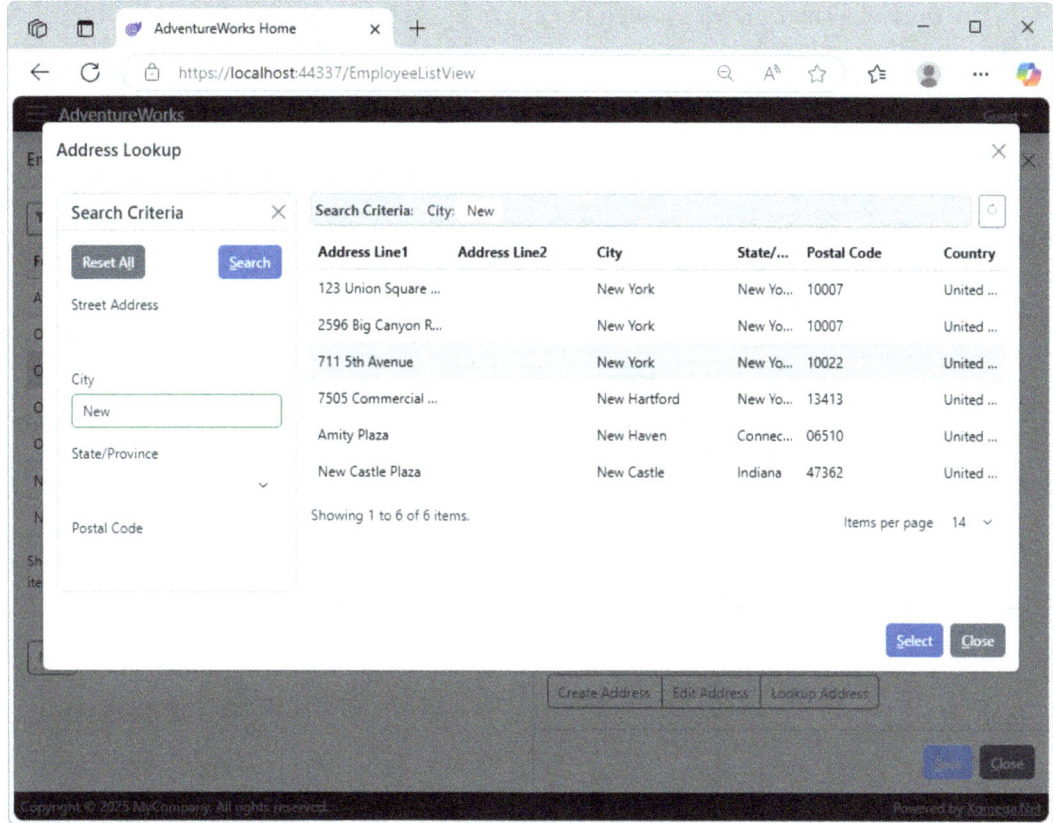

Figure 4-21. Employee address lookup link and view

Notice that the Address Lookup view has a *Select* button, which becomes enabled after you select a row in the results grid. Clicking it will return the selected address to the Employee Details view and populate the home address fields with the values from the selected address.

Using a full-scale lookup view, where the user can search records by multiple criteria and view several fields in the results grid, helps ensure they select the correct object, which may not always be possible with a simple drop-down list or an autocomplete field.

Employee Address Validation

With the current design of the Employee Details view, where the home address for the new employee is either created or selected via the address lookup view, we need a good way to inform the user that the address is required.

Chapter 4   Building Out a Details View

In the previous section, we marked the `address id` parameter as required in the inputs of the `create` and `update` operations. If you try to save a new employee without selecting a home address, you will get an error message saying "AddressId is required", which doesn't make much sense since the Address ID is not even shown on the screen.

Therefore, open the `Resources.resx` file in the `AdventureWorks.Client.Common` project and add a new resource `EmployeeView_Error_AddressRequired` with the value "Please create a new address or look up an existing address.", as shown in Figure 4-22.

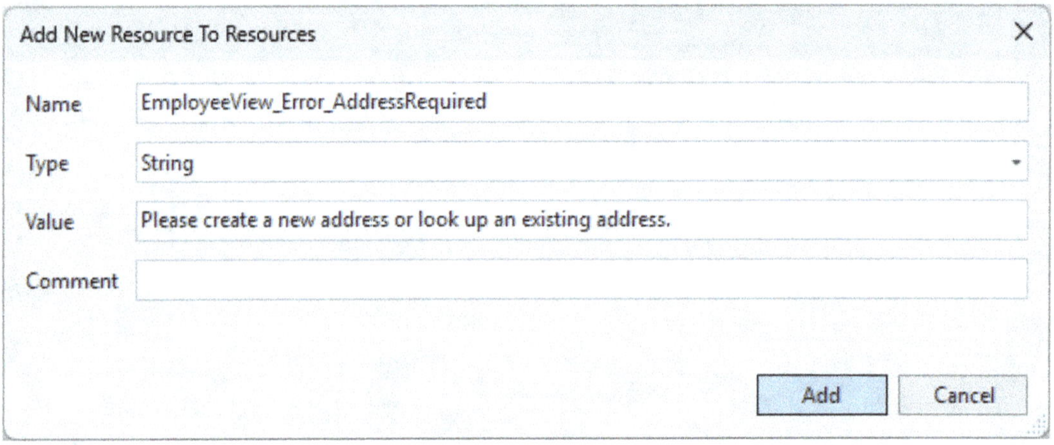

Figure 4-22. Adding an error message for the required address

Next, right-click the nested `Messages.tt` file, and select *Run Custom Tool* to regenerate the `Messages` class with string constants for the resources in the `Resources.resx` file.

You can add custom address validation in the `EmployeeAddressObjectCustomized` class. Normally, you would override the `Validate` method and add a validation error there, but in this case, we want to replace the default validation error for the `address id` parameter with a more user-friendly message.

Therefore, set the `Validator` property of the `AddressIdProperty` to a lambda function that checks if the address ID is null and adds a validation error with the custom message, as shown in Listing 4-65.

Listing 4-65. Adding address validation to the EmployeeAddressObject

```
protected override void OnInitialized()
{
    base.OnInitialized();

    Expression<Func<DataProperty, bool>> expEditAddr =
        addrId => !addrId.IsNull(null);
    EditAddressAction.SetComputedEnabled(
        expEditAddr, AddressIdProperty);

+   AddressIdProperty.Validator = (dp, val, row) => {
+       if (AddressIdProperty.IsNull())
+           AddressIdProperty.AddValidationError(row,
+               Messages.EmployeeView_Error_AddressRequired);
+   };
}
```

Note To avoid hardcoding the error message in the class, we use the constant EmployeeView_Error_AddressRequired, generated from the resource we added earlier.

Now, when you try to save a new employee without selecting an address, you will see a more user-friendly error message, as shown in Figure 4-23.

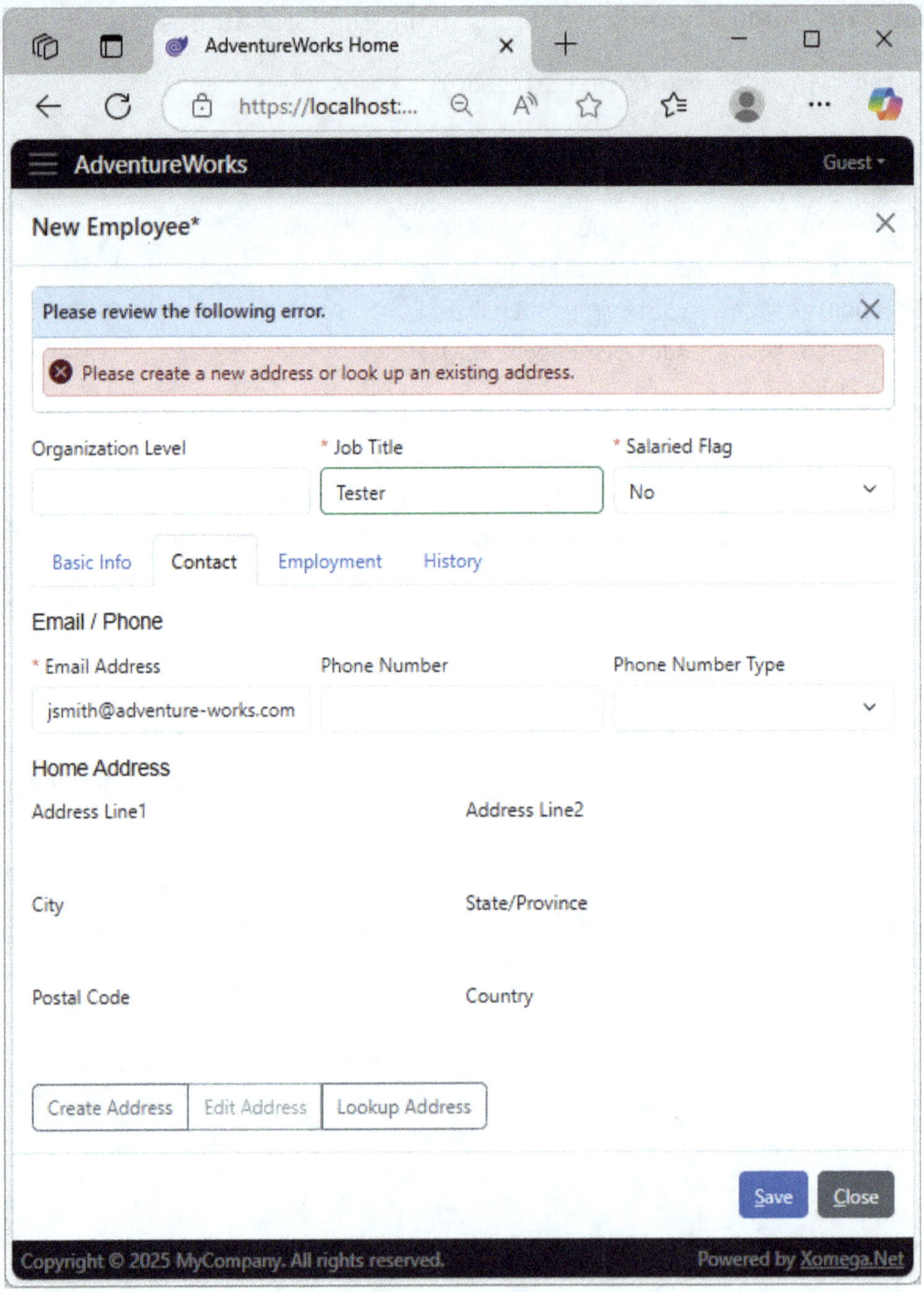

CHAPTER 4   BUILDING OUT A DETAILS VIEW

Figure 4-23. Improved employee address validation message

Computed UI Fields

At the beginning of this chapter, we added two child lists to the Employee Details view for the employee's pay history and department history, which we placed in the History tab. Effectively, those lists also store information about the current employee pay and department.

However, we also want to display the current pay rate and department in the main Employee Details view. This will also allow users to edit them, which will, in turn, create a new pay history record or department history record, respectively.

In this section, we will add the current pay and department information to the Employee Details view and include additional computed UI-only fields, whose values will be calculated based on the current pay and department information.

Adding Current Pay Info

We'll start by adding the employee's current pay info to the *Employment* tab. If you remember, the pay history record consists of the `pay rate`, `pay frequency`, and the `rate change date`, so we will need to show the pay rate and frequency with the latest rate change date.

We will also add a computed field for the *Annual Pay*, which will be calculated based on the pay rate and frequency.

Adding Pay Rate to Operations

As usual, we will start by adding the `pay rate` and `pay frequency` parameters to the CRUD operations of the `employee` object and making them required, as shown in Listing 4-66.

Listing 4-66. Adding pay rate to CRUD operations

```
<object name="employee">
  <operation name="read" type="read">
    <output>
+     <param name="pay rate" type="money"/>
+     <param name="pay frequency" type="pay frequency"/>
      ...
    </output>
```

```
    </operation>
    <operation name="create" type="create">
      <input arg="data">
+       <param name="pay rate" type="money" required="true"/>
+       <param name="pay frequency" type="pay frequency"
+               required="true"/>
        ...
      </input>
    </operation>
    <operation name="update" type="update">
      <input>
        <param name="business entity id"/>
        <struct name="data">
+         <param name="pay rate" type="money" required="true"/>
+         <param name="pay frequency" type="pay frequency"
+                 required="true"/>
          ...
        </struct>
      </input>
    </operation>
</object>
```

Since we add these parameters directly to the main input and output structures, they will be automatically added to the `EmployeeObject` data object.

Adding UI-Only Fields

We also want to show the *Annual Pay*, which is calculated on the UI from the pay rate and frequency. If it's not included in the CRUD operations, we need a way to add it to the `EmployeeObject` data object separately.

To do this, you can define a new structure `employee properties` with the annual pay parameter in the `employee.xom` and include the `xfk:add-to-object` configuration to add it to the `EmployeeObject`, as shown in Listing 4-67.

CHAPTER 4   BUILDING OUT A DETAILS VIEW

Listing 4-67. Adding UI-only annual pay field

```
  <enums>[...]
+ <structs>
+   <struct name="employee properties">
+     <param name="annual pay" type="money"/>
+     <config>
+       <xfk:add-to-object class="EmployeeObject"/>
+     </config>
+     <usage generic="true"/>
+   </struct>
+ </structs>
  <objects>[...]
```

Note We are not planning to use this structure in any operations, so to avoid an Xomega warning that the structure is not used, I also added a `usage` element with the `generic="true"` attribute to it.

Grouping Pay Properties

Now, let's define a new field group pay in the `EmployeeObject` data object and add the pay rate, pay frequency, and annual pay fields to it. We will also include the orphaned salaried flag field with a proper label in this group and then add this group to the *Employment* tab, as shown in Listing 4-68.

Listing 4-68. Adding a Pay field group

```
<xfk:data-object class="EmployeeObject" customize="true">
  <ui:display>
    <ui:fields>[...]
    <ui:fields group="name" title="Employee Name">[...]
    <ui:fields group="personal" title="Personal Info">[...]
    <ui:fields group="email phone" title="Email / Phone">[...]
    <ui:fields group="status">[...]
    <ui:fields group="benefits">[...]
```

241

```
+    <ui:fields group="pay">
+      <ui:field param="salaried flag" label="Is Salaried"/>
+      <ui:field param="pay rate"/>
+      <ui:field param="pay frequency"/>
+      <ui:field param="annual pay" editable="false"/>
+    </ui:fields>
     <ui:panel-layout>
       <ui:panel/>
       <ui:tabs>
         <ui:tab title="Basic Info">[...]</ui:tab>
         <ui:tab title="Contact">[...]</ui:tab>
         <ui:tab title="Employment">
           <ui:panel group="status" field-cols="1"
                                   panel-cols="2"/>
           <ui:panel group="benefits" field-cols="1"
                                     panel-cols="2"/>
+          <ui:panel group="pay"/>
         </ui:tab>
         <ui:tab title="History">[...]</ui:tab>
       </ui:tabs>
     </ui:panel-layout>
   </ui:display>
 </xfk:data-object>
```

Normally, Xomega determines if a field is display-only if it is part of the output structures but none of the input structures of the CRUD operations. We want the annual pay field to be display-only, since it's a computed field, but Xomega cannot infer that from the operations' structures, so we need to explicitly set the `editable="false"` attribute for it.

Service Logic to Update Pay

Let's build the model and implement the service logic to update the current pay rate and frequency. First, I'll add a new method `UpdatePayRateAsync` to the `EmployeeServiceExtended.cs` file, which checks if the supplied pay rate and frequency are different from the current ones, and, if so, creates a new `EmployeePayHistory` record with the current date as the rate change date, as shown in Listing 4-69.

Listing 4-69. Method to update pay rate

```
public partial class EmployeeService
{
+   protected async Task UpdatePayRateAsync(Employee employee,
+       decimal payRate, byte payFrequency,
+       CancellationToken token)
+   {
+       if (employee == null) return;
+       var curPayRate = employee.PayHistoryObjectList
+           .OrderByDescending(ph => ph.RateChangeDate)
+           .FirstOrDefault();
+
+       if (curPayRate != null && curPayRate.Rate == payRate
+           && curPayRate.PayFrequency == payFrequency)
+           return; // no change, nothing to do
+
+       await ctx.EmployeePayHistory.AddAsync(
+           new EmployeePayHistory
+           {
+               EmployeeObject = employee,
+               Rate = payRate,
+               PayFrequency = payFrequency,
+               RateChangeDate = DateTime.Now,
+               ModifiedDate = DateTime.Now
+           }, token);
+   }
    ...
}
```

Tip The `EmployeePayHistory` table in the database has some check constraints for the `RateFrequency` to be either 1 (monthly) or 2 (biweekly) and for the `Rate` to be between 6.5 and 200. You can also add these server-side validations to this method to return a user-friendly error message.

CHAPTER 4   BUILDING OUT A DETAILS VIEW

Reading and Updating Pay Info

Next, we need to add custom code to the ReadAsync, CreateAsync, and UpdateAsync methods of the EmployeeService to read the current pay rate and frequency from the latest pay history record and to update them using the UpdatePayRateAsync method, as shown in Listing 4-70.

Listing 4-70. Custom code for reading and updating pay info

```
public virtual async Task<Output<Employee_ReadOutput>>
    ReadAsync(int _businessEntityId,
            CancellationToken token = default)
{
    // CUSTOM_CODE_START: add custom code for Read operation below
    ...
+   var payRate = obj.PayHistoryObjectList
+       .OrderByDescending(ph => ph.RateChangeDate)
+       .FirstOrDefault();
+   res.PayRate = payRate?.Rate;
+   res.PayFrequency = payRate?.PayFrequency;
    // CUSTOM_CODE_END
}
public virtual async Task<Output<Employee_CreateOutput>> CreateAsync(
    Employee_CreateInput _data, CancellationToken token = default)
{
    // CUSTOM_CODE_START: add custom code for Create operation below
    ...
+   await UpdatePayRateAsync(obj,
+       _data.PayRate, _data.PayFrequency, token);
    // CUSTOM_CODE_END
}
public virtual async Task<Output> UpdateAsync(int _businessEntityId,
    Employee_UpdateInput_Data _data, CancellationToken token = default)
{
    // CUSTOM_CODE_START: add custom code for Update operation below
    ...
```

```
+       await UpdatePayRateAsync(obj,
+           _data.PayRate, _data.PayFrequency, token);
    // CUSTOM_CODE_END
}
```

> **Note** Since we didn't make the `pay rate` and `pay frequency` parameters required in the `read` operation, they use nullable types in the result structure, and we cannot copy them from the entity using the `ServiceUtils.CopyProperties` method.

Configuring Computed Fields

You can configure a computed value for the *Annual Pay* property on the UI, as well as set the minimum and maximum values for the *Pay Rate* property, in the `EmployeeObjectCustomized.cs` file.

Similar to how we configured conditional *Required* and *Enabled* attributes of the properties in the previous sections, you can use the `SetComputedValue` method on the `AnnualPayProperty` with a LINQ expression that computes the annual pay based on the pay rate and frequency, as shown in Listing 4-71.

Listing 4-71. Configuring computed annual pay and pay rate range

```
+ using static AdventureWorks.Services.Common.Enumerations.PayFrequency;
public class EmployeeObjectCustomized : EmployeeObject
{
    protected override void OnInitialized()
    {
        ...
+       PayRateProperty.MinimumValue = 6.5M;
+       PayRateProperty.MinimumAllowed = true;
+       PayRateProperty.MaximumValue = 200;
+       PayRateProperty.MaximumAllowed = true;
+
+       Expression<Func<EmployeeObject, object>> xAnnualPay =
```

CHAPTER 4   BUILDING OUT A DETAILS VIEW

```
+                obj => ComputeAnnualPay(
+                    obj.PayRateProperty.Value,
+                    obj.PayFrequencyProperty.Value);
+        AnnualPayProperty.SetComputedValue(xAnnualPay, this);
    }

+   private static decimal? ComputeAnnualPay(
+       decimal? payRate, Header payFrequency)
+   {
+       if (payRate == null) return null;
+       return (payFrequency?.Id) switch
+       {
+           Biweekly => payRate * 26,
+           Monthly => payRate * 12,
+           _ => null,
+       };
+   }
}
```

To simplify the LINQ expression, I added and used a separate method `ComputeAnnualPay`, which takes the values of the `PayRate` and `PayFrequency` properties. In this method, I was able to use the values of the `PayFrequency` static enumeration that we defined earlier.

Caution   Make sure that the values of all dependent properties are retrieved in the LINQ expression, rather than in the method it calls, for the computed value to be updated automatically when the dependent properties change.

Reviewing Pay Fields

Let's run the application and open the Employee Details view to review the changes. You should see the *Pay* panel in the *Employment* tab with the *Is Salaried* flag, moved down here from the top panel, as well as the *Pay Rate*, *Pay Frequency*, and the display-only *Annual Pay* fields, as shown in Figure 4-24.

CHAPTER 4 BUILDING OUT A DETAILS VIEW

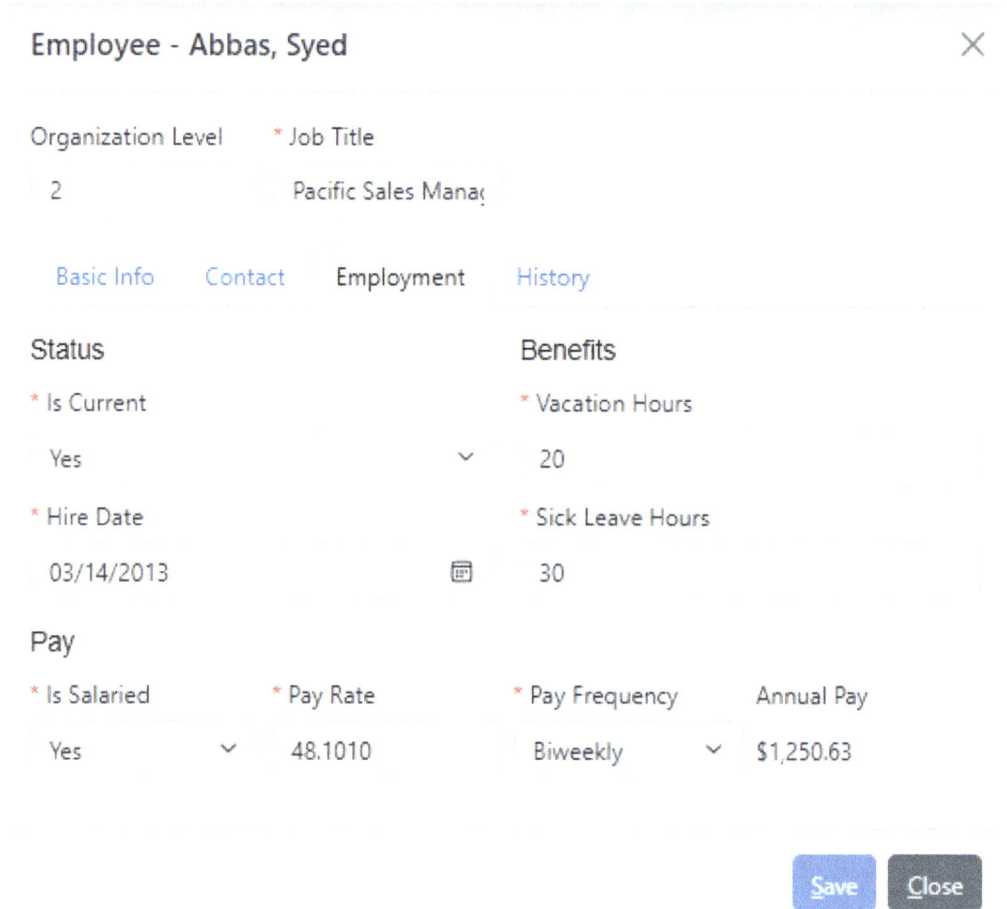

Figure 4-24. Employee pay info on the details view

If you change either the *Pay Rate* or *Pay Frequency,* the *Annual Pay* field should be updated automatically.

Note Being display-only, the *Annual Pay* field uses the display format for money with the currency symbol, while the *Pay Rate* field uses a numeric edit format.

Adding Current Department

Next, similar to the pay info, let's add some fields to the Employee Details view to let users see and edit the employee's current department information. We will show them in a new *Organization* tab, where we'll also include the *Job Title* and *Organization Level* fields remaining at the top of the view.

The department history record consists of the `department id` and `shift id`, as well as the `start date` and `end date`. The current department is the one with the end date set to `null`. Editing the current department or shift should set the `end date` of the current department history record to the current date and create a new record with the new department and shift.

Adding Department Parameters

As usual, we will start by adding the `department id` and `shift id` parameters for the current department to the CRUD operations of the `employee` object and making them required, as shown in Listing 4-72.

Listing 4-72. Adding department parameters to CRUD operations

```
<object name="employee">
  <operation name="read" type="read">
    <output>
+     <param name="department id" type="department"/>
+     <param name="shift id" type="shift"/>
      ...
    </output>
  </operation>
  <operation name="create" type="create">
    <input arg="data">
+     <param name="department id" type="department"
+             required="true"/>
+     <param name="shift id" type="shift" required="true"/>
      ...
    </input>
  </operation>
```

```
      <operation name="update" type="update">
        <input>
          <param name="business entity id"/>
          <struct name="data">
+           <param name="department id" type="department"
+                  required="true"/>
+           <param name="shift id" type="shift" required="true"/>
            ...
          </struct>
        </input>
      </operation>
    </object>
```

We have already created the department and shift dynamic enumerations, which allow users to select the department and shift from a drop-down list. However, when viewing or selecting the shift, users may also want to see the shift start and end times, which we can add as UI-only fields that are computed based on the selected shift.

Adding UI-Only Shift Fields

We already defined a structure employee properties to hold UI-only properties that are not part of the CRUD operations, so we can add the shift start and shift end parameters to it, as shown in Listing 4-73.

Listing 4-73. Adding UI-only shift fields

```
  <struct name="employee properties">
+   <param name="shift start" type="time"/>
+   <param name="shift end" type="time"/>
    <param name="annual pay" type="money"/>
    <config>
      <xfk:add-to-object class="EmployeeObject"/>
    </config>
    <usage generic="true"/>
  </struct>
```

Now that we have all the properties added to the EmployeeObject data object, we can configure the UI display for them.

Adding Organization Tab

For the current department info, I will create a new field group department and add to it the department and shift fields that we just added. I will also create another field group position for the current position of the employee in the organization and add the job title and organization level fields to it.

Finally, I will add a new *Organization* tab and include the department and position panels in it, as shown in Listing 4-74.

Listing 4-74. Adding Organization tab with field groups

```
<xfk:data-object class="EmployeeObject" customize="true">
  <ui:display>
    <ui:fields>[...]
    <ui:fields group="name" title="Employee Name">[...]
    <ui:fields group="personal" title="Personal Info">[...]
    <ui:fields group="email phone" title="Email / Phone">[...]
    <ui:fields group="status">[...]
    <ui:fields group="benefits">[...]
    <ui:fields group="pay">[...]
+   <ui:fields group="department">
+     <ui:field param="department id" label="Department"/>
+     <ui:field param="shift id" label="Shift"/>
+     <ui:field param="shift start" editable="false"/>
+     <ui:field param="shift end" editable="false"/>
+   </ui:fields>
+   <ui:fields group="position">
+     <ui:field param="job title"/>
+     <ui:field param="organization level" label="Org Level"/>
+   </ui:fields>
    <ui:panel-layout>
      <ui:panel/>
      <ui:tabs>
        <ui:tab title="Basic Info">[...]
        <ui:tab title="Contact">[...]
        <ui:tab title="Employment">[...]
```

```
+       <ui:tab title="Organization">
+         <ui:panel group="department"/>
+         <ui:panel group="position"/>
+       </ui:tab>
        <ui:tab title="History">[...]
      </ui:tabs>
    </ui:panel-layout>
  </ui:display>
</xfk:data-object>
```

Note I also configured proper labels for some of the fields and specified the `editable="false"` attribute for the UI-only computed `shift start` and `shift end` fields, similar to how we did it for the *Annual Pay* field earlier.

Update Department Method

Let's build the model and implement the service logic to update the current department and shift. I will add a new method `UpdateDepartmentAsync` to the `EmployeeServiceExtended.cs` file, which checks if the supplied department and shift are different from the current ones and, if so, closes the current department record and creates a new `EmployeeDepartmentHistory` record with the current date as the start date, as shown in Listing 4-75.

Listing 4-75. Method to update current department

```
public partial class EmployeeService
{
+   protected async Task UpdateDepartmentAsync(
+       Employee employee, short deptId, byte shiftId,
+       CancellationToken token)
+   {
+       if (employee == null) return;
+       var emplDpt = employee.DepartmentHistoryObjectList
+           .FirstOrDefault(d => d.EndDate == null);
```

```
+        if (emplDpt != null)
+        {
+            if (emplDpt.DepartmentId == deptId &&
+                emplDpt.ShiftId == shiftId)
+                return; // no change, nothing to do
+            // otherwise close the current department record
+            emplDpt.EndDate = DateTime.Now;
+        }
+
+        var dept = await ctx.FindEntityAsync<Department>(
+            currentErrors, token, deptId);
+        var shift = await ctx.FindEntityAsync<Shift>(
+            currentErrors, token, shiftId);
+        await ctx.EmployeeDepartmentHistory.AddAsync(
+            new EmployeeDepartmentHistory
+            {
+                EmployeeObject = employee,
+                DepartmentObject = dept,
+                ShiftObject = shift,
+                StartDate = DateTime.Now,
+                ModifiedDate = DateTime.Now
+            }, token);
+    }
     ...
 }
```

> **Note** Instead of storing the department and shift IDs directly in the EmployeeDepartmentHistory record, I used the FindEntityAsync method to resolve the Department and Shift entities, which will also throw a validation error if the department or shift does not exist.

CHAPTER 4 BUILDING OUT A DETAILS VIEW

Read and Update Department

To implement the reading and updating of the current department and shift, I will add custom code to the ReadAsync, CreateAsync, and UpdateAsync methods of the EmployeeService, similar to how we did it for the pay info, as shown in Listing 4-76.

Listing 4-76. Custom code for reading and updating department

```
public virtual async Task<Output<Employee_ReadOutput>>
    ReadAsync(int _businessEntityId,
              CancellationToken token = default)
{
    // CUSTOM_CODE_START: add custom code for Read operation below
    ...
+   var department = obj.DepartmentHistoryObjectList
+       .FirstOrDefault(d => d.EndDate == null);
+   res.DepartmentId = department?.DepartmentId;
+   res.ShiftId = department?.ShiftId;
    // CUSTOM_CODE_END
}
public virtual async Task<Output<Employee_CreateOutput>>
    CreateAsync(Employee_CreateInput _data,
                CancellationToken token = default)
{
    // CUSTOM_CODE_START: add custom code for Create operation below
    ...
+   await UpdateDepartmentAsync(obj,
+       _data.DepartmentId, _data.ShiftId, token);
    // CUSTOM_CODE_END
}
public virtual async Task<Output> UpdateAsync(
    int _businessEntityId,
    Employee_UpdateInput_Data _data,
    CancellationToken token = default)
{
    // CUSTOM_CODE_START: add custom code for Update operation below
    ...
```

253

CHAPTER 4 BUILDING OUT A DETAILS VIEW

```
+       await UpdateDepartmentAsync(obj,
+           _data.DepartmentId, _data.ShiftId, token);
        // CUSTOM_CODE_END
}
```

Computed Shift Fields

When we added a `read` enum for the `shift` object in the first section of this chapter, we included the `start time` and `end time` parameters in the output, which means they are available as attributes of the shift value.

To set up computed values for the *Shift Start* and *Shift End* properties, you can pass a LINQ expression to the `SetComputedValue` method, which will extract the values of these attributes from the shift value, as shown in Listing 4-77.

Listing 4-77. Configuring computed shift fields

```
+ using AdventureWorks.Services.Common.Enumerations;
public class EmployeeObjectCustomized : EmployeeObject
{
    protected override void OnInitialized()
    {
        ...
+       Expression<Func<EnumByteProperty, object>>
+           expShiftStart = shift => shift.Value == null ?
+               null : shift.Value[Shift.Attributes.StartTime];
+       ShiftStartProperty.SetComputedValue(
+           expShiftStart, ShiftIdProperty);
+
+       Expression<Func<EnumByteProperty, object>>
+           expShiftEnd = shift => shift.Value == null ?
+               null : shift.Value[Shift.Attributes.EndTime];
+       ShiftEndProperty.SetComputedValue(
+           expShiftEnd, ShiftIdProperty);
    }
}
```

CHAPTER 4　BUILDING OUT A DETAILS VIEW

Reviewing Organization Fields

Let's run the application and open the Employee Details view to review the changes. You should no longer see any orphaned fields at the top of the view. Instead, you will find the *Organization* tab with the *Department* and *Position* panels, showing the current department and shift, as well as the *Job Title* and *Org Level*, as shown in Figure 4-25.

Figure 4-25. Employee Organization tab with department

If you select a different shift, the *Shift Start* and *Shift End* fields should be updated automatically. To verify that the *Department* panel shows the current department, you can open the *History* tab and check the latest department history record, as shown in Figure 4-26.

CHAPTER 4 BUILDING OUT A DETAILS VIEW

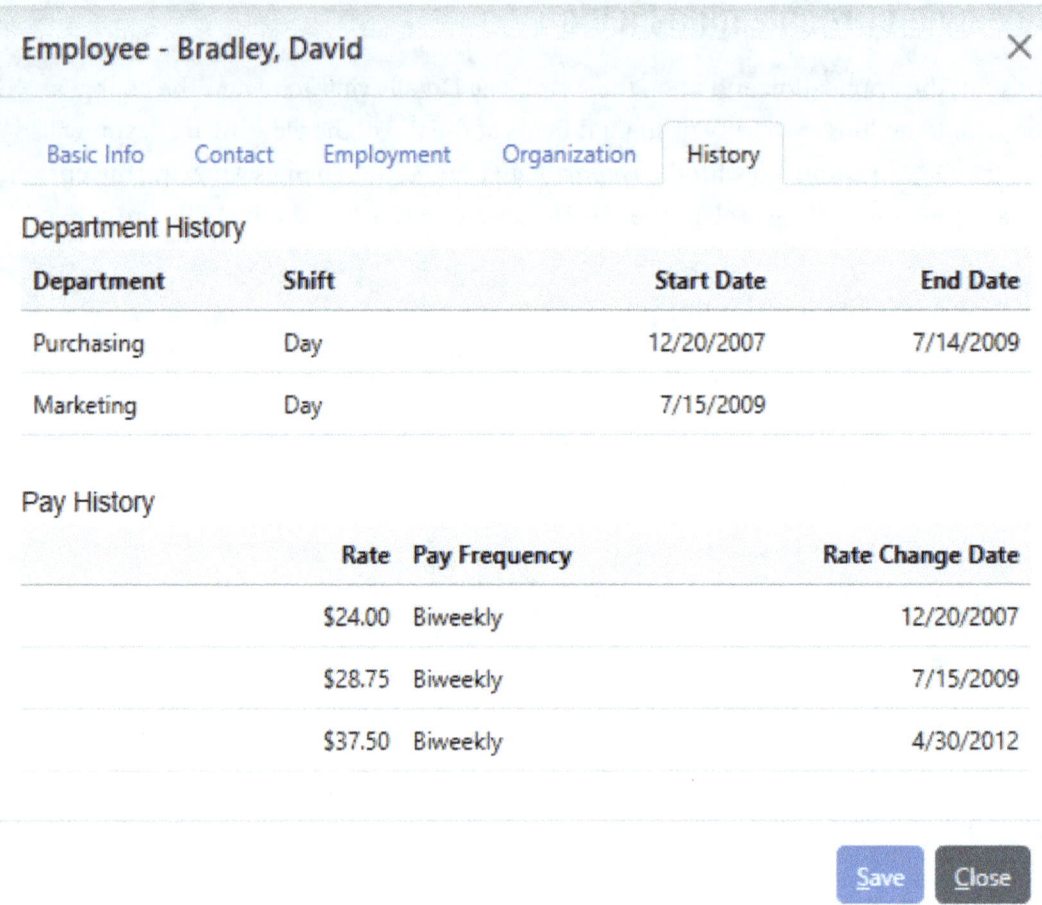

Figure 4-26. Employee History tab with Department History

Working with Hierarchies

In the previous section, we added the *Organization* tab for the employee's current department and position, which included the *Job Title* and *Org Level*. However, this doesn't quite paint the full picture of the employee's position in the organization. Typically, users would also want to see (and update) the employee's manager, as well as any direct reports the employee may have.

Traditionally, the organization hierarchy is modeled by storing the manager's ID in the employee record. However, the sample AdventureWorks database models the employee hierarchy by storing the employee's *OrganizationNode*, which uses the SQL Server-specific type `hierarchyid`.

In this section, we will use *OrganizationNode* to display the employee's manager and direct reports. We will make the *Manager* field editable with auto-complete control and the *Org Level* field read-only, as it will be derived from the manager's level.

Adding the Manager Field

Let's start by adding an editable *Manager* field to the *Position* panel, while making the *Org Level* read-only.

Adding Manager to Operations

Since we want the manager to be editable, we need to add a `manager id` parameter with type `employee` to the input of the `create` and `update` operations, in addition to the output of the `read` operation, as shown in Listing 4-78.

Listing 4-78. Adding manager to CRUD operations

```
  <object name="employee">
    <operation name="read" type="read">
      <output>
+       <param name="manager id" type="employee"/>
        ...
      </output>
    </operation>
    <operation name="create" type="create">
      <input arg="data">
+       <param name="manager id" type="employee"/>
        ...
-       <param name="organization level"/>
      </input>
    </operation>
    <operation name="update" type="update">
      <input>
        <param name="business entity id"/>
        <struct name="data">
+         <param name="manager id" type="employee"/>
          ...
```

```
        <param name="organization level"/>
      </struct>
    </input>
  </operation>
</object>
```

I also removed the `organization level` parameter from the `create` and `update` operations to make it read-only, as it will be derived from the manager's level.

Grouping Manager with Position

Next, let's add the `manager id` field to the `position` group and update its label to "Manager", as shown in Listing 4-79.

Listing 4-79. Adding manager to the position panel

```
<xfk:data-object class="EmployeeObject" customize="true">
  <ui:display>
    <ui:fields>[...]
    <ui:fields group="name" title="Employee Name">[...]
    <ui:fields group="personal" title="Personal Info">[...]
    <ui:fields group="email phone" title="Email / Phone">[...]
    <ui:fields group="status">[...]
    <ui:fields group="benefits">[...]
    <ui:fields group="pay">[...]
    <ui:fields group="department">[...]
-   <ui:fields group="position">
+   <ui:fields group="position" field-cols="3">
      <ui:field param="job title"/>
+     <ui:field param="manager id" label="Manager"/>
      <ui:field param="organization level" label="Org Level"/>
    </ui:fields>
    <ui:panel-layout>[...]
  </ui:display>
</xfk:data-object>
```

Since the `position` group now has three fields, I also set the `field-cols="3"` attribute to make the fields take up the full width of the panel.

Adding Employee Enumeration

To select the manager for an employee on the detail view, we can add a dynamic enumeration to the employee object, since the number of employees is not too large and can be cached on the client. To do this, right-click the employee.xom file, and select *Generate* ➤ *Model Enhancements* ➤ *Read Enum Operation*.

Updating the Employee Type

By default, the *Read Enum Operation* generator updates the key employee type to inherit from integer enumeration. However, since the employee object has a one-to-one relationship with the person object, its key type should inherit from the person type instead, so I will change the base type back to person.

Any configurations it would have inherited from integer enumeration can be added manually. So, I will add EnumIntProperty and set the Blazor control for this type to XAutoComplete, as shown in Listing 4-80.

Listing 4-80. Updating the employee type

```
- <type name="employee" base="integer enumeration">
+ <type name="employee" base="person">
+   <config>
+     <xfk:property class="EnumIntProperty"
+                   namespace="Xomega.Framework.Properties"/>
+     <ui:blazor-control>
+       <XAutoComplete/>
+     </ui:blazor-control>
+   </config>
    <enum ref="employee"/>
  </type>
```

Note Alternatively, you can set the *Make Key Type Enumerated* parameter of the *Read Enum Operation* generator to False, and it will not change the key type. In this case, you'd still need to add the proper configurations for the property and the Blazor control, as well as a reference to the employee enum.

Updating the Read Enum Operation

In the output of the read enum operation, we want to include the employee's full name, organization level, job title, and the current flag, so I will remove the other default parameters from the output, as shown in Listing 4-81.

Listing 4-81. Updating employee read enum operation

```
<object name="employee">
  <operation name="read enum">
    <output list="true">
      <param name="business entity id"/>
+     <param name="name" type="string"/>
+     <param name="national id number"/>
-     <param name="login id"/>
-     <param name="organization node"/>
      <param name="organization level"/>
      <param name="job title"/>
-     <param name="birth date"/>
-     <param name="marital status"/>
-     <param name="gender"/>
-     <param name="hire date"/>
-     <param name="salaried flag"/>
-     <param name="vacation hours"/>
-     <param name="sick leave hours"/>
      <param name="current flag"/>
-     <param name="rowguid"/>
-     <param name="modified date"/>
    </output>
    <config>
      <rest:method verb="GET" uri-template="employee/enum"/>
      <xfk:enum-cache enum-name="employee"
                      id-param="business entity id"
-                     desc-param="national id number"/>
+                     desc-param="name"
+                     is-active-param="current flag"/>
    </config>
```

CHAPTER 4 BUILDING OUT A DETAILS VIEW

```
    <doc>[...]
  </operation>
</object>
```

Note I also set the `desc-param` for the enumeration to the `name` parameter and the `is-active-param` to the `current` flag.

Adding Custom Code for the Enum

Let's build the model and add custom code to the `ReadEnumAsync` method of the `EmployeeService` to set the full name of the employee in the `Name` output parameter, as shown in Listing 4-82.

Listing 4-82. Adding custom code for employee's Read Enum

```
public virtual async Task<Output<ICollection<Employee_ReadEnumOutput>>>
    ReadEnumAsync(CancellationToken token = default)
{
    ...
    select new Employee_ReadEnumOutput() {
        BusinessEntityId = obj.BusinessEntityId,
        // CUSTOM_CODE_START: set the Name output parameter of ReadEnum
           operation below
-       // TODO: Name = obj.???, // CUSTOM_CODE_END
+       Name = obj.BusinessEntityObject.LastName + ", " +
+               obj.BusinessEntityObject.FirstName,
+       // CUSTOM_CODE_END
        OrganizationLevel = obj.OrganizationLevel,
        JobTitle = obj.JobTitle,
        CurrentFlag = obj.CurrentFlag,
    };
    ...
}
```

261

Reading and Updating the Manager

Now we need to add some code to read the manager of the employee and update it in the CreateAsync and UpdateAsync methods. What makes this a bit tricky is that the top manager (CEO) has a blank OrganizationNode and OrganizationLevel, so we need to handle that case separately.

EmployeeServiceExtended Functions

First, let's add a method to get the employee's manager in the EmployeeServiceExtended.cs file with special handling for the CEO and first-level employees, as shown in Listing 4-83.

Listing 4-83. Method to get employee's manager

```
public partial class EmployeeService
{
+    protected async Task<Employee> GetManagerAsync(
+        Employee obj, CancellationToken token)
+        => obj.OrganizationNode == null ? null :
+            obj.OrganizationLevel == 1 ?
+              await ctx.Employee.FirstOrDefaultAsync(e =>
+                  e.CurrentFlag &&
+                  e.OrganizationLevel == null) :
+              await ctx.Employee.FirstOrDefaultAsync(e =>
+                  e.OrganizationNode ==
+                  obj.OrganizationNode.GetAncestor(1));
    ...
}
```

Next, we will add a method to update the employee's manager in the same file. If the employee's manager is being changed, we will update the OrganizationNode and OrganizationLevel of the employee and all its descendants, accordingly, as shown in Listing 4-84.

CHAPTER 4   BUILDING OUT A DETAILS VIEW

Note We assume that there can be only one current employee with no Organization Level, which is the manager for all first-level employees. You can add such a validation to the update method below, but I skipped it for brevity.

Listing 4-84. Method to update employee's manager

```
public partial class EmployeeService
{
+   protected async Task UpdateManagerAsync(Employee employee,
+       int? managerId, CancellationToken token)
+   {
+       if (employee == null) return;
+       var curManager = await GetManagerAsync(
+           employee, token);
+       if (curManager != null &&
+           curManager.BusinessEntityId == managerId)
+           return; // no change, nothing to do
+       var descendants = await ctx.Employee.Where(
+           e => e.OrganizationNode.IsDescendantOf(
+               employee.OrganizationNode) &&
+           e.BusinessEntityId != employee.BusinessEntityId)
+           .ToListAsync(token);
+       if (managerId == null) // top-level employee
+       {
+           employee.OrganizationNode = null;
+           employee.OrganizationLevel = null;
+       }
+       else
+       {
+           var manager = await ctx.FindEntityAsync<Employee>(
+               currentErrors, token, managerId);
+           var mgrRpts = manager.OrganizationNode == null ?
+               ctx.Employee.Where(e =>
+                   e.OrganizationLevel == 1) :
```

```
            ctx.Employee.Where(e =>
                e.OrganizationNode.GetAncestor(1) ==
                manager.OrganizationNode);
        var maxNode = await mgrRpts.MaxAsync(e =>
                e.OrganizationNode, token);
        var mgrNode = manager.OrganizationNode ??
            HierarchyId.GetRoot();
        var curNode = employee.OrganizationNode;
        // generate a unique node
        // as the first after manager's max child
        employee.OrganizationNode =
            mgrNode.GetDescendant(maxNode);
        employee.OrganizationLevel =
            employee.OrganizationNode.GetLevel();

        foreach (var emp in descendants)
        {
            emp.OrganizationNode =
                emp.OrganizationNode.GetReparentedValue(
                    curNode, employee.OrganizationNode);
            emp.OrganizationLevel =
                emp.OrganizationNode.GetLevel();
        }
    }
}
    ...
}
```

Note In these methods, we use some special methods of the HierarchyId type, such as GetAncestor, GetDescendant, and GetReparentedValue, to navigate the hierarchy and update the employee's organization node and level. This type is specific to SQL Server, and you can read more about it in the official Microsoft documentation.

Updating CRUD Operations

Now that we have everything in place, we can update the `ReadAsync`, `CreateAsync`, and `UpdateAsync` methods in the `EmployeeService.cs` file to read and update the manager's ID using the methods we just added, as shown in Listing 4-85.

Listing 4-85. Updating CRUD operations for employee manager

```
public virtual async Task<Output<Employee_ReadOutput>>
    ReadAsync(int _businessEntityId,
              CancellationToken token = default)
{
    // CUSTOM_CODE_START: add custom code for Read operation below
    ...
+   var mgr = await GetManagerAsync(obj, token);
+   res.ManagerId = mgr?.BusinessEntityId;
    // CUSTOM_CODE_END
}
public virtual async Task<Output<Employee_CreateOutput>>
    CreateAsync(Employee_CreateInput _data,
              CancellationToken token = default)
{
    // CUSTOM_CODE_START: add custom code for Create operation below
    ...
+   await UpdateManagerAsync(obj, _data.ManagerId, token);
    // CUSTOM_CODE_END
}
public virtual async Task<Output> UpdateAsync(
    int _businessEntityId,
    Employee_UpdateInput_Data _data,
    CancellationToken token = default)
{
    // CUSTOM_CODE_START: add custom code for Update operation below
    ...
+   await UpdateManagerAsync(obj, _data.ManagerId, token);
    // CUSTOM_CODE_END
}
```

CHAPTER 4 BUILDING OUT A DETAILS VIEW

If the user saves an employee with a new manager, the *OrganizationLevel* field will be updated automatically by the service logic. However, if the user changes the manager on the UI, we need the *Org Level* to show the new value even before the employee is saved, to be consistent with the manager field.

Configure UI Logic

To auto-update the *Org Level* field based on the selected manager, I will add a method GetOrgLevel to the EmployeeObjectCustomized.cs file, which gets the employee's organization level based on the supplied manager. I will then use this method in a LINQ expression to set the computed value of the OrganizationLevelProperty, as shown in Listing 4-86.

Listing 4-86. UI logic for Org Level and Manager format

```
  public class EmployeeObjectCustomized : EmployeeObject
  {
      protected override void OnInitialized()
      {
          ...
+         Expression<Func<EnumIntProperty, object>>
+             expOrgLevel = mgr => GetOrgLevel(mgr.Value);
+         OrganizationLevelProperty.SetComputedValue(
+             expOrgLevel, ManagerIdProperty);
+
+         ManagerIdProperty.KeyFormat = Header.FieldText;
      }
+     private static object GetOrgLevel(Header mgr)
+     {
+         if (mgr == null) return null;
+         var mgrLvlAttr = mgr[Employee.Attributes
+             .OrganizationLevel];
```

CHAPTER 4   BUILDING OUT A DETAILS VIEW

```
+            if (mgrLvlAttr == null) return 1;
+            if (int.TryParse(mgrLvlAttr.ToString(),
+                             out int mgrLvl))
+                return mgrLvl + 1;
+            return null; // bad data
+        }
}
```

> **Note** Because we use auto-complete control for the manager field, we also need to set the `KeyFormat` of the `ManagerIdProperty` to display the employee's name in the text box after selection, rather than the internal employee ID.

Review the Manager Field

Let's run the application and review the changes we made. When you open the *Organization* tab of the Employee Detail view, you should see the *Manager* field with an auto-complete control that shows a filtered list of employees based on what you type in the text box, as shown in Figure 4-27.

CHAPTER 4   BUILDING OUT A DETAILS VIEW

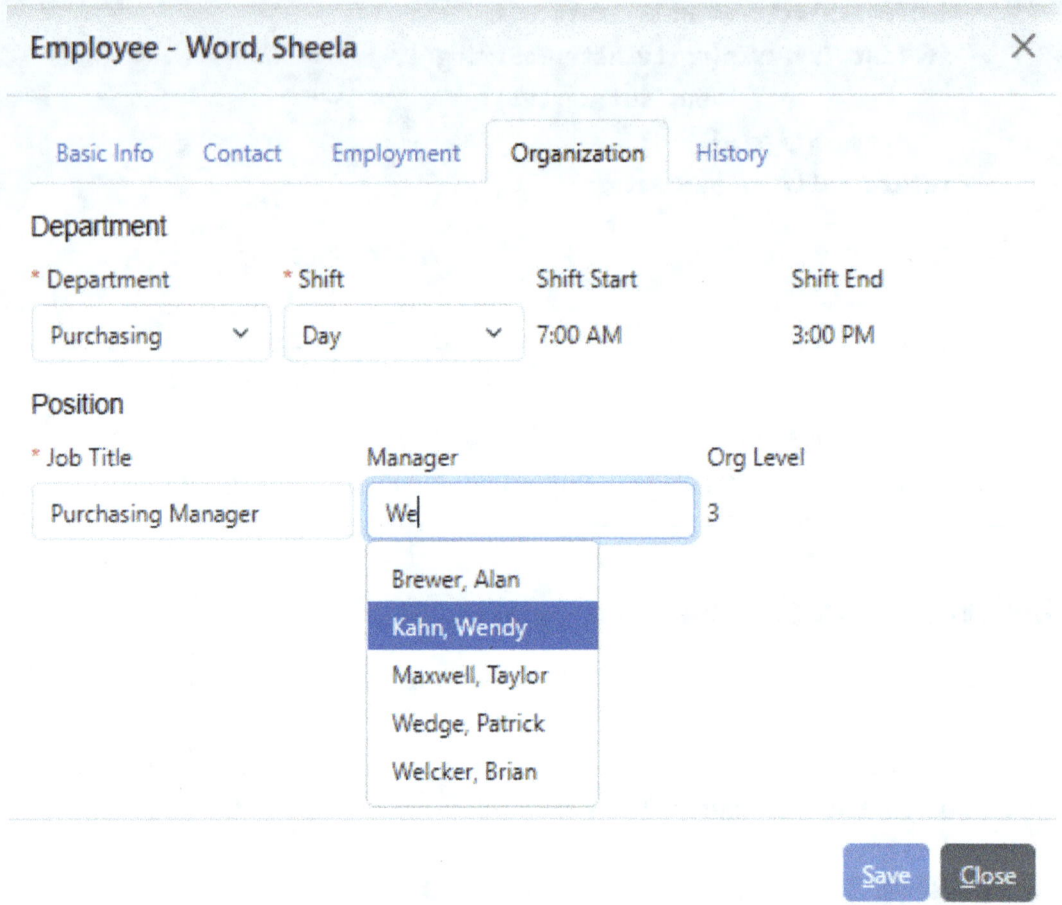

Figure 4-27.   Manager field in the Organization tab

Notice also that the *Org Level* field is now read-only and will be updated automatically when you select a new manager, based on the manager's level.

Refreshing the Lookup Cache

Presumably, it's not very frequent that a new employee is added or their organization level is changed, which allows us to cache employees returned by the `read enum` operation in the lookup cache and use it to resolve the manager's name from the `manager id` field on the client side or to provide a list of employees in the auto-complete control.

CHAPTER 4 BUILDING OUT A DETAILS VIEW

However, users who add or update employees often, such as HR staff, will want their changes to be applied immediately and reflected when they select a manager for an employee. To achieve this, we can clear the employee lookup cache when any employee is saved, and it will be refreshed the next time it is accessed.

To do this, we will override the SaveAsync method in the EmployeeObjectCustomized class and remove the employee lookup table from the cache after a successful save, as shown in Listing 4-87.

Listing 4-87. Refreshing the employee lookup cache

```
public class EmployeeObjectCustomized : EmployeeObject
{
+   public override async Task<ErrorList> SaveAsync(
+       object options, CancellationToken token = default)
+   {
+       var errLst = await base.SaveAsync(options, token);
+       if (!errLst.HasErrors())
+       {
+           LookupCache.Get(ServiceProvider,
+                           LookupCache.Global)
+                   .RemoveLookupTable(Employee.EnumName);
+       }
+       return errLst;
+   }
}
```

Note Other users will need to restart the application to refresh their lookup cache, but you can implement various strategies to refresh the cache automatically, such as using a timer or a signal from the server.

CHAPTER 4 ■ BUILDING OUT A DETAILS VIEW

Adding Direct Reports

Now that we have the employee's manager, let's complete the employee's organization hierarchy by adding a list of the employee's direct reports, showing their first and last names, as well as their job titles.

Direct Reports List Object

I'll start by defining a new list data object, `EmployeeReportsList`, and adding it to the `EmployeeObject` as a child named `reports`. I will also add a new panel to the *Organization* tab for that child list with the title "Direct Reports", as shown in Listing 4-88.

Listing 4-88. Adding a child list object for direct reports

```
<xfk:data-objects>
  <xfk:data-object class="EmployeeObject" customize="true">
+    <xfk:add-child name="reports"
+                   class="EmployeeReportsList"/>
    ...
    <ui:display>
      ...
      <ui:panel-layout>
-        <ui:panel/>
        <ui:tabs>
          <ui:tab title="Basic Info">[...]
          <ui:tab title="Contact">[...]
          <ui:tab title="Employment">[...]
          <ui:tab title="Organization">
            <ui:panel group="department"/>
            <ui:panel group="position"/>
+           <ui:panel child="reports" title="Direct Reports"/>
          </ui:tab>
          <ui:tab title="History">[...]
        </ui:tabs>
```

```
      </ui:panel-layout>
    </ui:display>
  </xfk:data-object>
+ <xfk:data-object class="EmployeeReportsList" list="true"/>
</xfk:data-objects>
```

Note Since all the fields in the `EmployeeObject` have been added to their own groups and panels by now, I also removed the default `ui:panel` from the `ui:panel-layout`, which was showing ungrouped fields.

Reading Direct Reports

So far, we have read child lists, such as the pay history or department history, from a separate `read list` operation, which was defined on the respective subobject. You can also read direct reports in a separate operation of type `readlist`, if you prefer.

However, to avoid multiple server calls, I will just add a list structure named `reports` to the output of the existing `read` operation and will add its parameters to the `EmployeeReportsList` data object, as shown in Listing 4-89.

Listing 4-89. Adding reports to the output of the read operation

```
<object name="employee">
  <operation name="read" type="read">
    <input>[...]
    <output>
      ...
+     <struct name="reports" list="true">
+       <param name="employee id" type="employee"/>
+       <param name="last name" type="name"/>
+       <param name="first name" type="name"/>
+       <param name="job title"/>
+       <config>
+         <xfk:add-to-object class="EmployeeReportsList"/>
+       </config>
+     </struct>
```

```
      </output>
    </operation>
</object>
...
    <xfk:data-object class="EmployeeReportsList" list="true">
+     <ui:display>
+       <ui:fields>
+         <ui:field param="employee id" hidden="true"/>
+       </ui:fields>
+     </ui:display>
+   </xfk:data-object>
```

I also updated the `EmployeeReportsList` data object to hide the internal `employee id` field.

Method for Reading Direct Reports

Next, let's build the model and add a method to the `EmployeeServiceExtended.cs` file to get the employee's direct reports. For the top-level employee (CEO), we will return all employees at the first level, while for other employees, we will return only immediate descendants of their `OrganizationNode`, as shown in Listing 4-90.

Listing 4-90. Adding a method to read direct reports

```
public partial class EmployeeService
{
+   protected async Task<List<Employee_ReadOutput_Reports>>
+       GetReportsAsync(Employee obj, CancellationToken token)
+   {
+       var reports = ctx.Employee.Where(e => e.CurrentFlag);
+       reports = (obj.OrganizationNode == null) ?
+           reports.Where(e => e.OrganizationLevel == 1) :
+           reports.Where(e => obj.OrganizationNode ==
+                         e.OrganizationNode.GetAncestor(1));
+       return await reports.Select(
+           e => new Employee_ReadOutput_Reports
```

CHAPTER 4   BUILDING OUT A DETAILS VIEW

```
+            {
+                EmployeeId = e.BusinessEntityId,
+                FirstName = e.BusinessEntityObject.FirstName,
+                LastName = e.BusinessEntityObject.LastName,
+                JobTitle = e.JobTitle
+            }).ToListAsync(token);
+    }
     ...
}
```

Custom Code for Reading Reports

Once we have the method to get direct reports, we can call it in the custom code of the ReadAsync method in the EmployeeService to populate the reports list in the output, as shown in Listing 4-91.

Listing 4-91. Updating the ReadAsync method to read reports

```
public virtual async Task<Output<Employee_ReadOutput>>
    ReadAsync(int _businessEntityId,
              CancellationToken token = default)
{
    // CUSTOM_CODE_START: add custom code for Read operation below
    ...
+   res.Reports = await GetReportsAsync(obj, token);
    // CUSTOM_CODE_END
}
```

Reviewing Direct Reports

Let's run the application and review the results. When you open the *Organization* tab for a mid-level manager, you should see the *Direct Reports* panel with a list of employees who report directly to this employee, as shown in Figure 4-28.

CHAPTER 4   BUILDING OUT A DETAILS VIEW

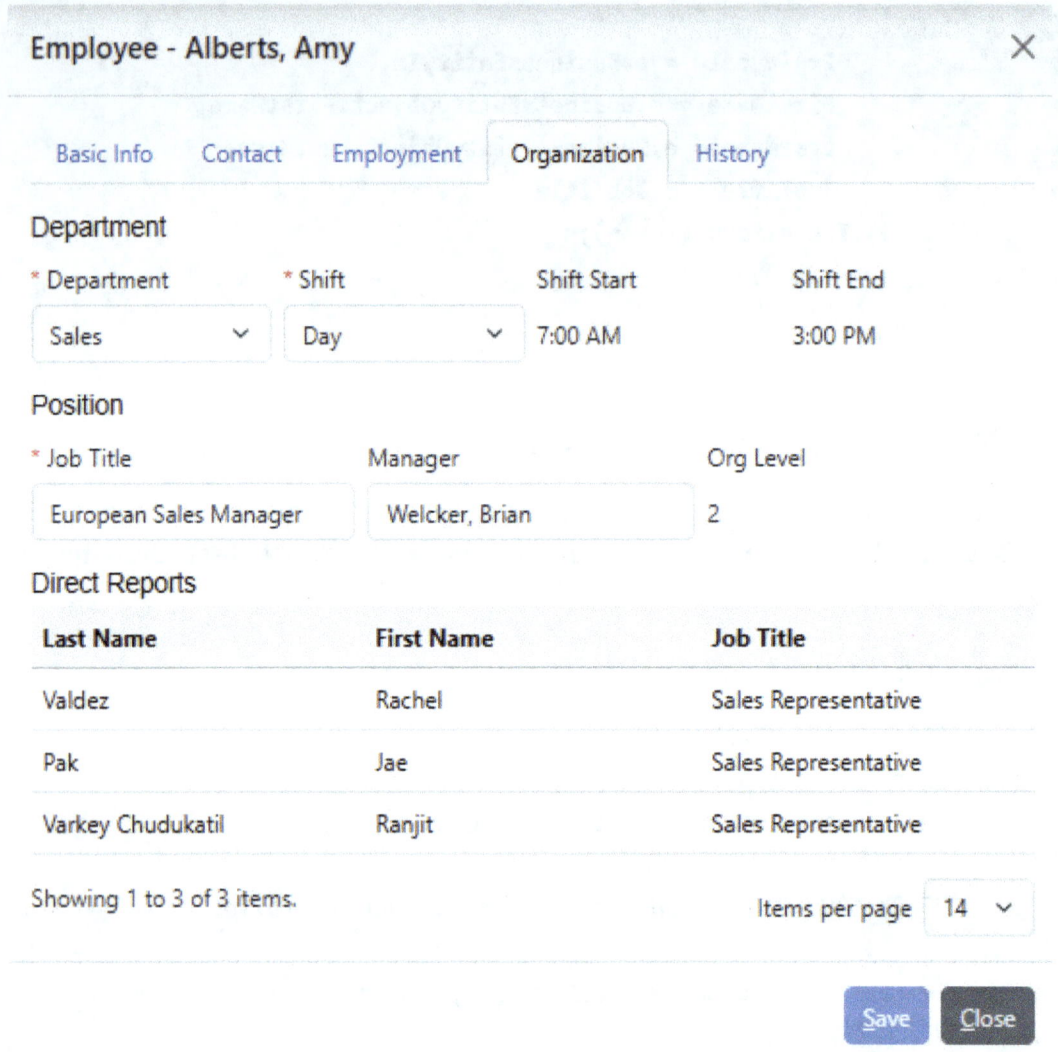

Figure 4-28.   Organization tab with direct reports

Tip   If you want to remove the pagination from the direct reports list or change the default page size, you can do that in the customized `EmployeeReportsList` data object.

Summary

In this chapter, you learned how to take the default Details View for all the fields of the Employee entity and turn it into a complex, full-fledged Employee Details view. You saw how to add child lists, fields from related entities, and UI-only fields whose values are computed from other fields. Along the way, you practiced enriching the model by defining subobjects, enums, and new logical types.

In addition to displaying new data, you also learned various ways to edit, validate, and save new fields using custom service logic, including some specialized logic for hierarchical data. You saw how to build and use a Lookup View for selecting an existing Address entity or how to open a separate Details View to create or update an employee's home address.

Finally, you learned how to customize the Details View layout by grouping fields into tabs and panels and configuring their layout. You saw how easy it is to make the Details View use a master-detail layout when opening it from the List View and how to display dynamic information in the title of the Details View.

In the next chapter, you will learn best practices for securing Xomega applications at different levels, including authentication, various access levels to screens and services, protecting sensitive data, and more.

CHAPTER 5

Implementing Security

In the previous chapters, we created a solution for our application and built complete, fully functional Employee List and Employee Details views. When creating the solution, we selected the password authentication option.

This set up the default plumbing and infrastructure for user authentication, including the login screen and back-end authentication services, but it did not provide any real logic for securing the application beyond that. Currently, a user can log in with any username and the default password and can access any screen or service in the application.

In this chapter, you will learn best practices for securing Xomega applications with multiple layers of defense, using clear logic and well-structured code that is easy to maintain and extend. We'll show you how to implement username and password validation, secure access to screens and services based on user roles, and protect private or sensitive data from unauthorized access.

We will define realistic security requirements for our application based on the structure of the sample AdventureWorks database and show you how to implement them using Xomega. In addition to internal users, we will also allow external users, such as customers or vendors, to access the application to view their orders and other relevant information.

Access to the employee screens will be limited to internal users, and you will need additional privileges to view the details of an employee other than yourself. Creating and editing employees, as well as viewing private or sensitive information such as pay and benefits, will be allowed only for Human Resources personnel.

Without further ado, let's start by implementing username and password validation.

CHAPTER 5   IMPLEMENTING SECURITY

Implement Password Validation

As mentioned earlier, when we selected the password authentication option while initially creating the solution, the solution template set up the login screen and various services to allow authentication in both Blazor Server and WebAssembly modes and secured the REST API calls.

For validation of the user's credentials, it uses a generated `PasswordLoginService`, which was customized with a default implementation of the `LoginAsync` method that checks if the supplied password is the default value "password." This is where you need to add the proper validation logic for the username and password.

Password Validation Service Logic

For each record in the Person table, the sample AdventureWorks database allows storing the hashed password in the corresponding record of the Password table. To allow any person in the system to log in, we will use their email address as the username, since the `LoginId` field in the Employee table would allow authentication only for internal employees.

To validate the password, you should also read the Password record for the person with the given email address and then hash the supplied password using the salt from that record. The resulting hash should be compared with the stored password hash to determine if the credentials are valid.

However, to be able to log in under different accounts for security testing, we will continue to check the password for the default word "password" for now, since we don't know the passwords used in the sample database, nor how exactly they were hashed. You can also surround it with the `#if DEBUG` conditions to ensure that it's not used in production. Listing 5-1 illustrates the changes you need to make to the `PasswordLoginServiceCustomized` class to implement the validation of the username and password.

Listing 5-1. Username validation service logic

```
+ using Microsoft.EntityFrameworkCore;
+ using System.Linq;
public override async Task<Output<UserInfo>> LoginAsync(
    PasswordCredentials _credentials,
```

```
      CancellationToken token = default)
{
    ...
-   // TODO: validate _credentials.Username and _credentials.Password here
+   // look up password
+   var pwdQry = from em in ctx.EmailAddress
+       join pw in ctx.Password
+           on em.BusinessEntityId equals pw.BusinessEntityId
+       where em.EmailAddress1 == _credentials.UserName
+       select pw;
+   var pwd = await pwdQry.FirstOrDefaultAsync(token);
+
+   // validate password. TODO:
+   // hash _credentials.Password using pwd.PasswordSalt,
+   // and compare it with pwd.PasswordHash instead
-   bool passwordValid = _credentials.Password == "password";
+   bool passwordValid = pwd != null &&
+                        _credentials.Password == "password";
    if (!passwordValid)
        currentErrors.AddValidationError(
            Messages.InvalidCredentials);
    ...
}
```

Note For security reasons, the validation error returned from the service generically states "Invalid credentials" without specifying whether the username or password was incorrect.

Remove Default User and Password

So far, every time we were running the application, we had the username and password pre-populated in the Login screen with the default values to help us test the functionality we were developing without slowing us down by having to enter credentials every time.

CHAPTER 5 IMPLEMENTING SECURITY

Now that you have implemented username and password validation, you should remove the default user and password from the `LoginObjectCustomized` class, as shown in Listing 5-2.

Listing 5-2. Removing the default user and password from the login screen

```
public class LoginObjectCustomized : LoginObject
{
    protected override void Initialize()
    {
        base.Initialize();

        // disable modification tracking to avoid unsaved changes prompts
        TrackModifications = false;
        IsNew = false;

-       // TODO: remove the following code after implementing security
-       UserNameProperty.SetValue("Guest");
-       PasswordProperty.SetValue("password");
    }
}
```

Tip If you need to continue developing other non-security-related features and want to expedite the login process, you can temporarily set your own username and password locally. To take it a step further, you can implement auto-login in the `ActivateAsync` method of the `LoginViewModelCustomized` class to skip the login screen altogether by uncommenting the corresponding code there.

Review Email-Based Login

If you run the application now, you will need to enter a valid email address for a person in the system with a password stored in the Password table. After logging in, you will see the email address of the current user in the top right corner of the screen, as shown in Figure 5-1.

CHAPTER 5   IMPLEMENTING SECURITY

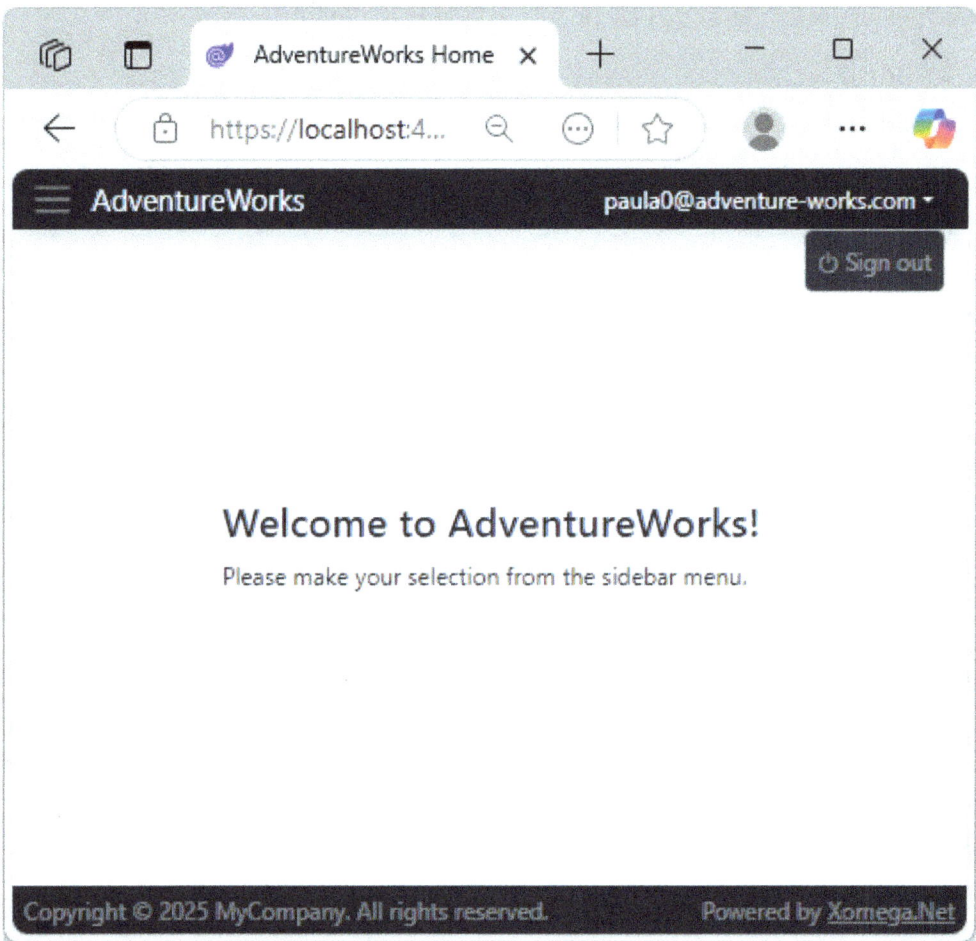

Figure 5-1. Email-based login

Populate User Claims

Now that we have implemented validation of the user credentials, we need to come up with a set of user claims for our application. User claims are usually included in the security token, such as an authentication cookie or a JWT, that is passed around or stored locally to keep the security context of the current user.

CHAPTER 5 IMPLEMENTING SECURITY

Generally, user claims can be categorized using the following types:

- Identity claims that are used to uniquely identify the user, such as their username or user ID

- Claims used to display information about the current user, such as their first and last name or email address

- Claims used to determine user's access to various data and actions in the application, such as their roles and associations with different entities

We need to determine which claims from the above categories we need to include to implement the security requirements for our application, and make sure they are populated correctly when the user logs in.

Enhancing User Info for Claims

Within the password-based security framework that was set up by the solution template, the user claims are modeled by the `user info` structure that is returned as the output of the `login` operation. By default, that structure had only the `authentication type` and the `user name` parameters.

We need to add the internal `business entity id` as the user identifying claim, as well as the `first name` and `last name` as the claims used to display information about the user.

For security claims, we will add the `person type` to distinguish between internal and external users, as well as the `job title` and `org level` for internal employees to determine their access to various screens and services, as shown in Listing 5-3.

Listing 5-3. Enhancing user info for user claims in login.xom

```
<types>
-   <type name="user name" base="string" size="50"/>
+   <type name="user name" base="name"/>
</types>
<structs>
-   <struct name="user info">
+   <struct name="user info" object="person">
        <param name="authentication type" type="string"/>
```

```
          <param name="user name" type="user name"/>
+         <param name="first name"/>
+         <param name="last name"/>
+         <param name="business entity id"/>
+         <param name="person type"/>
+         <param name="job title" type="string"/>
+         <param name="org level" type="small int"/>
      </struct>
  </structs>
```

Note I also updated the user name type to be based on the name type that we defined earlier.

Reading User Info for Claims

Let's build the model to regenerate the classes and then implement the logic to read the additional user info from the database in the LoginAsync method of the PasswordLoginServiceCustomized class. I will create a LINQ query to read the user info from the Person entity left-joined with the Employee entity, as shown in Listing 5-4.

Listing 5-4. Reading user info in the Login operation

```
public override async Task<Output<UserInfo>> LoginAsync(
    PasswordCredentials _credentials,
    CancellationToken token = default)
{
    ...
    // TODO: read user info here
-   var userInfo = new UserInfo()
-   {
-       UserName = _credentials.UserName,
-   };
+   var usrQry = from p in ctx.Person
+       join e in ctx.Employee on p.BusinessEntityId
```

```
+              equals e.BusinessEntityId into eg
+          // left join to include non-employees
+          from emp in eg.DefaultIfEmpty()
+          where p.BusinessEntityId == pwd.BusinessEntityId
+          select new UserInfo
+          {
+              UserName = _credentials.UserName,
+              FirstName = p.FirstName,
+              LastName = p.LastName,
+              BusinessEntityId = p.BusinessEntityId,
+              PersonType = p.PersonType,
+              JobTitle = emp.JobTitle,
+              OrgLevel = emp.OrganizationLevel
+          };
+      var userInfo = await usrQry.FirstOrDefaultAsync(token);
       return await Task.FromResult(
           new Output<UserInfo>(currentErrors, userInfo));
   }
```

Note The authentication type is set automatically by the framework based on the service that is being called, so we don't need to set it explicitly.

User Info Conversion to IPrincipal

While the `user info` is a custom structure that we defined for our application to hold the user security information, .NET applications use the standard `Claim`, `ClaimsIdentity`, and `ClaimsPrincipal` classes to represent user claims. Therefore, the Xomega Framework defines the `IPrincipalConverter<T>` interface to convert between a custom user info structure and the standard `ClaimsPrincipal`.

Our solution template already included a default implementation of this interface called `UserInfoPrincipalConverter` in the `AdventureWorks.Services.Common` project, which is available to both the server and client projects. You need to enhance this converter to include the additional user info parameters that we defined earlier.

UserInfo to ClaimsPrincipal Conversion

To convert the UserInfo structure to a ClaimsPrincipal, you need to update the ToPrincipal method of the UserInfoPrincipalConverter class to include the new claims that we defined. For the user info parameters that map to standard claims, I will use constants from the ClaimTypes class to create the claims.

For any custom claims, such as job title and org level, I will define constants for the custom claim types in the converter class and use them to add the corresponding claims if their values are specified in UserInfo, as shown in Listing 5-5.

Listing 5-5. Converting UserInfo to ClaimsPrincipal

```
 public class UserInfoPrincipalConverter :
             IPrincipalConverter<UserInfo>
 {
+    public const string ClaimTypeJobTitle =
+        "http://adventure-works.com/jobTitle";
+    public const string ClaimTypeOrgLevel =
+        "http://adventure-works.com/orgLevel";

     public UserInfo FromPrincipal(
         ClaimsPrincipal principal)[...]

     public ClaimsPrincipal ToPrincipal(UserInfo userInfo)
     {
-        Claim[] claims = new[] {
-            new Claim(ClaimTypes.Name, userInfo.UserName),
-        };
+        var claims = new List<Claim>([
+            new Claim(ClaimTypes.NameIdentifier,
+                    userInfo.BusinessEntityId.ToString(),
+                    ClaimValueTypes.Integer),
+            new Claim(ClaimTypes.Name,
+                $"{userInfo.FirstName} {userInfo.LastName}"),
+            new Claim(ClaimTypes.GivenName,
+                    userInfo.FirstName),
```

CHAPTER 5 IMPLEMENTING SECURITY

```
+            new Claim(ClaimTypes.Surname, userInfo.LastName),
+            new Claim(ClaimTypes.Email, userInfo.UserName),
+            new Claim(ClaimTypes.Role, userInfo.PersonType),
+        ]);
+
+        if (userInfo.JobTitle != null) claims.Add(
+            new Claim(ClaimTypeJobTitle, userInfo.JobTitle));
+        if (userInfo.OrgLevel != null) claims.Add(
+            new Claim(ClaimTypeOrgLevel,
+                      userInfo.OrgLevel.ToString(),
+                      ClaimValueTypes.Integer));
         return new ClaimsPrincipal(new ClaimsIdentity(
                 claims, userInfo.AuthenticationType));
    }
}
```

Note For the standard Name claim, which is used by the Identity.Name field and is displayed by default in the UI for the current user, I am using concatenation of the FirstName and LastName values. If you find this redundant, you can update the LoginDisplay component to use the individual FirstName and LastName claims instead of the identity name.

UserInfo from ClaimsPrincipal Conversion

To convert from a ClaimsPrincipal to a UserInfo structure, you need to update the FromPrincipal method of the UserInfoPrincipalConverter class to read the additional claims using either the standard or custom claim types, as shown in Listing 5-6.

Listing 5-6. Converting ClaimsPrincipal to UserInfo

```
public class UserInfoPrincipalConverter :
            IPrincipalConverter<UserInfo>
{
    public UserInfo FromPrincipal(ClaimsPrincipal principal)
```

CHAPTER 5 IMPLEMENTING SECURITY

```
    {
        var username = principal.FindFirst(
-           ClaimTypes.Name)?.Value;
+           ClaimTypes.Email)?.Value;

        if (username != null)
        {
-           return new UserInfo
+           var userInfo = new UserInfo
            {
                AuthenticationType = principal.Identity
                    .AuthenticationType,
                UserName = username,
+               FirstName = principal.FindFirst(
+                   ClaimTypes.GivenName)?.Value,
+               LastName = principal.FindFirst(
+                   ClaimTypes.Surname)?.Value,
+               PersonType = principal.FindFirst(
+                   ClaimTypes.Role)?.Value,
+               JobTitle = principal.FindFirst(
+                   ClaimTypeJobTitle)?.Value,
+           };
+           if (int.TryParse(principal.FindFirst(
+             ClaimTypes.NameIdentifier)?.Value, out int id))
+               userInfo.BusinessEntityId = id;
+           if (short.TryParse(principal.FindFirst(
+             ClaimTypeOrgLevel)?.Value, out short lvl))
+               userInfo.OrgLevel = lvl;
+           return userInfo;
        }
        return null;
    }
}
```

287

CHAPTER 5   IMPLEMENTING SECURITY

Note   Claim values are always strings, so you need to parse them to the appropriate types, such as `int` or `short`, when reading them from the claims.

Reviewing Claims in the UI

If you run the application now and log in using a valid email address, you should see the full name of the user in the top right corner of the screen, instead of the email address, as shown in Figure 5-2.

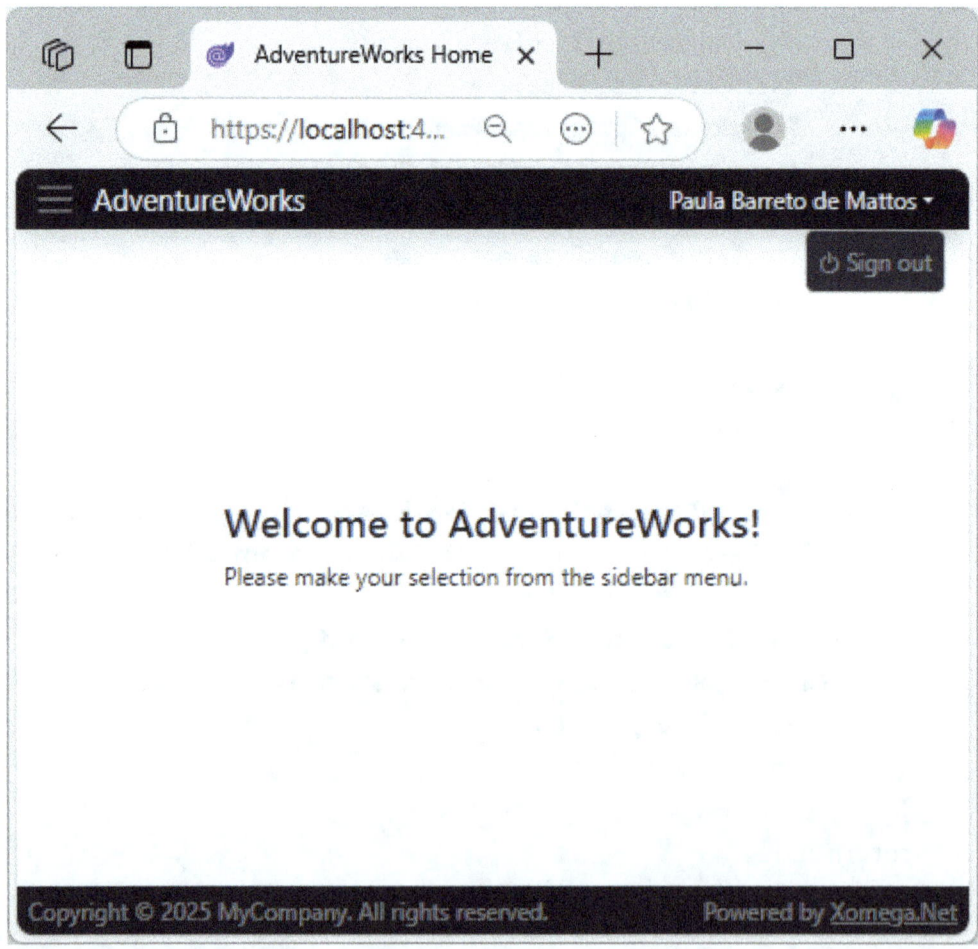

Figure 5-2. *Updated identity name in the UI*

Claims IPrincipal Extensions

In Xomega business services and data objects, the current user is available as the CurrentPrincipal property, which is of the standard type IPrincipal that has a list of claims.

Instead of working with the claims directly, it is more convenient to define a number of extension methods for the IPrincipal interface to retrieve specific security information about the current user. For this, I will create a static class PrincipalExtensions in the *ServiceContracts/Auth* folder of the AdventureWorks.Services.Common project and add the following extension methods to it.

Employee Check

First, I will add an extension method to check if the current user is an employee by checking if their person type, which we used as role, is either Employee or SalesPerson, as shown in Listing 5-7.

Listing 5-7. Checking if the current user is an employee

```
+ namespace AdventureWorks.Services.Common;
+
+ public static class PrincipalExtensions
+ {
+     public static bool IsEmployee(this IPrincipal principal)
+         => principal.IsInRole(PersonType.Employee) ||
+             principal.IsInRole(PersonType.SalesPerson);
+ }
```

Note To check the person type of the user, I used generated constants from the PersonType static enum that we defined earlier.

CHAPTER 5   IMPLEMENTING SECURITY

Executive Check

We may want to allow certain things only for high-level employees, such as executives. To check if the current user is an executive, I will add another extension method that checks if the user is an employee and has an organization level of 1 or less, as shown in Listing 5-8.

Listing 5-8. Checking if the current user is an executive

```
public static class PrincipalExtensions
{
    ...
+   public static bool IsExecutive(this IPrincipal principal)
+   {
+       if (principal?.Identity is ClaimsIdentity ci)
+       {
+           var orgLvlClaim = ci.Claims.FirstOrDefault(
+               c => c.Type == UserInfoPrincipalConverter
+                               .ClaimTypeOrgLevel);
+           return principal.IsEmployee() &&
+               (orgLvlClaim == null ||
+                   short.Parse(orgLvlClaim.Value) < 2);
+       }
+       return false;
+   }
}
```

Note   The top manager (CEO) has no organization level, so we check if the `org level` claim is not present for them.

Human Resources Check

Editing employees and viewing their private information, such as pay and benefits, should be allowed only for Human Resources personnel. To check if the current user is in Human Resources, I will add an extension method that checks if the user has a job title starting with "Human Resources", as shown in Listing 5-9.

Listing 5-9. Checking if the current user is in Human Resources

```
public static class PrincipalExtensions
{
    ...
+   public static bool IsHR(this IPrincipal principal,
+                           bool manager = false)
+   {
+       var hrTitle = "Human Resources" +
+                       (manager ? " Manager" : "");
+       if (principal.Identity is ClaimsIdentity ci)
+           return ci.HasClaim(c =>
+               c.Type == UserInfoPrincipalConverter
+                           .ClaimTypeJobTitle &&
+               c.Value.StartsWith(hrTitle,
+                   StringComparison.OrdinalIgnoreCase));
+       return false;
+   }
}
```

Note You can also check if the user is a Human Resources Manager by passing `true` to the `manager` parameter. Such users have more privileges than regular Human Resources personnel.

Person ID Retrieval

Finally, let's add an extension method to retrieve the internal person ID of the current user, which is stored in the `NameIdentifier` claim, as shown in Listing 5-10.

Listing 5-10. Retrieving the person ID from the current user

```
public static class PrincipalExtensions
{
    ...
+   public static int? GetPersonId(this IPrincipal principal)
+   {
+       Claim idClaim = null;
+       if (principal.Identity is ClaimsIdentity ci &&
+           (idClaim = ci.Claims.FirstOrDefault(
+               c => c.Type == ClaimTypes.NameIdentifier))
+               != null)
+           return int.Parse(idClaim.Value);
+       return null;
+   }
}
```

You can use this method in your application code to determine whether the user is accessing their own details or those of another user and to enforce the security rules accordingly.

Define Application Permissions

All the previous work we've done on defining and populating user claims and adding extension methods on the `IPrincipal` interface to access the values of those claims was laying the groundwork to help us define and implement security rules for our application.

Traditionally, with role-based authorization (RBA), developers have been checking user roles in various places in the code to determine whether a user has access to a particular functionality or data. This approach can make it difficult to maintain and extend the security logic, especially in large applications with complex security requirements.

To find out what a specific role allows the user to do, you would have to search through the code to find all the places where that role is checked, which makes it hard to understand the overall security model. Similarly, adding new roles or changing the security rules would require modifying multiple places in the code, which can lead to inconsistencies and bugs.

CHAPTER 5 IMPLEMENTING SECURITY

Therefore, for Xomega applications, we recommend defining a set of application permissions that represent the specific actions or data access levels in your application. Then you can create an extension method `HasPermission` on the `IPrincipal` interface to check whether the user has a specific permission, which you will call in your code to check the relevant permissions.

This approach allows you to centralize the security logic in one place, making it easier to maintain and extend. Let's see how to implement this in our application.

AppPermissions Enumeration

First, we will define an enumeration `AppPermissions` that will contain all the application permissions we need. Just like with the other common security classes that we added, I will add it in the same folder *ServiceContracts/Auth* in the shared `AdventureWorks.Services.Common` project to make sure that it's accessible to both the client and service logic.

To make the meaning of each permission very clear, we can use a naming convention that reflects the action and the entity or data being accessed.

For example, we can define permission `Employee_View` to allow searching for employees and viewing their details in general and a special permission `Employee_View_Others` to allow viewing details of employees other than yourself.

Similarly, we can define `Employee_View_Others_Pay` and `Employee_View_Others_Private` to protect access to sensitive information on other employees, assuming that the user can always view their own pay and private information.

In terms of making changes to the employee data, we can define `Employee_Create` and `Employee_Update` permissions to allow creating and updating employees, respectively, as shown in Listing 5-11.

Listing 5-11. Defining application permissions

```
+ namespace AdventureWorks.Services.Common;
+
+ public enum AppPermissions
+ {
+     Employee_View,
+     Employee_View_Others,
+     Employee_View_Others_Pay,
```

```
+       Employee_View_Others_Private,
+       Employee_Create,
+       Employee_Update,
+ }
```

> **Note** Remember, employees cannot be deleted in the sample AdventureWorks database, so we don't need permission for that. However, you can define a separate permission for making an employee not current if this requires a special privilege in your application.

Application Permission Rules

Next, we will implement the `HasPermission` extension method on the `IPrincipal` interface to check whether the user has a specific permission. You can put it in the existing `IPrincipalExtensions` class that we created earlier, but it is preferable to create a separate static class, `AppPermissionRules`, to keep all permission rules in one place, as shown in Listing 5-12.

Listing 5-12. Specifying application permission rules

```
+ namespace AdventureWorks.Services.Common;
+
+ public static class AppPermissionRules
+ {
+     public static bool HasPermission(
+         this IPrincipal p,
+         AppPermissions permission
+     )
+     {
+         return permission switch
+         {
+             AppPermissions.Employee_View
+                 => p.IsEmployee(),
+             AppPermissions.Employee_View_Others
```

```
+                    => p.IsExecutive() || p.IsHR(),
+                AppPermissions.Employee_View_Others_Pay
+                    => p.IsHR(),
+                AppPermissions.Employee_View_Others_Private
+                    => p.IsHR(),
+                AppPermissions.Employee_Create
+                    => p.IsHR(true),
+                AppPermissions.Employee_Update
+                    => p.IsHR(),
+                _ => false,
+            };
+    }
+ }
```

By looking at the code above, you can easily see who has access to each permission. Human Resources personnel have full access to employee data, except that only Human Resources managers can create new employees. Top-level executives can view details of other employees, but they cannot view their pay or private information, and regular employees can only view their own data.

Securing Business Services

Now that we have defined the application permissions and associated security rules, we can start implementing them in our application. Best practices for securing Xomega applications include a multi-layered approach, where you provide multiple layers of protection by securing each individual layer.

In this section, we will focus on securing the business services that provide access to the data and functionality of our application. This will ensure that users cannot call services they are not authorized to use or read data they should not access, regardless of how they access the services—whether through the UI or directly via REST API calls.

Securing Operation Access

For any operation in the service that requires a specific permission, you should check that permission before executing the operation and return a security error if the user does not have the required permission.

Adding a Security Error Message

For simplicity, we will use a generic error message, "Operation not allowed," whenever the user does not have access to a specific service operation. You can add this message to the `Resources.resx` file under the `AdventureWorks.Services.Entities` project, as shown in Figure 5-3.

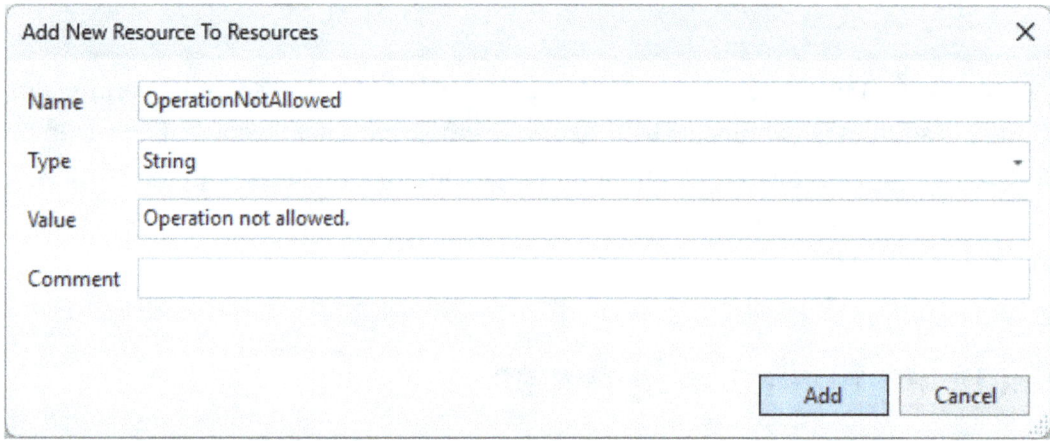

Figure 5-3. *Adding OperationNotAllowed message*

To regenerate the `Messages` class, right-click the nested `Messages.tt` file and select *Run Custom Tool*.

Tip You can also add more specific messages for each operation as needed, but make sure not to disclose any information that could help an attacker compromise your application.

CHAPTER 5 IMPLEMENTING SECURITY

Security Checks in CRUD Operations

At the start of each method for the operations in the generated service class, you will find a placeholder for custom code where you can add your security checks for that operation. You can access the principal for the currently logged-in user using the `CurrentPrincipal` property and check if they have the required permission using the `HasPermission` extension method defined earlier.

For our `EmployeeService`, I will add security checks for the `Employee_View` permission in the `ReadAsync` and `ReadListAsync` operations, and for the `Employee_Create` and `Employee_Update` permissions in the `CreateAsync` and `UpdateAsync` operations, respectively. If the user does not have the required permission, I will add a critical security error using the generated constant `Messages.OperationNotAllowed`, as shown in Listing 5-13.

Listing 5-13. Adding security checks to CRUD operations

```
public virtual async Task<Output<Employee_ReadOutput>>
    ReadAsync(int _businessEntityId,
              CancellationToken token = default)
{
    // CUSTOM_CODE_START: add custom security checks for Read
    operation below
+   if (!CurrentPrincipal.HasPermission(
+           AppPermissions.Employee_View))
+       currentErrors.CriticalError(ErrorType.Security,
+           Messages.OperationNotAllowed);
    // CUSTOM_CODE_END
}
public virtual async Task<Output<Employee_CreateOutput>>
    CreateAsync(Employee_CreateInput _data,
                CancellationToken token = default)
{
    // CUSTOM_CODE_START: add custom security checks for Create
    operation below
+   if (!CurrentPrincipal.HasPermission(
+           AppPermissions.Employee_Create))
```

297

CHAPTER 5 IMPLEMENTING SECURITY

```
+           currentErrors.CriticalError(ErrorType.Security,
+               Messages.OperationNotAllowed);
    // CUSTOM_CODE_END
}
public virtual async Task<Output> UpdateAsync(
    int _businessEntityId,
    Employee_UpdateInput_Data _data,
    CancellationToken token = default)
{
    // CUSTOM_CODE_START: add custom security checks for Update
    operation below
+   if (!CurrentPrincipal.HasPermission(
+           AppPermissions.Employee_Update))
+       currentErrors.CriticalError(ErrorType.Security,
+           Messages.OperationNotAllowed);
    // CUSTOM_CODE_END
}
public virtual async Task<Output<ICollection<Employee_ReadListOutput>>>
    ReadListAsync(Employee_ReadListInput_Criteria _criteria,
                  CancellationToken token = default)
{
    // CUSTOM_CODE_START: add custom security checks for ReadList
    operation below
+   if (!CurrentPrincipal.HasPermission(
+           AppPermissions.Employee_View))
+       currentErrors.CriticalError(ErrorType.Security,
+           Messages.OperationNotAllowed);
    // CUSTOM_CODE_END
}
```

Note Adding a critical error will abort the operation immediately and return the specified error message to the caller. Using `ErrorType.Security` will also set the appropriate HTTP status code for the response, such as 403 Forbidden.

CHAPTER 5 IMPLEMENTING SECURITY

Reviewing Operation Security

Since we started securing the application with business services, we can use the UI to test the security of the operations by logging in with different users and trying to access the employee services.

Non-employee User

First, let's log in as a customer Kim Abercrombie with a person type of "Store Contact" using their email address kim2@adventure-works.com. The system allows this user to log in to view their orders, but they should have no access to the employee services.

If you open the Employee List screen under this user and try to search for employees, you will get the "Operation not allowed" error message that we added, as shown in Figure 5-4.

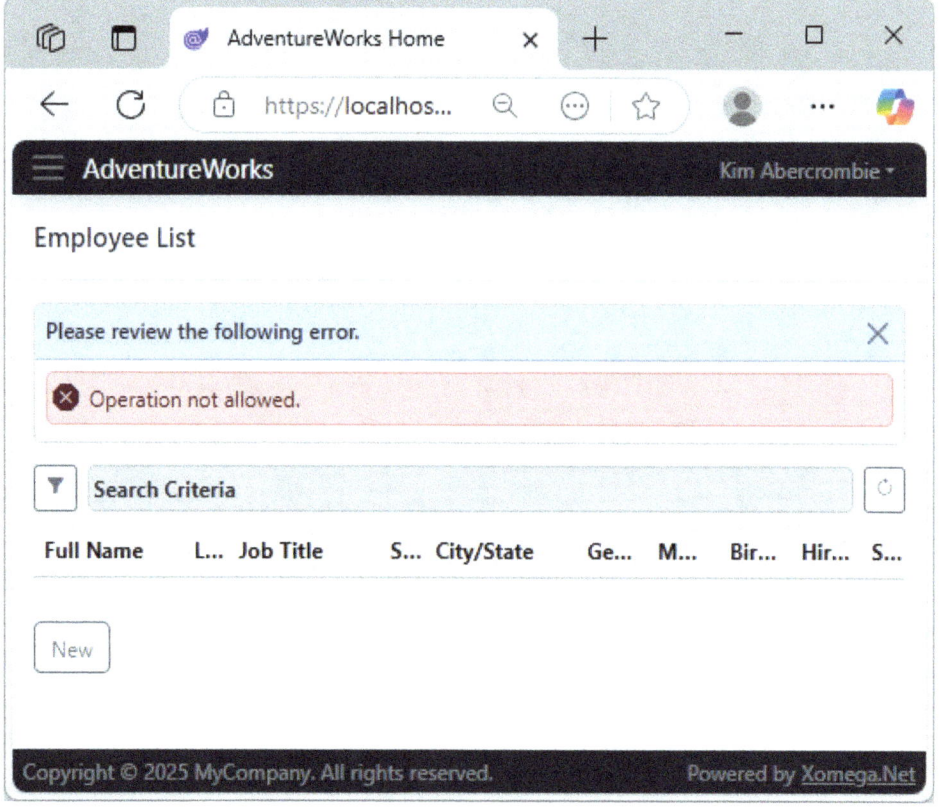

Figure 5-4. Employee List search for non-employee user

299

Of course, in the final system, they should not even have access to the Employee List screen. Yet, this shows that they will not be able to browse employees even if the UI is not fully secured or they bypass the UI and call the service directly.

Non-HR Employee User

Next, to test that only a Human Resources user can update employee information, let's log in as an employee Chris Norred, whose job title is "Control Specialist" using their email address chris1@adventure-works.com.

As an employee, Chris can view the Employee List, search for employees, and view their details. However, if Chris tries to update any information on the details screen, even their own, and hit *Save*, they will get the same "Operation not allowed" error message, as shown in Figure 5-5.

CHAPTER 5　IMPLEMENTING SECURITY

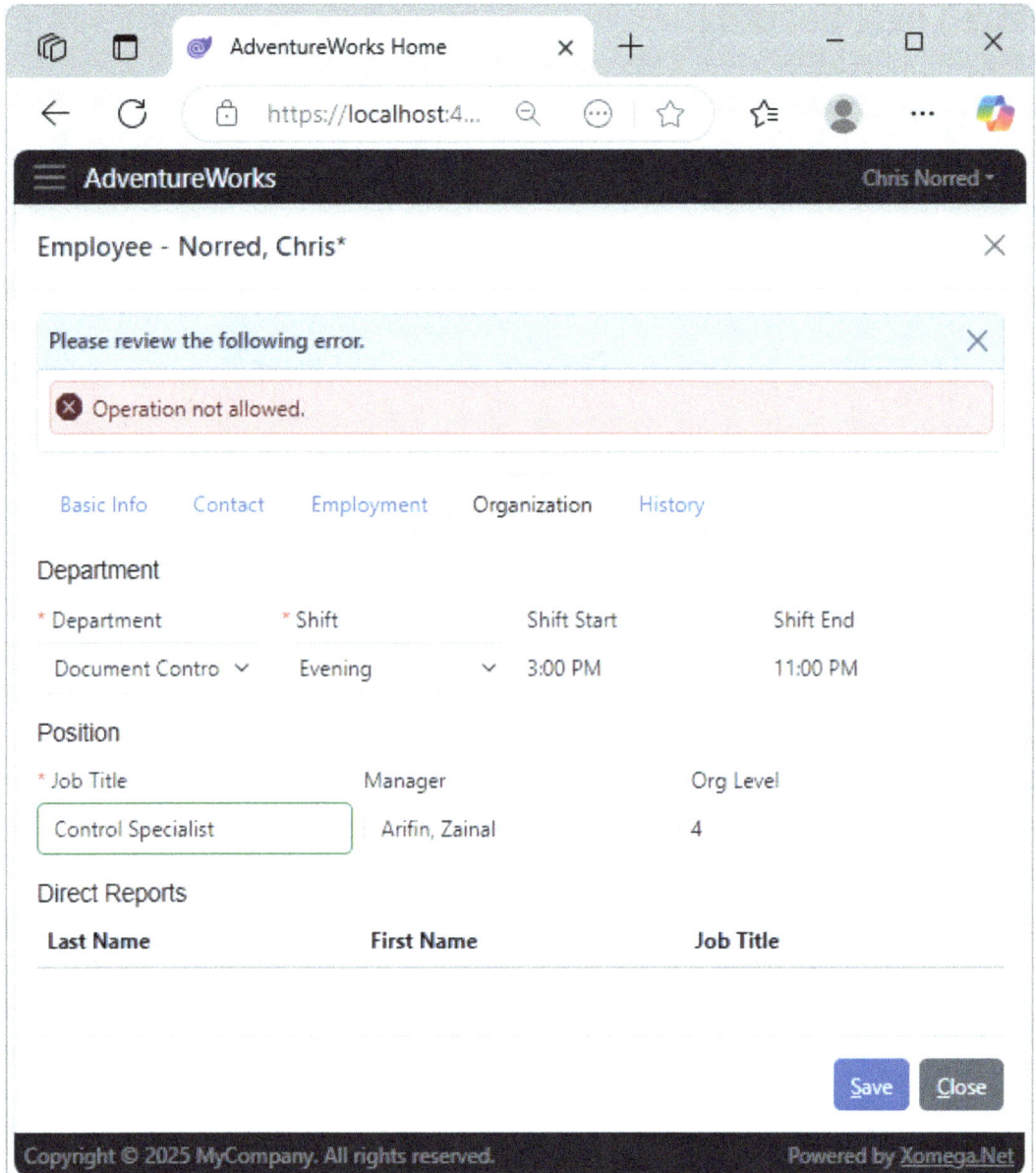

Figure 5-5. Saving employee as non-HR user

This proves that the read operations are accessible to all employees, but only HR personnel can update employee information. Similarly, you can test the `CreateAsync` operation by trying to create a new employee, which should also fail with the same error message.

CHAPTER 5   IMPLEMENTING SECURITY

Row-Level Security

Even though all employees can read the employee data, they should not be able to view details of other employees without special permission. Therefore, you need to add some additional security checks to the read operations to implement row-level security.

Row Access in Read Operation

An employee should always be able to read their own details. However, to read details of another employee, they should have Employee_View_Others permission, so we need to update the security checks in the ReadAsync operation to account for that.

You can determine if the employee is trying to read their own details by comparing the _businessEntityId parameter with the ID of the currently logged in employee, which you can get from the principal using the GetPersonId extension method.

Then, you can add a condition to the security check to throw a security error if the user does not have the Employee_View_Others permission and is not reading their own details, as shown in Listing 5-14.

Listing 5-14. Adding row access security to Read operation

```
public virtual async Task<Output<Employee_ReadOutput>>
    ReadAsync(int _businessEntityId,
            CancellationToken token = default)
{
    // CUSTOM_CODE_START: add custom security checks for Read
       operation below
+   bool self = _businessEntityId == CurrentPrincipal
+                                    .GetPersonId();
    if (!CurrentPrincipal.HasPermission(
-         AppPermissions.Employee_View))
+       || !self && !CurrentPrincipal.HasPermission(
+         AppPermissions.Employee_View_Others))
        currentErrors.CriticalError(ErrorType.Security,
            Messages.OperationNotAllowed);
    // CUSTOM_CODE_END
}
```

After this change, let's run the application to test it in the UI.

CHAPTER 5 IMPLEMENTING SECURITY

Access to Details of Another Employee

Let's log in as Chris Norred, run a search for employees, and try to view details of another employee. You should see the "Operation not allowed" error message, and the data for the employee should not be populated, as shown in Figure 5-6.

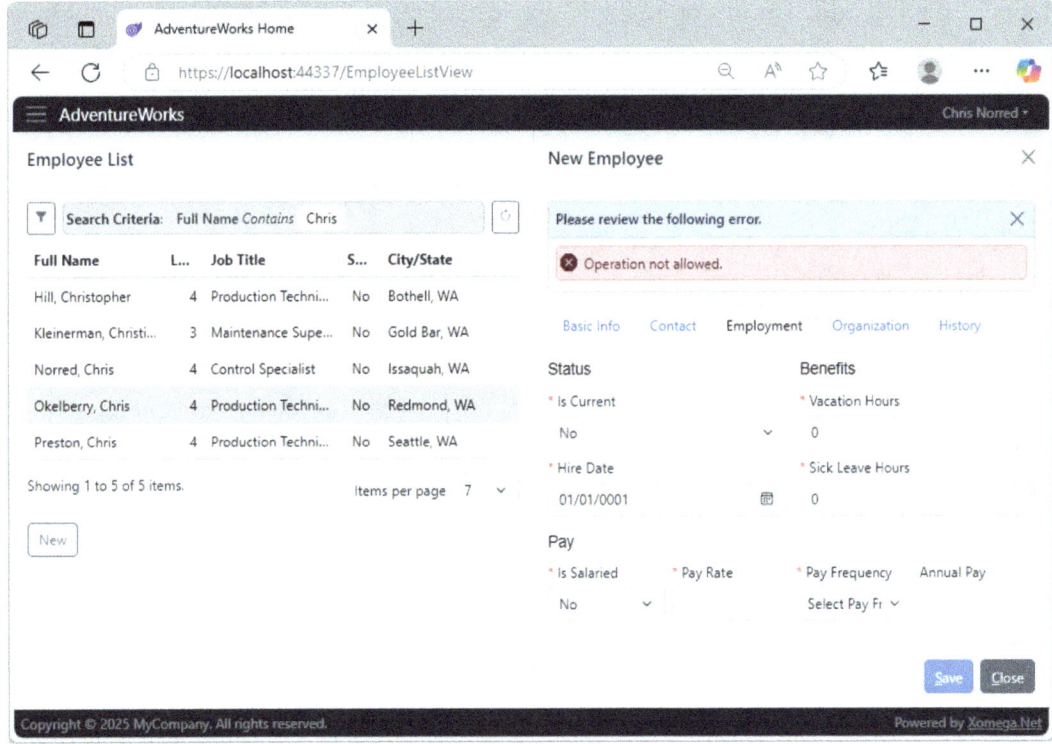

Figure 5-6. Employee details for another employee

Note If you click on the employee record for the current employee though, you will see the details for Chris Norred without any errors.

Row Access in ReadList Operation

While employee users cannot read full details of other employees now, they can still read some information about them in the Employee List, so we also need to implement row-level security in the `ReadListAsync` operation.

Unlike the ReadAsync operation, where we throw an error if the user tries to read another employee's details, in the ReadListAsync operation, we need to add custom filter criteria to restrict the results based on the user's permissions.

The generated ReadListAsync method has a placeholder for custom code where you can add your custom filter criteria to the source query. I will get the personId of the current user and add a condition to the source query for that ID if the user does not have the Employee_View_Others permission, as shown in Listing 5-15.

Listing 5-15. Adding row access security to ReadList operation

```
public virtual async Task<Output<ICollection<Employee_ReadListOutput>>>
ReadListAsync(
    Employee_ReadListInput_Criteria _criteria, CancellationToken token =
    default)
{
    // CUSTOM_CODE_START: add custom filter criteria to the source query
    for ReadList operation below
-   // src = src.Where(o => o.FieldName == VALUE);
+   int? personId = CurrentPrincipal.GetPersonId();
+   if (!CurrentPrincipal.HasPermission(
+           AppPermissions.Employee_View_Others))
+       src = src.Where(o => o.BusinessEntityId == personId);
    // CUSTOM_CODE_END
}
```

Let's run the application again to test the changes in the UI.

Employee List for Non-HR User

If you log in as the same employee Chris Norred, open the Employee List, and run the search with no criteria, you should see only one record for the current user in the list, as shown in Figure 5-7.

CHAPTER 5   IMPLEMENTING SECURITY

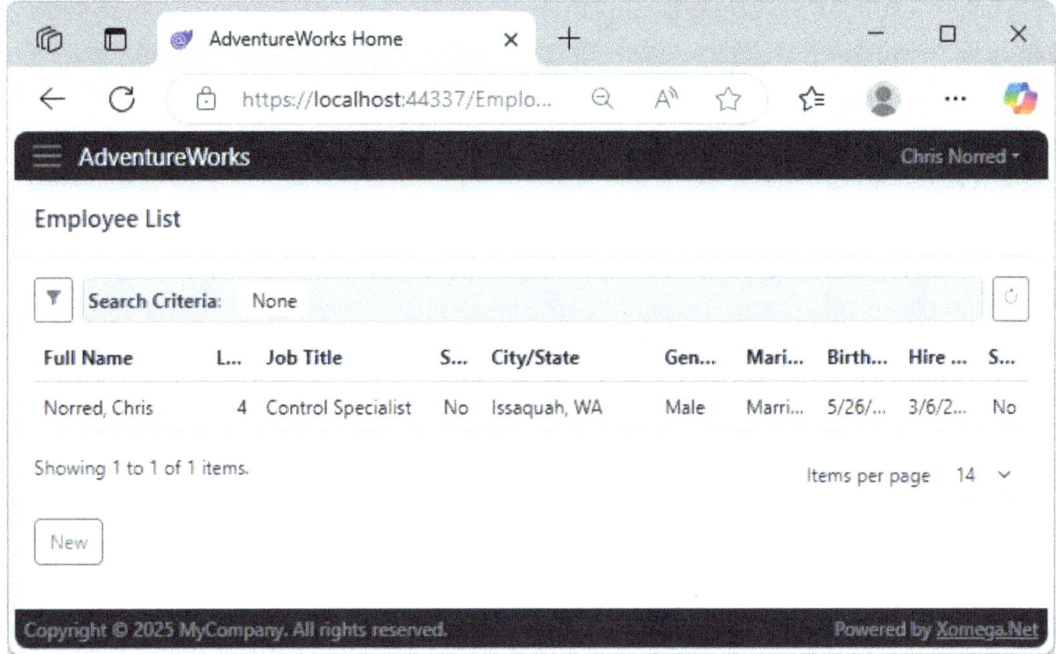

Figure 5-7. Employee List for non-HR user

Note Had we added row-level security to the `ReadListAsync` operation first, we would not have been able to use UI to test row-level security in the `ReadAsync` operation, since we would not be able to select another employee to view their details.

Secure Sensitive Data

In addition to securing access to the operations and row-level security, we also need to protect sensitive data from unauthorized access. This includes private information about employees, such as their national ID number, birth date, marital status, as well as their pay and benefits information.

CHAPTER 5 IMPLEMENTING SECURITY

This data should be accessible only to the employees themselves and to the users that have permissions `Employee_View_Others_Private` or `Employee_View_Others_Pay`. Currently, both permissions are granted only to Human Resources personnel, but it provides some flexibility to allow access to the pay information to other users, such as top-level executives, if needed.

We will implement this protection in the `ReadAsync` and `ReadListAsync` operations of the `EmployeeService`, which must return the result with other information, so we cannot just throw a security error or filter the results like we did for row-level security. Instead, we will have to leave the sensitive data blank or set it to a default value if the user does not have the required permission.

Sensitive Data in Read Operation

In the `ReadAsync` operation, we will update the custom code to check if the user has `Employee_View_Others_Pay` permission to either set the pay rate and frequency or clear the benefits information, which has been automatically copied to the result earlier. Similarly, we will clear the private information, if the user cannot view it.

Finally, we also need to add a security check to the `PayHistory_ReadListAsync` method to return an empty list if the user does not have permission to view pay information, as shown in Listing 5-16.

Listing 5-16. Protecting sensitive data in Read operation

```
public virtual async Task<Output<Employee_ReadOutput>>
    ReadAsync(int _businessEntityId,
              CancellationToken token = default)
{
    // CUSTOM_CODE_START: add custom code for Read operation below
    ...
+   if (self || CurrentPrincipal.HasPermission(
+       AppPermissions.Employee_View_Others_Pay))
+   {
        var payRate = obj.PayHistoryObjectList
            .OrderByDescending(ph => ph.RateChangeDate)
            .FirstOrDefault();
```

CHAPTER 5 IMPLEMENTING SECURITY

```
              res.PayRate = payRate?.Rate;
              res.PayFrequency = payRate?.PayFrequency;
+         }
+         else
+         {
+             res.SalariedFlag = false;
+             res.VacationHours = 0;
+             res.SickLeaveHours = 0;
+         }
+         if (!self && !CurrentPrincipal.HasPermission(
+             AppPermissions.Employee_View_Others_Private))
+         {
+             res.NationalIdNumber = null;
+             res.LoginId = null;
+             res.BirthDate = DateTime.MinValue;
+             res.MaritalStatus = null;
+         }
          ...
          // CUSTOM_CODE_END
      }
      ...
      public virtual async Task<
        Output<ICollection<EmployeePayHistory_ReadListOutput>>>
          PayHistory_ReadListAsync(
              int _businessEntityId,
              CancellationToken token = default)
      {
          ...
          // CUSTOM_CODE_START: add custom security checks for
          // PayHistory_ReadList operation below
+         var self = _businessEntityId == CurrentPrincipal
+                                           .GetPersonId();
+         if (!self && !CurrentPrincipal.HasPermission(
+                 AppPermissions.Employee_View_Others_Pay))
+             return new Output<ICollection<
```

CHAPTER 5   IMPLEMENTING SECURITY

```
+                EmployeePayHistory_ReadListOutput>>(
+                    currentErrors, [], totalCount);
     // CUSTOM_CODE_END
     ...
}
```

> **Note**   We return an empty list for the `PayHistory_ReadListAsync` method instead of throwing a security error, since this operation is called by the UI as part of reading the employee details. Otherwise, you would need to add custom UI code to handle the security error without displaying it to the user.

Let's run the application to test these changes in the UI.

Sensitive Data for Executive Users

Log in as the executive user Jean Trenary, whose job title is "Information Services Manager," using the email address `jean0@adventure-works.com`. This account allows you to view details of other employees, but not their pay or private information.

If you open the details for another employee, you will see that private information in the *Basic Info* tab is not populated, as shown in Figure 5-8.

CHAPTER 5   IMPLEMENTING SECURITY

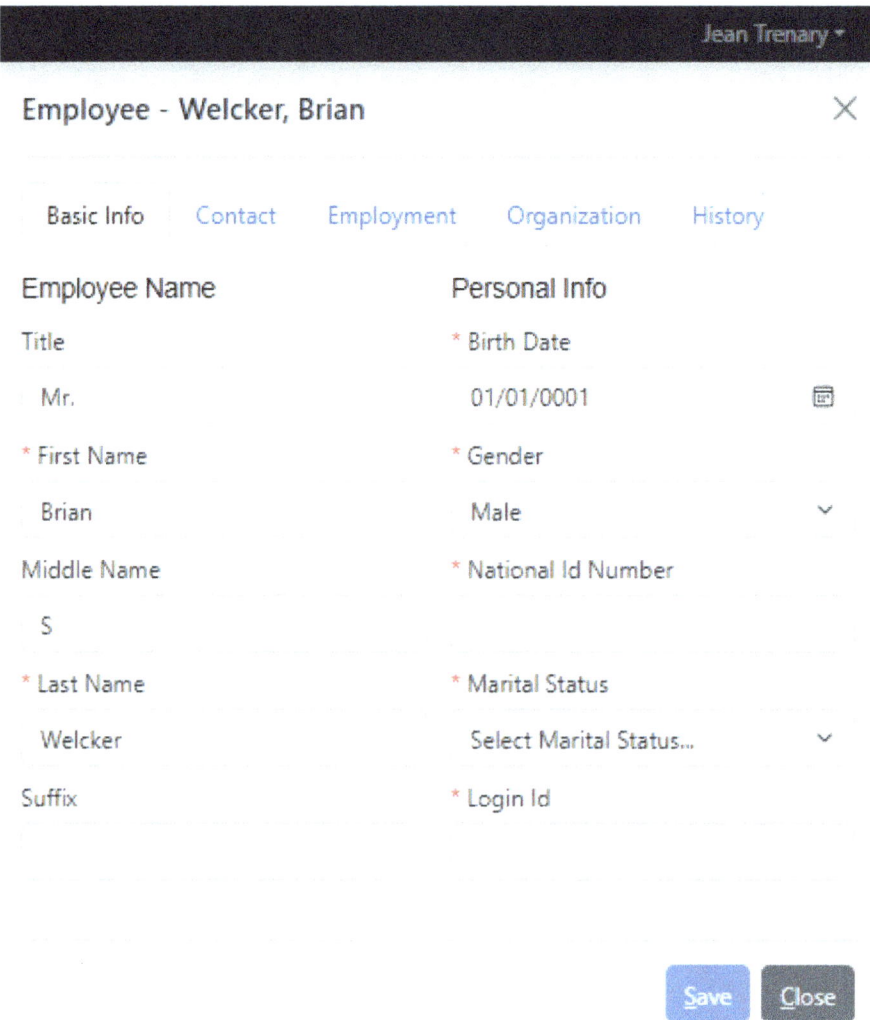

Figure 5-8. Personal info of another employee for executive user

---

Note   Even though *Gender* is part of the *Personal Info* panel, it is not considered private information, so it is still populated.

If you switch to the *Employment* tab, you will see that the employee benefits and pay information are also not populated, as shown in Figure 5-9.

309

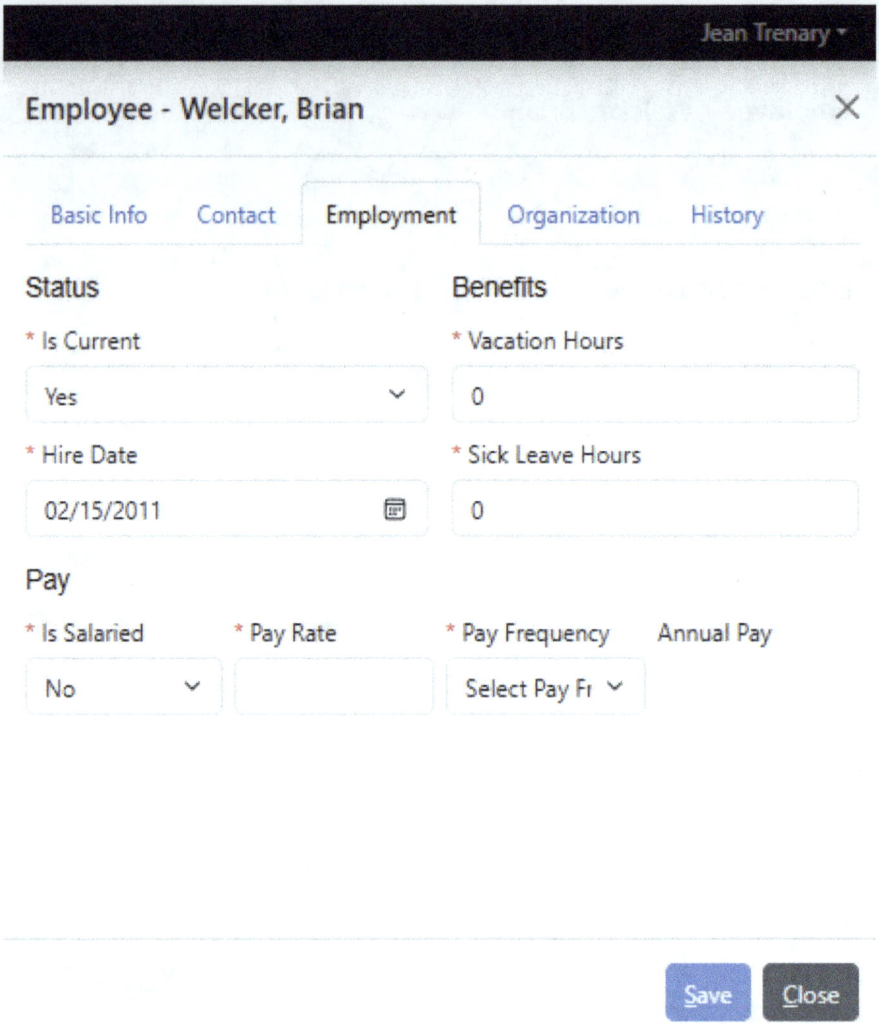

CHAPTER 5   IMPLEMENTING SECURITY

Figure 5-9. Benefits and pay info of another employee for executive user

This takes care of protecting sensitive data on the Employee Details screen, but some of this data, such as marital status, birth date, and salaried flag, is also displayed on the Employee List screen, so we need to update the `ReadListAsync` operation to protect that data as well.

Sensitive Data in ReadList Operation

The problem with reading sensitive data in the read list operation is that those output parameters use the same names as the corresponding fields in the employee object, which allows Xomega to automatically populate them from their respective fields in the generated ReadListAsync method.

One way to provide custom code for populating these parameters is to change their names in the read list operation, so that it no longer matches the names of the fields in the employee object. So, let's change the names of the parameters to include the private prefix, as shown in Listing 5-17.

Listing 5-17. Renaming parameter for sensitive data in ReadList operation

```
 <object name="employee">
     <operation name="read list" type="readlist">
       <output list="true">
-        <param name="marital status"/>
+        <param name="private marital status"
+               type="marital status"/>
-        <param name="birth date"/>
+        <param name="private birth date" type="date"/>
-        <param name="salaried flag" type="yesno"
-               required="true"/>
+        <param name="private salaried flag" type="yesno"/>
       </output>
     </operation>
 </object>
 <xfk:data-object class="EmployeeList" list="true">
   <ui:display>
     <ui:fields>
-      <ui:field param="salaried flag" label="Salaried"/>
+      <ui:field param="private salaried flag"
+                label="Salaried"/>
+      <ui:field param="private marital status"
+                label="Marital Status"/>
```

CHAPTER 5 IMPLEMENTING SECURITY

```
+       <ui:field param="private birth date"
+                 label="Birth Date"/>
    </ui:fields>
  </ui:display>
</xfk:data-object>
```

> **Note** To keep the original column headers for these parameters, we need to set the labels for these fields in the `EmployeeList` data object. I also made the `private salaried flag` parameter not required to allow returning a blank value for it.

If you build the model now, you will see that these parameters have placeholders for custom code in the generated `ReadListAsync` method of the `EmployeeService`.

Since we populate their values in a LINQ query, we need to store the results of the permission checks in local variables `canViewOthersPrivate` and `canViewOthersPay` and use them along with the `personId` that we added earlier to set the values of these sensitive parameters, as shown in Listing 5-18.

Listing 5-18. Custom code for populating sensitive data in ReadList operation

```
public virtual async
    Task<Output<ICollection<Employee_ReadListOutput>>>
      ReadListAsync(Employee_ReadListInput_Criteria _criteria,
                    CancellationToken token = default)
{
    // CUSTOM_CODE_START: add custom filter criteria to the source query
    //   for ReadList operation below
+   bool canViewOthersPrivate, canViewOthersPay;
+   canViewOthersPrivate = CurrentPrincipal.HasPermission(
+       AppPermissions.Employee_View_Others_Private);
+   canViewOthersPay = CurrentPrincipal.HasPermission(
+       AppPermissions.Employee_View_Others_Pay);
    int? personId = CurrentPrincipal.GetPersonId();
```

```
    if (!CurrentPrincipal.HasPermission(
            AppPermissions.Employee_View_Others))
        src = src.Where(o => o.BusinessEntityId == personId);
    // CUSTOM_CODE_END
    ...
    select new Employee_ReadListOutput() {
        ...
        // CUSTOM_CODE_START: set the PrivateMaritalStatus output parameter
            of ReadList operation below
-       // TODO: PrivateMaritalStatus = obj.???, // CUSTOM_CODE_END
+       PrivateMaritalStatus = (obj.BusinessEntityId == personId
+           || canViewOthersPrivate) ? obj.MaritalStatus : null,
+       // CUSTOM_CODE_END
        // CUSTOM_CODE_START: set the PrivateBirthDate output parameter of
            ReadList operation below
-       // TODO: PrivateBirthDate = obj.???, // CUSTOM_CODE_END
+       PrivateBirthDate = obj.BusinessEntityId == personId
+           || canViewOthersPrivate ? obj.BirthDate : null,
+       // CUSTOM_CODE_END
        HireDate = obj.HireDate,
        // CUSTOM_CODE_START: set the PrivateSalariedFlag output parameter
            of ReadList operation below
-       // TODO: PrivateSalariedFlag = obj.???, // CUSTOM_CODE_END
+       PrivateSalariedFlag = obj.BusinessEntityId == personId
+           || canViewOthersPay ? obj.SalariedFlag : null,
+       // CUSTOM_CODE_END
    };
}
```

Review Private Data in Employee List

If you run the application now and log in as the same executive user, Jean Trenary, you will see that the Employee List screen shows values for the *Marital Status*, *Birth Date*, and *Salaried* flag only for the current employee, and not for other employees, as shown in Figure 5-10.

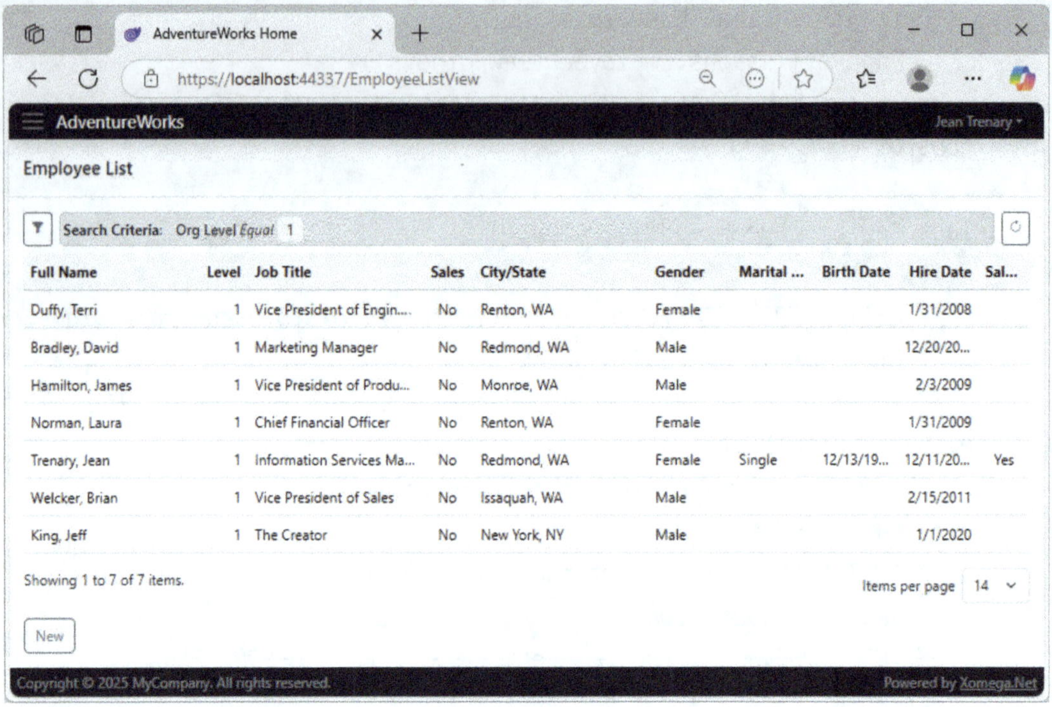

CHAPTER 5   IMPLEMENTING SECURITY

Figure 5-10. Employee List with private data

Secure UI Views and Fields

So far, we have secured business services for our application by protecting access to service operations, implementing row-level security, and guarding sensitive data. While technically it secures our application's functionality and data at its core, it does not provide good user experience on the UI.

You don't want to give users access to a list screen, which always returns an error "Operation not allowed" when they try to run the search or allow them to edit fields on a details screen to always show them the same security error when they hit *Save*.

Similarly, you don't want to show users fields they are not allowed to see, populated with some default values, or links to screens they cannot access. In this section, you will learn how to implement security on the UI—both in a platform-independent way and specifically for Blazor views, as needed.

Secure Editing on the UI

We will start by making the Employee Details screen uneditable for the users that don't have the corresponding permissions, i.e., non-HR employees. Thanks to Xomega Framework, you can do this very easily in customized data objects, which means that in addition to Blazor it will work for any other platform supported by Xomega Framework, such as WPF or even legacy ASP.NET Web Forms.

Making Data Object Read-Only

Just like the business services, data objects allow you to access the principal of the current user and check its permissions using the CurrentPrincipal property. Since we added extension methods to the IPrincipal interface in a shared project, we can use the HasPermission extension method to check the user's permissions on the UI as well.

Let's open the EmployeeObjectCustomized class that we created earlier, and check if the user has permission to create or update employees in the OnInitialized method. If they don't, we will set the AccessLevel property of the data object to AccessLevel.ReadOnly, as shown in Listing 5-19, which will make the entire object read-only, including all its fields and child objects.

Listing 5-19. Making the Employee object read-only

```
public class EmployeeObjectCustomized : EmployeeObject
{
    protected override void OnInitialized()
    {
        base.OnInitialized();
+       if (!CurrentPrincipal.HasPermission(
+               AppPermissions.Employee_Create) &&
+           !CurrentPrincipal.HasPermission(
+               AppPermissions.Employee_Update))
+       {
+           AccessLevel = AccessLevel.ReadOnly;
+           //SaveAction.AccessLevel = AccessLevel.None;
+       }
    }
}
```

CHAPTER 5 IMPLEMENTING SECURITY

> **Tip** You can also set `SaveAction.AccessLevel = AccessLevel.None;` to hide the *Save* button on the UI, as shown in the commented line above. Otherwise, the *Save* button will be just disabled by default, since it's enabled only when the data object is modified.

Let's run the application and log in as a non-HR employee Jean Trenary. If you open the Employee Details screen for any employee, you will see that all fields are disabled, as illustrated for the *Basic Info* tab in Figure 5-11.

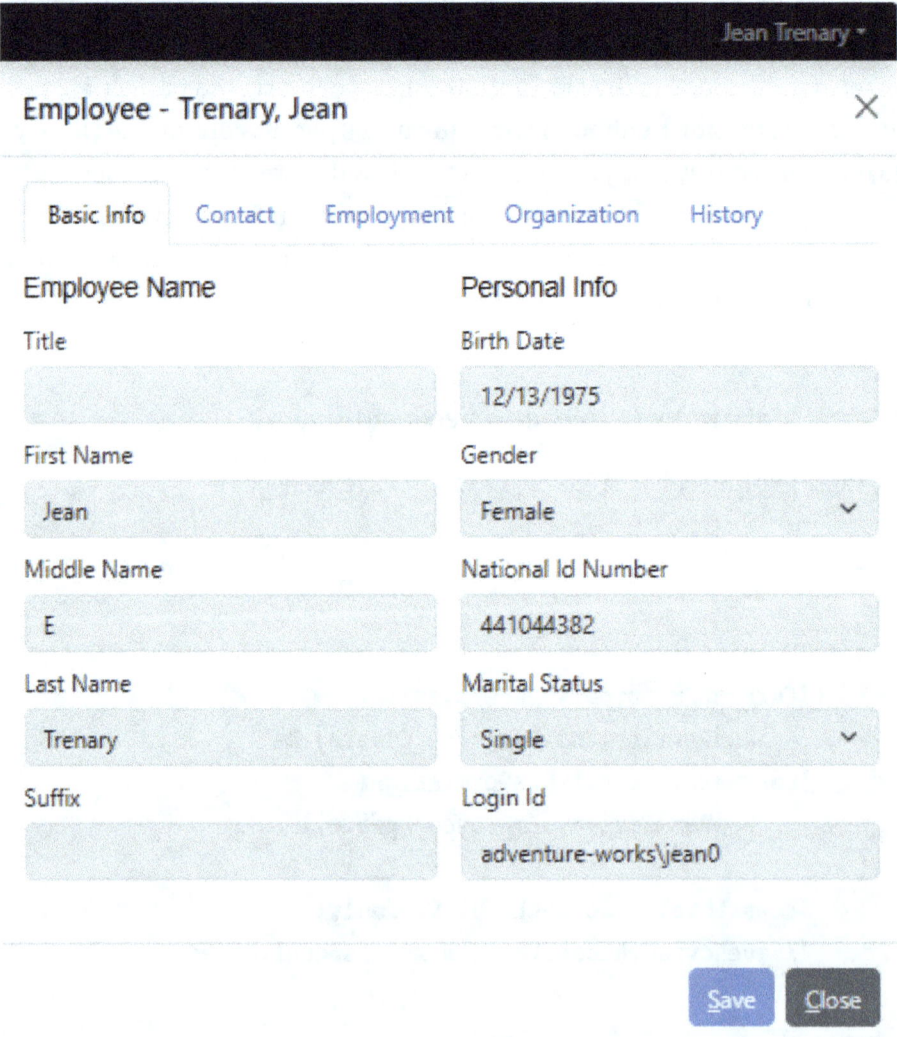

Figure 5-11. *Read-only fields on the Basic Info tab of the Employee Details screen*

CHAPTER 5 IMPLEMENTING SECURITY

If you switch to the *Contact* tab, you will see that the email and phone fields are also disabled, but we still have the *Create Address*, *Edit Address*, and *Lookup Address* links, which allow us to create or edit addresses, as shown in Figure 5-12.

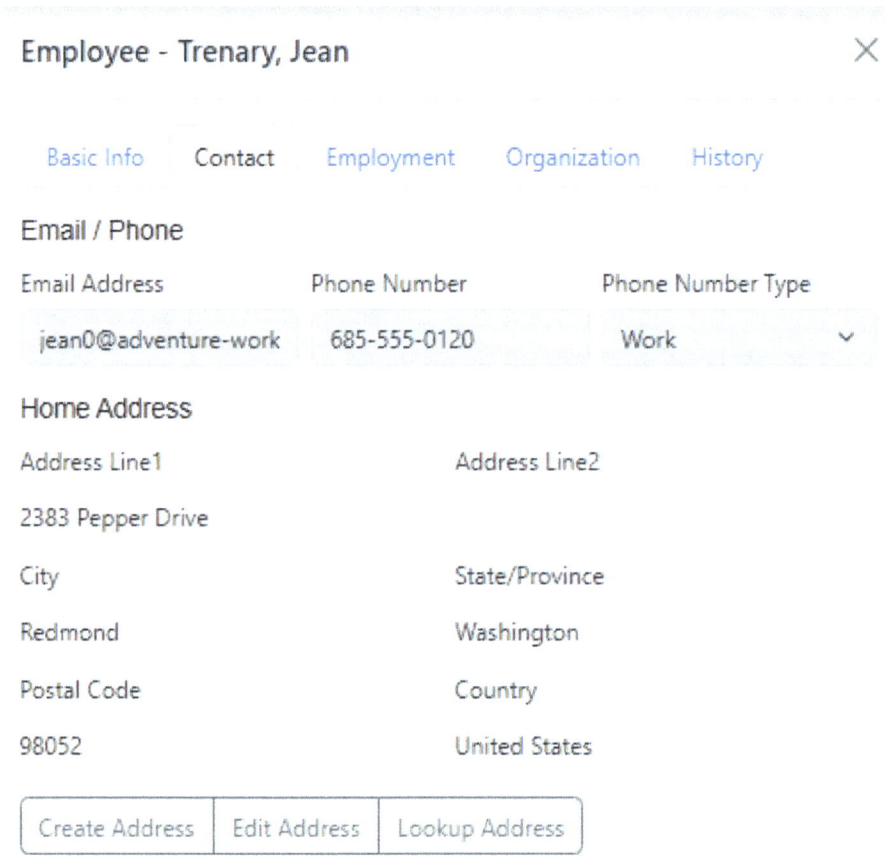

Figure 5-12. *Address edit links on the Contact tab of the Employee Details screen*

Actions on a read-only data objects are not automatically disabled or hidden, since they may just open another view and not necessarily modify the data object. Therefore, in our case, we need to explicitly hide the editing links for the address.

Hiding Editing Links

To hide the editing links for the address, you need to set the AccessLevel on the actions of the child EmployeeAddressObject to AccessLevel.None. You can either do this in the child EmployeeAddressObjectCustomized class, or just add it in the parent EmployeeObjectCustomized class, as shown in Listing 5-20.

317

CHAPTER 5   IMPLEMENTING SECURITY

Listing 5-20. Hiding editing links for the employee address

```
public class EmployeeObjectCustomized : EmployeeObject
{
    protected override void OnInitialized()
    {
        base.OnInitialized();
        if (!CurrentPrincipal.HasPermission(
                AppPermissions.Employee_Create) &&
            !CurrentPrincipal.HasPermission(
                AppPermissions.Employee_Update))
        {
            AccessLevel = AccessLevel.ReadOnly;
            //SaveAction.AccessLevel = AccessLevel.None;
+           AddressObject.CreateAddressAction.AccessLevel =
+               AccessLevel.None;
+           AddressObject.EditAddressAction.AccessLevel =
+               AccessLevel.None;
+           AddressObject.LookupAddressAction.AccessLevel =
+               AccessLevel.None;
        }
        ...
    }
}
```

Tip   Doing this in the `EmployeeObjectCustomized` parent class is better as you keep all the security logic in one place. Adding it to the `EmployeeAddressObjectCustomized` child class makes sense only if you add that child multiple times, e.g., as a Home and Work address.

Let's run the application again as a non-HR user and open the *Contact* tab. You will see that the *Create Address*, *Edit Address*, and *Lookup Address* links are no longer available, as shown in Figure 5-13.

318

CHAPTER 5 IMPLEMENTING SECURITY

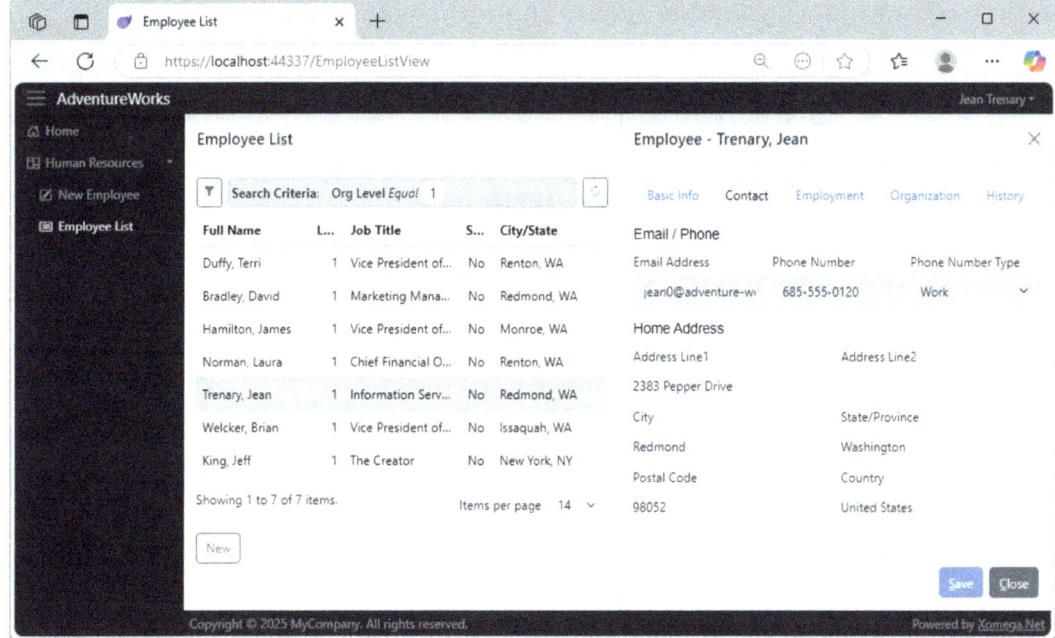

***Figure 5-13.** Contact tab of the Employee Details screen without edit links*

This takes care of the read-only access to the Employee Details screen for non-HR users. However, if you look at Figure 5-13, you will see that the *New* button is present on the Employee List screen, and the *New Employee* link is still available in the main menu, even though non-HR users are not allowed to create new employees.

Hiding Creation Links

Let's hide the links to create new employees for the users that don't have the necessary permissions. For the main menu, this will require a Blazor-specific solution, but for the Employee List screen, we can do it in the customized data object.

Updating Presentation Model

To implement security for the employee creation links, we need to make a couple of updates to the model, as shown in Listing 5-21:

- Add a `customize="true"` attribute to the `EmployeeList` data object to generate a customized data object for it.

- Add a `policy` attribute to the `ui:main-link` element for the *New Employee* link and set it to `Employee_Create`.

319

CHAPTER 5 IMPLEMENTING SECURITY

Listing 5-21. Model updates to secure employee creation links

```
<xfk:data-object class="EmployeeList" list="true"
+                customize="true">[...]
...
<ui:view name="EmployeeView" title="Employee">
  <ui:view-model data-object="EmployeeObject"
                 customize="true"/>
  <ui:main-link name="new employee"
+               policy="Employee_Create">
    <ui:params>
      <ui:param name="_action" value="create"/>
    </ui:params>
  </ui:main-link>
</ui:view>
```

Now let's build the model to regenerate all the necessary classes from the updated model.

Hiding the New link of Employee List

To hide the *New* button on the Employee List screen, we will check the `Employee_Create` permission in the `OnInitialized` method of the `EmployeeListCustomized` class and set the `AccessLevel` to `AccessLevel.None` for the *New* action, accordingly, as shown in Listing 5-21.

Listing 5-22. Hiding the New link of Employee List

```
public class EmployeeListCustomized : EmployeeList
{
    protected override void OnInitialized()
    {
        base.OnInitialized();
+       if (!CurrentPrincipal.HasPermission(
+               AppPermissions.Employee_Create))
+       {
+           NewAction.AccessLevel = AccessLevel.None;
+       }
    }
}
```

Note This is similar to what we did to hide the editing links on the Employee Details screen.

Adding Policies for App Permissions

The policy that we added to the main links in the model uses an Asp.Net Core authorization policy, which makes them Blazor-specific. These policies need to be defined separately and registered in the Startup.cs file of the Blazor application.

The Xomega Solution template already created a special AuthConfig class with a static method AddAppPolicies that you can use to register your policies. Since we used a policy name that matches the permission name, we can add a generic code to register all the application permissions as policies, as shown in Listing 5-23.

Listing 5-23. Adding policies for app permissions

```
public static class AuthConfig
{
    public static void AddAppPolicies(
        this AuthorizationOptions opts)
    {
-       // TODO: configure app policies here
+       foreach (var p in Enum.GetValues<AppPermissions>())
+       {
+           opts.AddPolicy(p.ToString(), policy =>
+               policy.RequireAssertion(ctx =>
+                   ctx.User.HasPermission(p)));
+       }
    }
}
```

Tip Using such permission-based policies in Blazor applications allows you to continue using permissions in the business services and data objects that are platform-agnostic and don't have a dependency on Asp.Net Core.

CHAPTER 5   IMPLEMENTING SECURITY

Reviewing Creation Links

Now let's run the application and log in as a non-HR employee Jean Trenary again. You will see that the *New Employee* link is no longer available on the main menu, and the *New* button is not present on the Employee List screen, as shown in Figure 5-14.

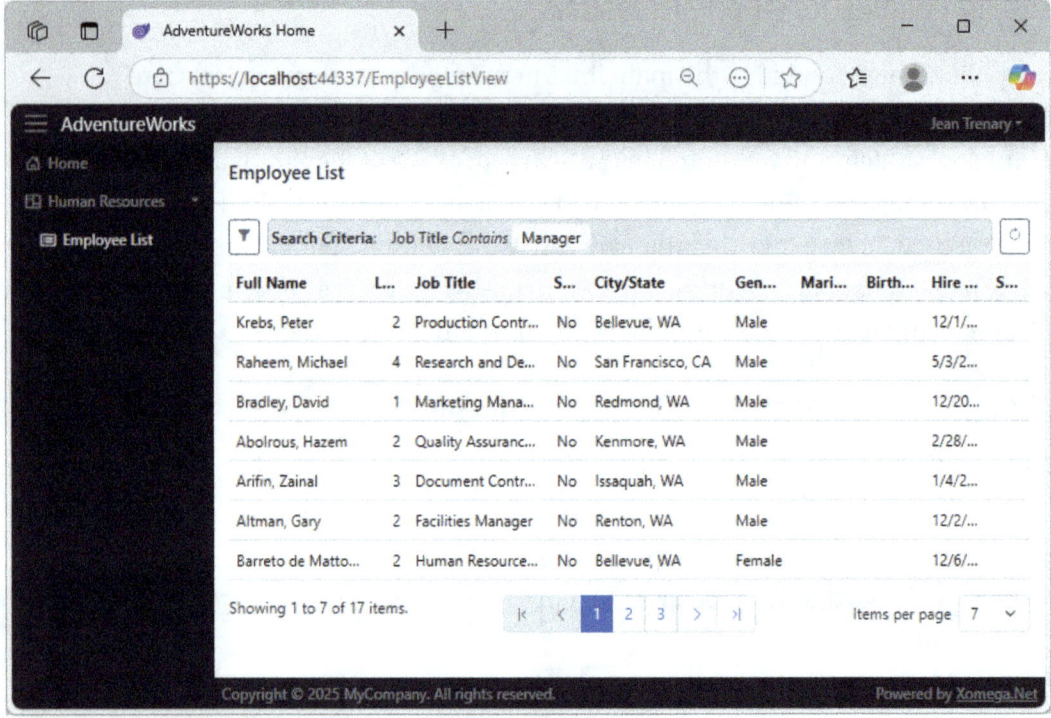

Figure 5-14.* Secured employee creation links*

Hiding Sensitive Data

Now that we have disabled editing for non-HR users, let's see how we can hide fields containing sensitive data, such as pay and private information, from the users that are not allowed to see them.

Hiding Sensitive Fields

To hide sensitive employee fields, you can set the `AccessLevel` to `AccessLevel.None` on the corresponding properties of the customized `EmployeeObject` for the users that are not allowed to see them.

322

However, the problem is that the security check for this includes checking the value of the BusinessEntityIdProperty to determine if the user is viewing their own employee details, which is not yet set when the OnInitialized method is called.

Therefore, instead of setting the AccessLevel directly in the OnInitialized method, we will add a Change event listener to the BusinessEntityIdProperty, where we can compare the value of the BusinessEntityIdProperty with the current user's person ID to determine if they are viewing their own employee details.

Next, we will determine the access level for the pay and private info fields based on whether the user is viewing their own details or has the corresponding permissions, and set it on the relevant properties, as shown in Listing 5-24.

Listing 5-24. Hiding sensitive fields in the Employee object

```
public class EmployeeObjectCustomized : EmployeeObject
{
    protected override void OnInitialized()
    {
        base.OnInitialized();
        ...
+       BusinessEntityIdProperty.Change += (sender, e) => {
+           if (!e.Change.IncludesValue()) return;
+           bool self = BusinessEntityIdProperty.Value?.Id ==
+               CurrentPrincipal.GetPersonId()?.ToString();
+           AccessLevel alPay = self ||
+               CurrentPrincipal.HasPermission(
+                   AppPermissions.Employee_View_Others_Pay)
+               ? AccessLevel.Full : AccessLevel.None;
+           AccessLevel alPrivate = self ||
+               CurrentPrincipal.HasPermission(
+                   AppPermissions.Employee_View_Others_Private)
+               ? AccessLevel.Full : AccessLevel.None;
+
+           SalariedFlagProperty.AccessLevel = alPay;
+           PayRateProperty.AccessLevel = alPay;
+           PayFrequencyProperty.AccessLevel = alPay;
+           AnnualPayProperty.AccessLevel = alPay;
```

```
+            VacationHoursProperty.AccessLevel = alPay;
+            SickLeaveHoursProperty.AccessLevel = alPay;
+            BirthDateProperty.AccessLevel = alPrivate;
+            NationalIdNumberProperty.AccessLevel = alPrivate;
+            LoginIdProperty.AccessLevel = alPrivate;
+            MaritalStatusProperty.AccessLevel = alPrivate;
+        };
         ...
    }
}
```

If you run the application and log in as an executive non-HR user, such as Jean Trenary, which can view other employees' details, but not their pay or private information, you will see that the private fields are hidden in the *Basic Info* tab, as shown in Figure 5-15.

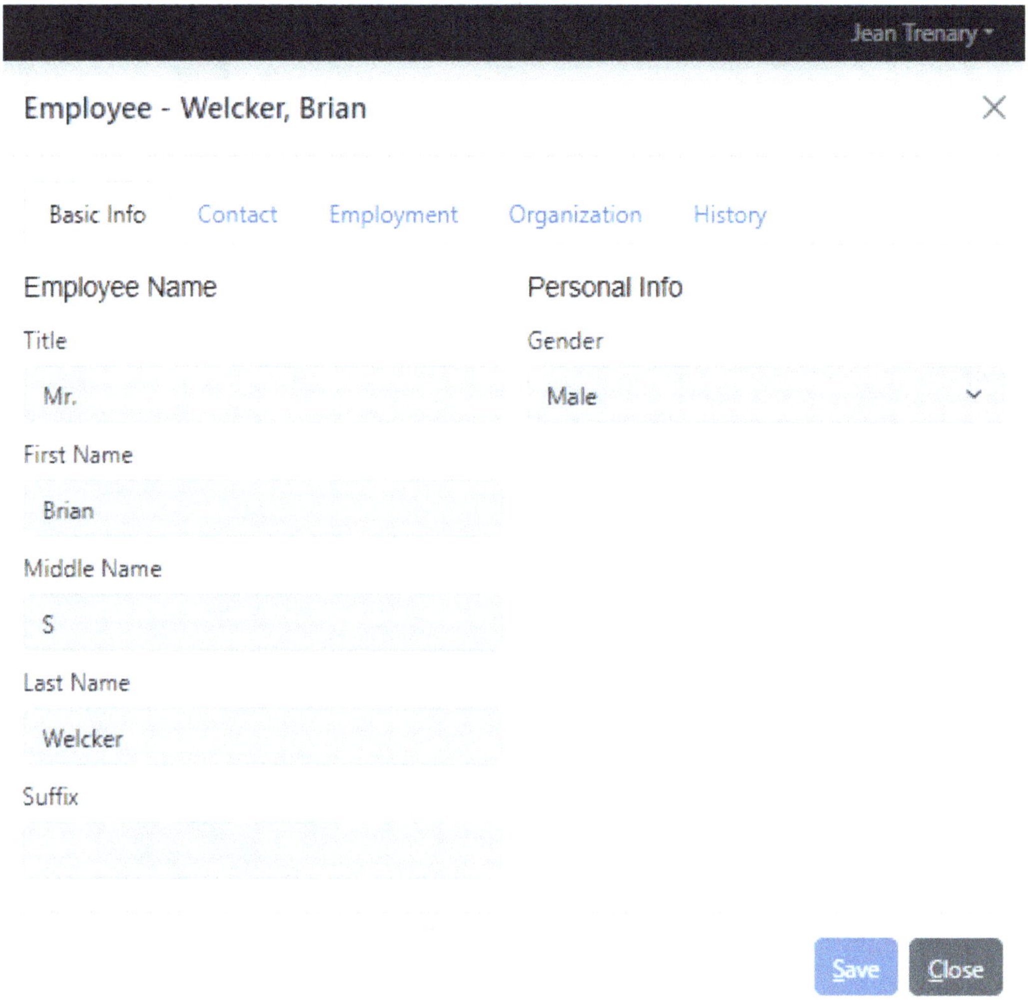

CHAPTER 5 IMPLEMENTING SECURITY

Figure 5-15. Employee details with private fields hidden

Similarly, if you switch to the *Employment* tab, you will see that the pay fields are also hidden, as shown in Figure 5-16.

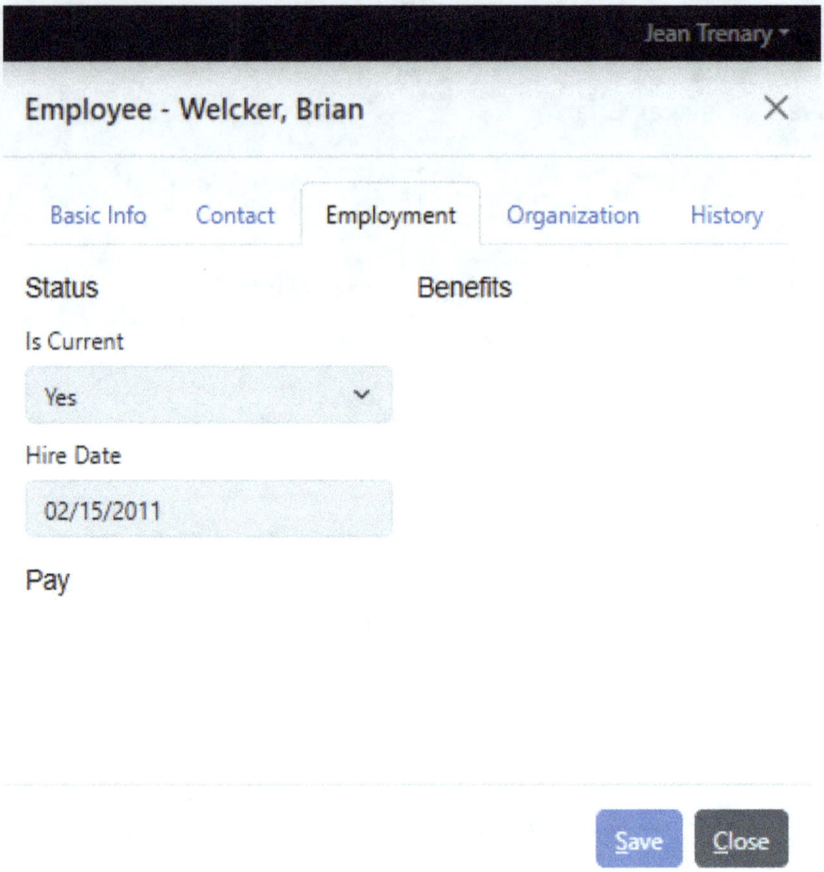

CHAPTER 5   IMPLEMENTING SECURITY

Figure 5-16. *Employee details with pay fields hidden*

Given that we hid all the fields in the *Benefits* and *Pay* panels, we also want to hide these entire panels to avoid dangling panel titles with no fields in them.

Note   Even though hiding entire panels may render setting `AccessLevel` on the individual fields unnecessary, it is still a good practice to also set `AccessLevel` on the individual properties as an added layer of security in case you decide to move some of them to a different panel or tab in the future.

Hiding UI Panels

Panels group fields on the UI, and the underlying data objects know nothing about the panels that their properties are bound to. Therefore, hiding panels on the UI involves binding their visibility to a flag that can be set in the view model based on the required visibility conditions.

Marking Panels with Conditional Visibility

To help you control the visibility of panels on the generated views, Xomega model allows you to indicate which panels or tabs should be conditionally visible by adding a visible-flag attribute to the ui:panel or ui:tab element in the model.

This will generate a property in the view model that you can override to control the visibility of the panel or tab. You can set the value of the visible-flag attribute to provide a custom name for that property, or leave it empty to have it generated automatically based on the panel or tab title.

In our case, we will add an empty visible-flag attribute to the *Benefits*, *Pay* and *Pay History* panels to allow hiding them for unauthorized users. To demonstrate other cases of conditional panel visibility, we will also add it to the *Direct Reports* panel and the *History* tab, which should not be visible when creating a new employee, as shown in Listing 5-25.

Listing 5-25. Marking panels with conditional visibility

```
<xfk:data-object class="EmployeeObject" customize="true">
  <ui:display>
    ...
    <ui:panel-layout>
      <ui:tabs>
        <ui:tab title="Basic Info">[...]
        <ui:tab title="Contact">[...]
        <ui:tab title="Employment">
          <ui:panel group="status" field-cols="1"
                    panel-cols="2"/>
          <ui:panel group="benefits" field-cols="1"
-                   panel-cols="2"/>
+                   panel-cols="2" visible-flag=""/>
```

CHAPTER 5 IMPLEMENTING SECURITY

```
-            <ui:panel group="pay"/>
+            <ui:panel group="pay" visible-flag=""/>
         </ui:tab>
         <ui:tab title="Organization">
           <ui:panel group="department"/>
           <ui:panel group="position"/>
           <ui:panel child="reports" title="Direct Reports"
+                    visible-flag=""/>
         </ui:tab>
-        <ui:tab title="History">
+        <ui:tab title="History" visible-flag="">
           <ui:panel child="department history"/>
-          <ui:panel child="pay history"/>
+          <ui:panel child="pay history" visible-flag=""/>
         </ui:tab>
       </ui:tabs>
     </ui:panel-layout>
   </ui:display>
</xfk:data-object>
```

Let's build the model to regenerate the view model with the new visibility flags.

Visibility Flags in Custom View Model

Now you can open the `EmployeeViewModelCustomized` class that we created earlier and override the visibility properties for the panels that we marked with the visible-flag attribute in the model.

I will add a helper method `IsSelf` to check if the current user is viewing their own employee details and use it to determine the visibility of the *Pay*, *Benefits*, and *Pay History* panels. I will also set the *Reports* panel and *History* tab to be visible only for existing employees, as shown in Listing 5-26.

Listing 5-26. Customizing visibility flags in the view model

```
public class EmployeeViewModelCustomized : EmployeeViewModel
{
    public override string BaseTitle =>
        base.BaseTitle + (MainObj.IsNew ? "" :
        $" - {MainObj.LastNameProperty.Value}, {MainObj.FirstNameProperty.
        Value}");
+   private bool IsSelf() =>
+       MainObj.BusinessEntityIdProperty.Value?.Id ==
+       MainObj.CurrentPrincipal.GetPersonId()?.ToString();
+   public override bool PanelPay_Visible => IsSelf() ||
+       MainObj.CurrentPrincipal.HasPermission(
+           AppPermissions.Employee_View_Others_Pay);
+
+   public override bool PanelBenefits_Visible
+       => PanelPay_Visible;
+
+   public override bool PanelPayHistory_Visible
+       => PanelPay_Visible;
+
+   public override bool PanelReports_Visible
+       => !MainObj.IsNew;
+
+   public override bool PanelHistory_Visible
+       => !MainObj.IsNew;
}
```

Now let's run the application and log in as a non-HR employee Jean Trenary. If you open the *Employment* tab of the Employee Details screen, you will see that the *Benefits* and *Pay* panels are now completely hidden, as shown in Figure 5-17.

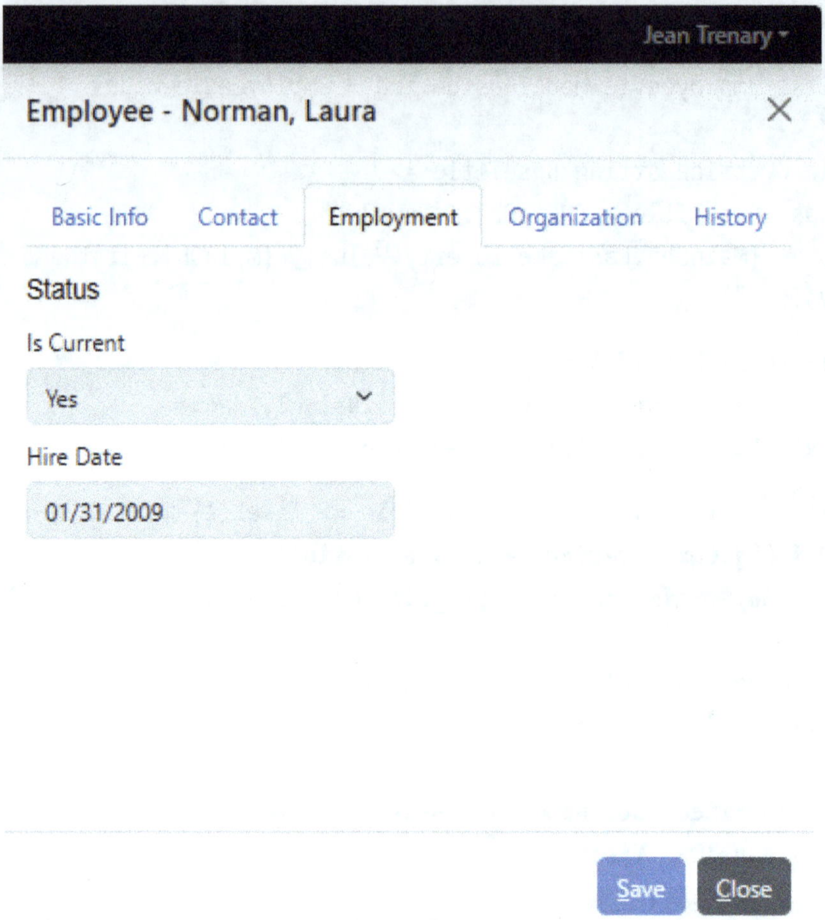

CHAPTER 5 IMPLEMENTING SECURITY

Figure 5-17. Employee pay and benefits panels hidden for non-HR users

If you switch to the *History* tab, you will see that the *Pay History* panel is also hidden, as shown in Figure 5-18.

CHAPTER 5 IMPLEMENTING SECURITY

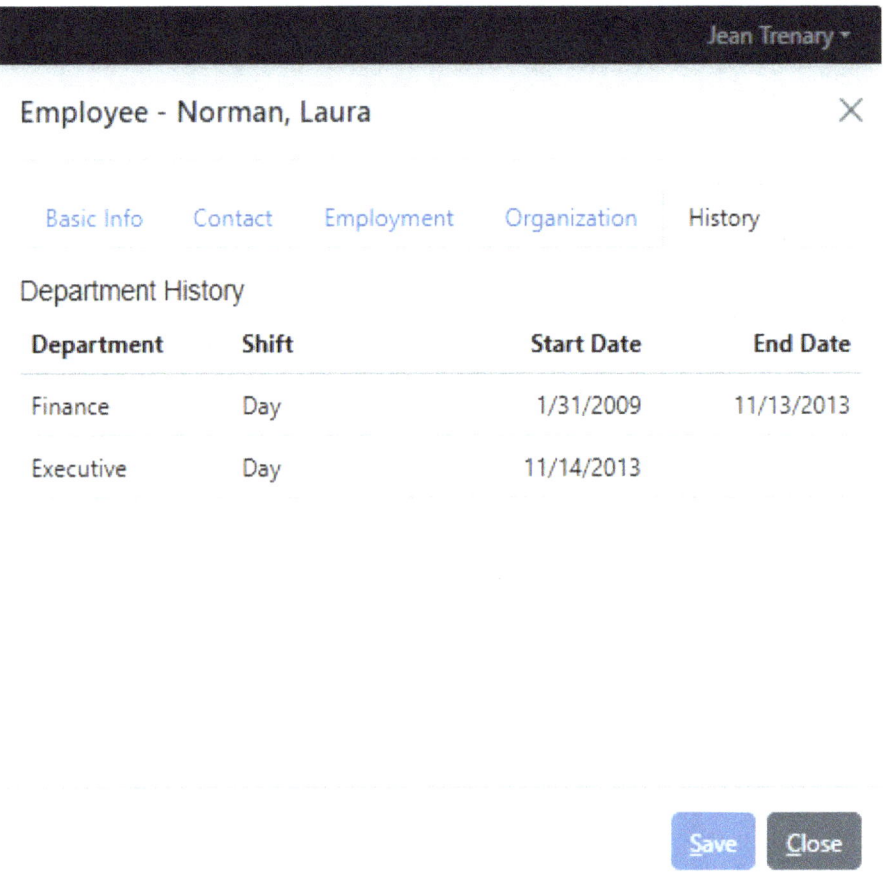

Figure 5-18. Employee pay history panel hidden for non-HR users

Finally, let's sign out and log back in as a Human Resources Manager user Paula Barreto de Mattos, which has a permission to create employees, using their email paula0@adventure-works.com. If you click the *New* link on the Employee List screen, you will see that the *History* tab and the *Direct Reports* panel on the *Organization* tab are both hidden, as shown in Figure 5-19.

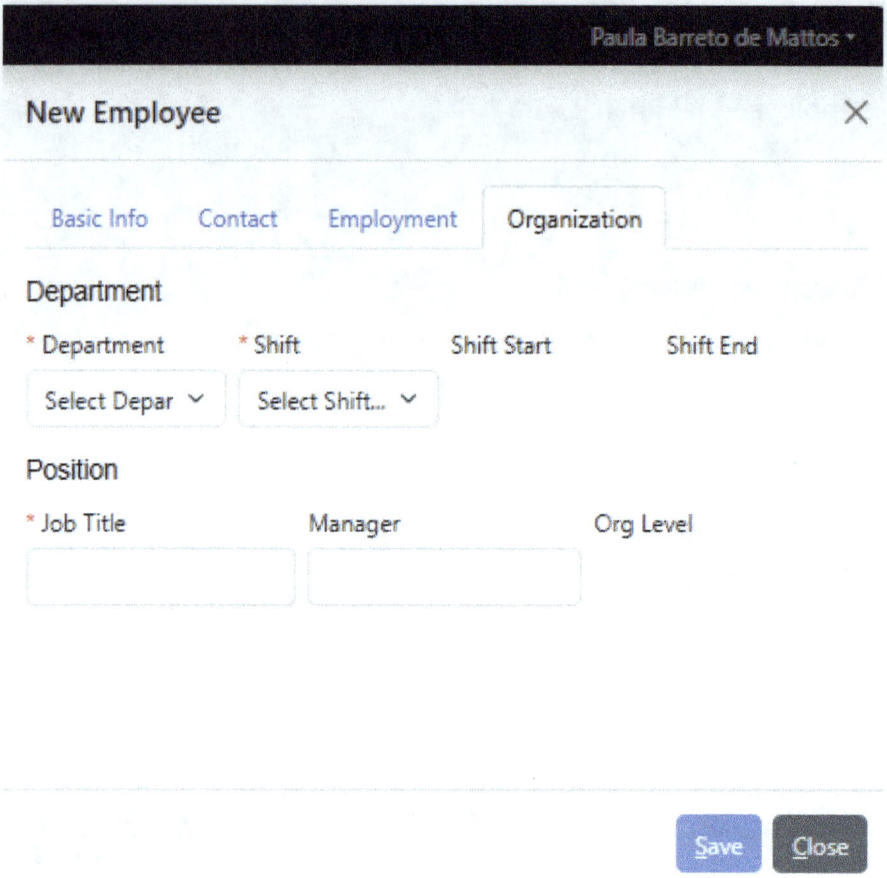

Chapter 5 Implementing Security

Figure 5-19. History tab and Direct Reports panel hidden when creating an employee

Securing Page Access

Hiding a link or a button on the UI is not enough to secure access to a page, since users can still access it by typing the URL directly in the browser. Therefore, we also need to secure access to the pages themselves, so that unauthorized users cannot access them even if they know the URL.

Setting View Policies

Earlier, we configured authorization policies based on all the application permissions in the `AuthConfig` class. Now we can use these policies to set the `policy` attribute on the `ui:view` elements in the model to secure access to the views.

To access employee views, users need to have the `Employee_View` permission, so we will set it on the `policy` attribute of the `ui:view` elements for the *EmployeeView* and *EmployeeListView* views, as shown in Listing 5-27.

Listing 5-27. Setting policies for employee views

```
<ui:view name="EmployeeView" title="Employee"
+       policy="Employee_View">[...]
<ui:view name="EmployeeListView" title="Employee List"
+       policy="Employee_View">[...]
```

This will prevent the users that don't have `Employee_View` permission from accessing the employee views directly by URL and will hide any main menu links to these views that don't have the `policy` attribute set explicitly.

If you build the model, run the application, and log in as customer user `kim2@adventure-works.com`, which has no permissions to view employees, you will see that the *New Employee* and *Employee List* links are not available in the main menu.

If you try to access the Employee Details view for a specific employee directly by typing the URL, e.g., `https://localhost:44337/EmployeeView?BusinessEntityId=1`, you will get an error message saying, "You are not authorized to access this page", as shown in Figure 5-20.

CHAPTER 5   IMPLEMENTING SECURITY

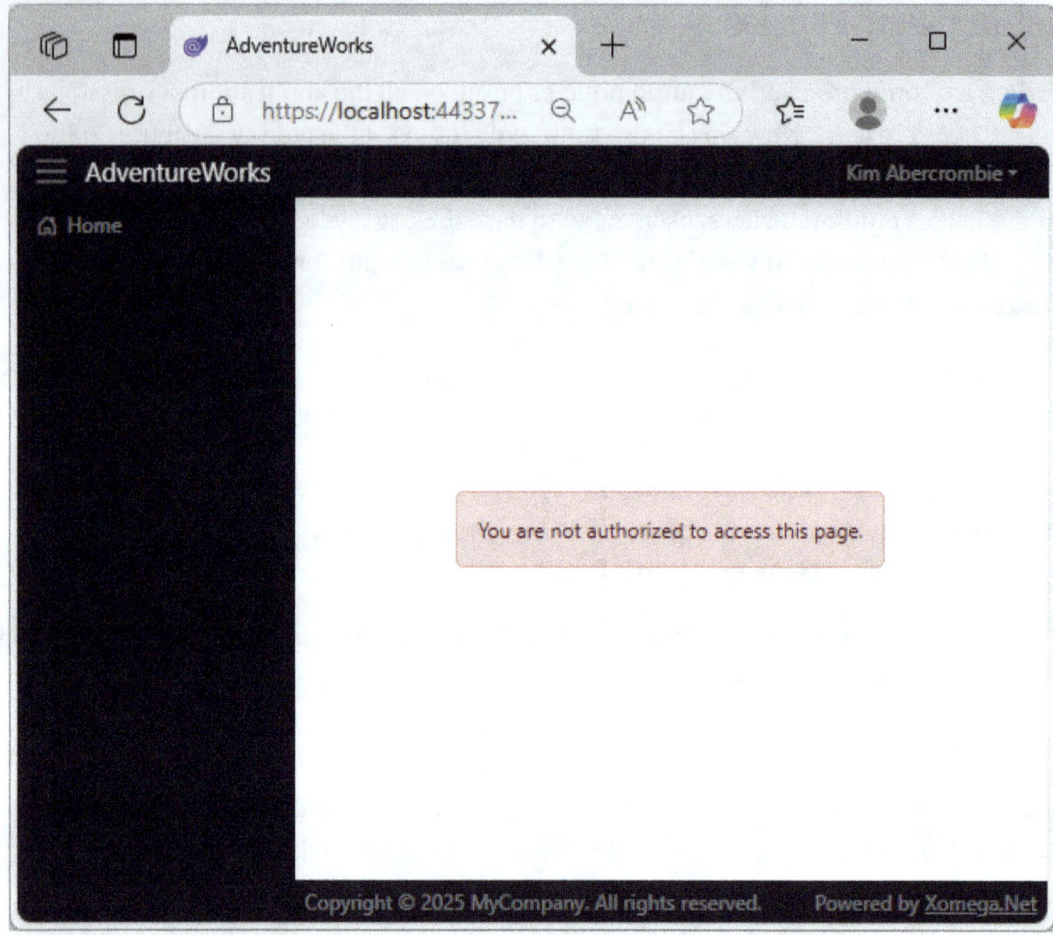

Figure 5-20. *Unauthorized access to Employee Details by URL*

Note You will get a similar error if you try to access the Employee List view by URL.

Parameter-Based Policy

Having `Employee_View` permission is the minimum requirement to access the Employee Details view, which allows users to view their own employee details. However, if they want to view other employees' details, they also need the `Employee_View_Others` permission.

CHAPTER 5 IMPLEMENTING SECURITY

So, if you log in as a regular employee user, such as Chris Norred, which is neither HR nor an executive user, and try to access the Employee Details view for another employee, you will see the "Operation not allowed" security error from the business service, as shown in Figure 5-21.

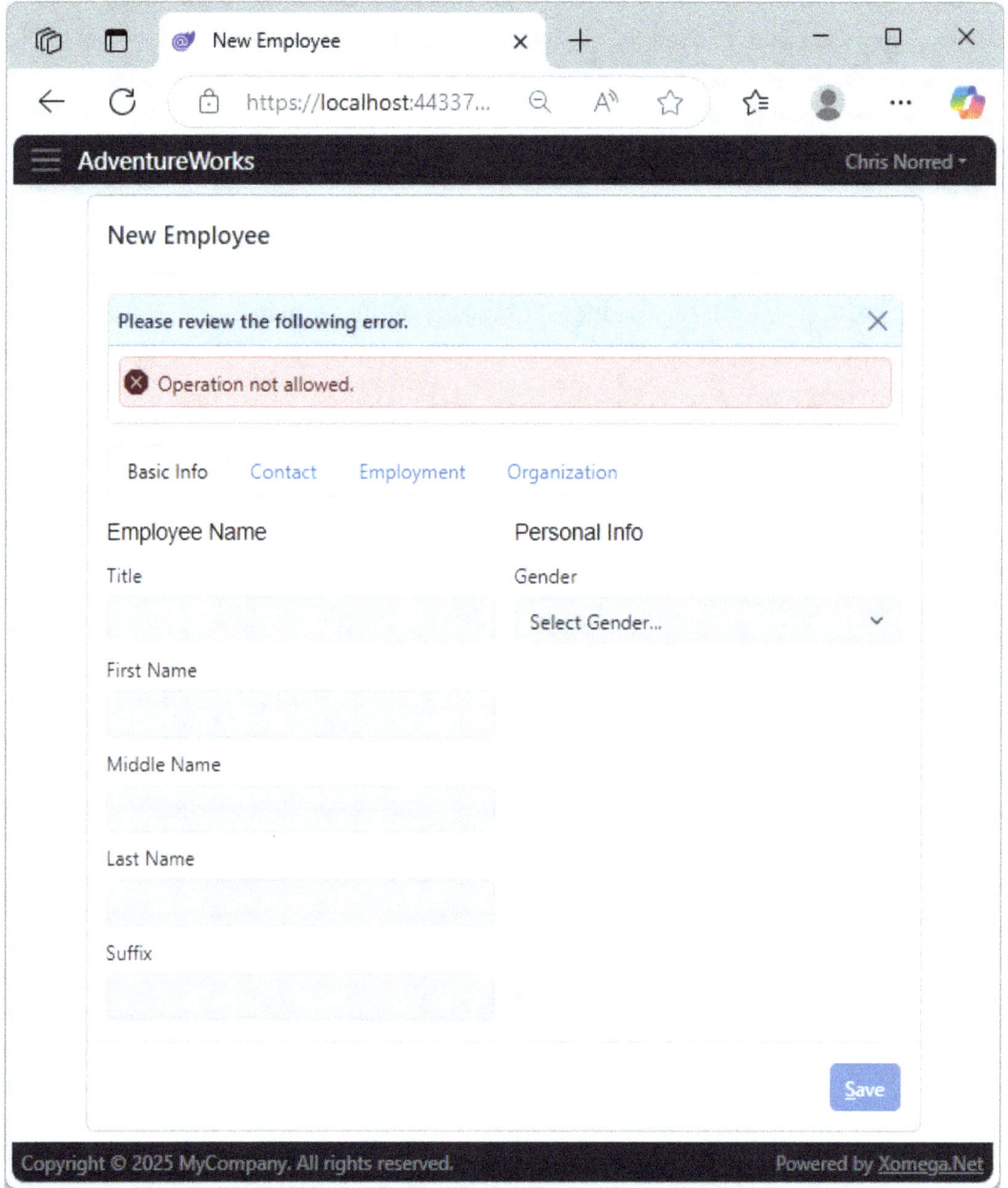

Figure 5-21. *Unauthorized access to Employee Details view for another employee*

CHAPTER 5 IMPLEMENTING SECURITY

To really polish the user experience and give the users a consistent security error message, even when they try to access the Employee Details view for another employee directly by URL, you can set the `policy` for the `EmployeeView` based on the specified `BusinessEntityId` parameter.

To do this, you can add a new file `EmployeeViewPage.razor.cs` in the *Views ➤ Human Resources* folder of the `AdventureWorks.Client.Blazor.Common` project with a partial class `EmployeeViewPage`. You can inject the `IServiceProvider` to access the current principal and then set the `AuthPolicy` property in the `SetAuthPolicy` to one of the following values:

- `Employee_Create` if the `action` parameter is set to `create`, which allows creating a new employee.

- `Employee_View` if the `BusinessEntityId` parameter matches the current user's person ID.

- `Employee_View_Others` if the `BusinessEntityId` parameter does not match the current user's person ID.

Listing 5-28 demonstrates how to implement this logic in the `EmployeeViewPage` partial class.

Listing 5-28. Setting parameter-based policy for EmployeeView

```
+ namespace AdventureWorks.Client.Blazor.Common.Views;
+
+ public partial class EmployeeViewPage
+ {
+     [Inject] IServiceProvider ServiceProvider { get; set; }
+
+     partial void SetAuthPolicy()
+     {
+         var qry = QueryHelpers.ParseQuery(
+             Navigation.ToAbsoluteUri(Navigation.Uri).Query);
+
```

```
+            if (qry.TryGetValue(ViewParams.Action.Param,
+                            out var action)
+                && action == ViewParams.Action.Create)
+            AuthPolicy = Enum.GetName(
+                AppPermissions.Employee_Create);
+
+            if (qry.TryGetValue(EmployeeObject.BusinessEntityId,
+                            out var id))
+            {
+                var usr = ServiceProvider.GetCurrentPrincipal();
+                var empId = usr.GetPersonId()?.ToString();
+                AuthPolicy = id == empId
+                    ? Enum.GetName(AppPermissions.Employee_View)
+                    : Enum.GetName(
+                        AppPermissions.Employee_View_Others);
+            }
+        }
+ }
```

If you run the application, log in as a regular employee user Chris Norred, and try to access the Employee Details view for another employee by URL, you will see the standard security error message "You are not authorized to access this page", without any fields or controls, as shown in Figure 5-22.

CHAPTER 5　IMPLEMENTING SECURITY

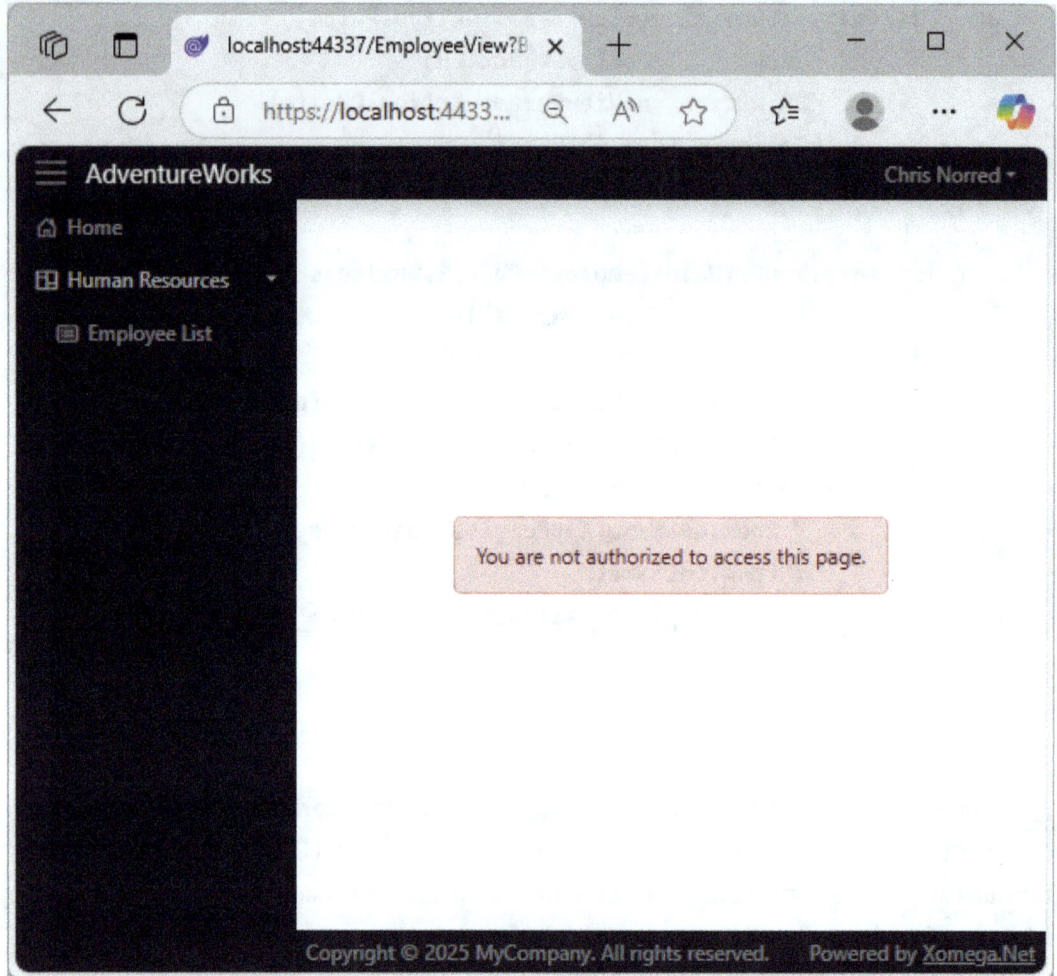

Figure 5-22. *Unauthorized access to Employee Details view for another employee*

However, if Chris Norred tries to access their own employee details by URL, they will still see the Employee Details view with all fields populated and disabled, as shown in Figure 5-23.

CHAPTER 5   IMPLEMENTING SECURITY

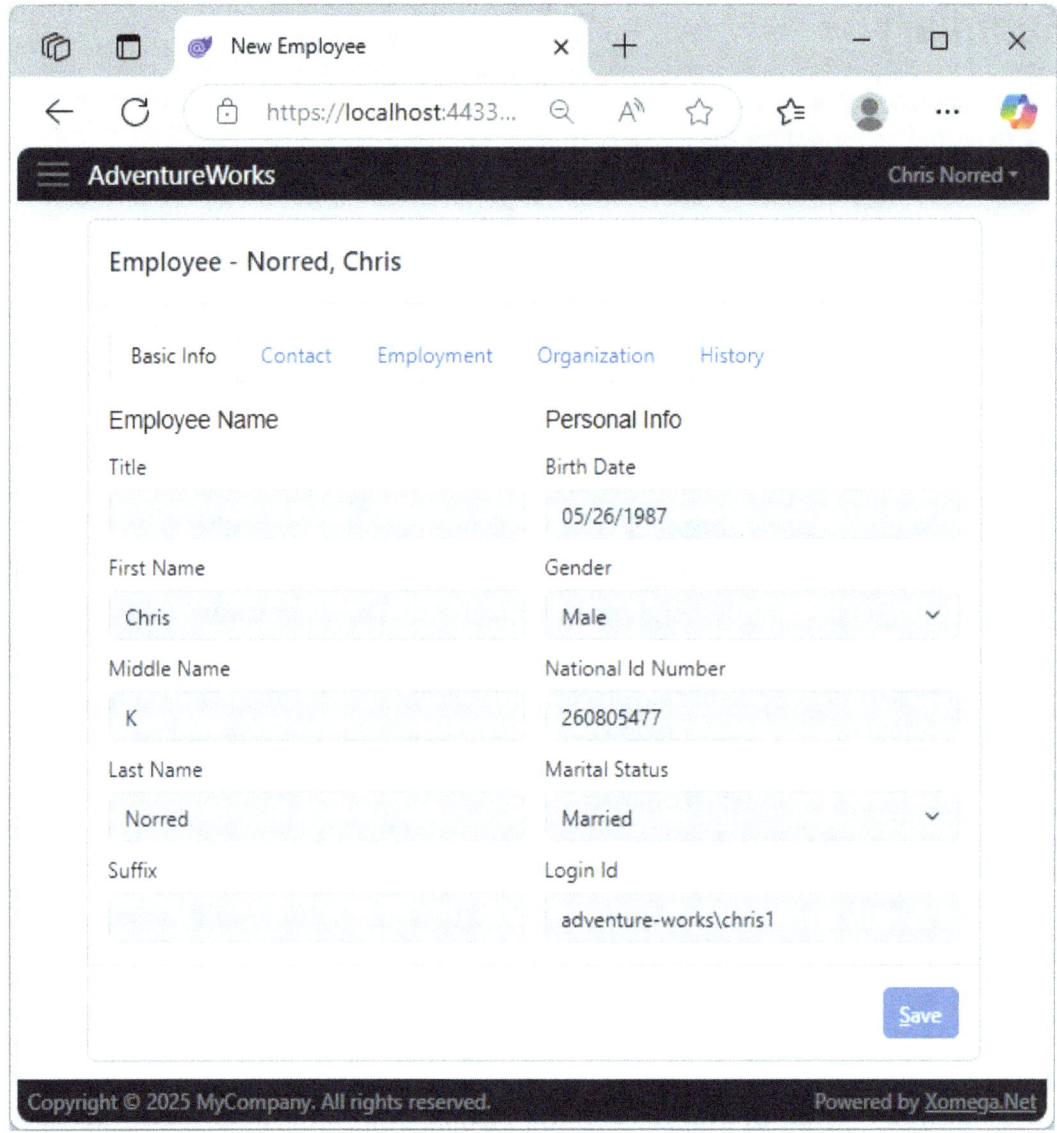

Figure 5-23. Employee Details view for self

As you can see, Xomega provides many options to secure access to UI views and fields, allowing you to deliver consistent user experience for different scenarios.

CHAPTER 5   IMPLEMENTING SECURITY

Summary

In this chapter, you learned how to secure your Xomega .NET applications using best practices that include multiple layers of protection in both the business services and the client UI. You saw how easy it is to implement username and password validation in an Xomega Solution, but you can also use other authentication methods, such as OAuth or OpenID Connect, for third-party identity providers.

You learned how to define a clear and easy-to-maintain security model for your application by specifying application permissions and security rules using claims-based extension methods on the IPrincipal interface. You then saw how to use these permissions to secure access to screens and services in the application, implement row-level security, and protect sensitive data from unauthorized access.

Implementing security checks directly in the business services, rather than in the API controllers, allows you to keep the security logic platform-agnostic regardless of how you invoke the services—whether directly, through a REST API, or via any other protocol such as gRPC.

Similarly, security checks in data objects and view models are also platform-agnostic, which allows you to reuse these objects and their presentation and security logic across different UI frameworks and platforms. This will help future-proof your application and make it easier to upgrade to newer technologies as they become available.

Thank you for reading this book through to the end. I hope it has given you a solid understanding of the Xomega platform and how to use it to quickly build high-quality, modern .NET applications.

With the open source Xomega Framework taking care of much of the common functionality that enterprise-grade applications require, and Xomega generators consistently producing the bulk of high-quality code from the model, all you need to do is craft the model based on your business requirements and implement any custom logic as needed.

With the rapid advancements in the Generative AI space, it's only a matter of time before most model updates and custom logic will be generated automatically as well, leading to even greater efficiency and productivity.

I invite you to try building your next application with Xomega and see how much faster you can develop it compared to other approaches. You can also contribute to the Xomega Framework open source project on GitHub, where we welcome any feedback, suggestions, and ideas. Visit https://xomega.net for more information about Xomega, and don't hesitate to reach out with any questions or comments. Happy coding!

Index

A

Above operator, 117, 119
AccessLevel property, 315
Add and Edit Employee Address
    links to address details
        create address link, 220, 221
        disabling edit link conditionally, 222, 223
        Edit Address Link, 221
    saving employee address
        add address input structures, 223, 224
        review employee address, 227, 228
        service logic, 225, 226
AddAppPolicies method, 321
AddCriteriaClause method, 130
Add/edit related objects
    Add and Edit Employee Address (*see* Add and Edit Employee Address)
    display the employee's home address (*see* Display the employee's home address, employee details screen)
Adding non-field criteria, 107
Address Details screen
    Address Details view, 219, 220
    custom code, AddressService, 216, 217
    customizing AddressObject, 217–219
    generate address details view, 214
Address Details view, 219, 220
Address fields
    configuring address fields, 211, 212
    reading address details, 210

AddressObject data object, 217–219
AdventureWorks.Client.Blazor.Common project, 336
AdventureWorks.Client.Common project, 136
AdventureWorks.Model, *see* Xomega model project structure
AdventureWorks.Services.Common project, 284, 289, 293
AdventureWorks.Services.Entities project, 119, 296
Application permissions
    AppPermissions enumeration, 293
    HasPermission method, 293
    rules, 294, 295
Associations between domain objects
    complex association, 30, 31
    simple association, 29, 30
    subtype associations, 32, 33
AuthConfig class, 321, 333

B

Base operators enumeration, 108, 109, 113, 117
Blazor solution structure
    AdventureWorks.Client.Blazor, 7
    AdventureWorks.Client.Blazor.Common, 7
    AdventureWorks.Client.Blazor.Wasm, 7
    AdventureWorks.Client.Common, 6
    AdventureWorks.Model, 6

INDEX

Blazor solution structure (*cont.*)
    AdventureWorks.Model.Diagrams, 6
    AdventureWorks.Services.Common, 6
    AdventureWorks.Services.Entities, 6
    AdventureWorks.Services.Rest, 6
    Xomega, 6
Boolean fields, 78, 171, 172
BuildExpression method, 119
BusinessEntityAddress object, 87–89
BusinessEntityIdProperty, 323
BusinessEntity object, 87, 90, 184

C

Cascading selection
    adding country criteria, 140–142
    configuration, 142–144
    country dynamic enumeration, 139
Checkbox options criteria, 125
Child lists
    department history child list (*see* Department history child list)
    pay history child list (*see* Pay history child list)
Child subobjects
    as a child list, 88–91
    city/state column, 93
    city/state result field, 84, 85
    entity model, 84–88
    reading subobject fields, 91–93
ClaimsPrincipal classes, 284
ComputeAnnualPay, 246
Computed shift fields, 254
Computed UI fields
    add current department (*see* Current department information, computed UI fields)
    add current pay info (*see* Current pay info, computed UI fields)
Conditionally required fields, 201, 202
Configure panel layout, details view
    custom view layout, 175
    grouping fields into panels, 166, 167
    lay out panels and fields
        editing Boolean fields, 171, 172
        employment tab, 171
        lay out employment tab, 173
        updated layout, Employment tab, 174
    organizing panels with tabs, 168
        employee details view, 168
        employment tab, 170, 171
        history tab, 169, 170
        personal info tab, 169
    responsive layout, 174
Contact tab, 189
    with Address, 213, 214
    with email address, 193
    with phone number, 202, 203
Copilot, 165
Create operation, 151–152, 182, 184, 190, 192, 200, 216, 226, 244, 253, 265, 297
Create address link, 220, 221, 227
CreateAsync and UpdateAsync methods, 226, 262
CreateAsync operation, 301
CRUD operations, 37
    add, 54, 55
    default, 55
Current department information, computed UI fields
    add department parameters, 248, 249
    add organization tab, 250

computed shift fields, 254
department history record, 248
employee history tab with department history, 256
employee organization tab with department, 255
read and update department, 253
review organization fields, 255
UI-only shift fields, 249
update department method, 251
Current pay info, computed UI fields
adding pay rate to operations, 239, 240
adding UI-only fields, 240, 241
configure computed annual pay and pay rate range, 245
configure computed fields, 245
grouping pay properties, 241, 242
reading and updating pay info, 244
review pay fields, 246, 247
service logic to update pay, 242, 243
CurrentPrincipal property, 289, 297, 315
Custom address service code, 232, 233
Custom field population logic, 80, 81
Custom operator display, 116
Custom operator logic
adding custom operator, 117–119
implementing operator's logic, 119–121
sample AdventureWorks database, 116
Custom range operators, 113–116
Custom search result fields
add, 79, 80
configure key field and links, 81, 82
custom field population logic, 80, 81
with details link, 83
employee list view, 82
employee object, 78
Custom view layout, 48–49, 175

D

Data transfer objects (DTO), 35
Default details view, 148
add/edit related objects (*see* Add/edit related objects)
computed UI Fields (*see* Computed UI fields)
configuring panel layout (*see* (Configure panel layout, details view)
display child lists (*see* Display child lists)
employee fields, 147
fields from related objects (*see* Fields from related objects)
lookup selection form (*see* Lookup selection form)
master-detail layout (*see* Master-detail layout)
Default operation, 151
Default operator contains, 111
Default operators configuration, 109–111
Default range operators, 113
Delete operation, employee object, 149
Department dynamic enumeration, 162, 163
Department history child list
add department dynamic enumeration, 162, 163
add shift dynamic enumeration, 163
department history child table, 164, 165
department history read list, 161, 162
department history subobject, 160, 161
update column names, 164
Department history child table, 164, 165
Department history read list, 161, 162
Department history subobject, 160, 161

INDEX

Direct reports
    custom code, reading reports, 273
    direct reports list object, 270
    list object, 270
    method, reading direct reports, 272
    Organization tab, 274
    reading direct reports, 271, 272
    review direct reports, 273

Display child lists
    add pay history child list
        pay history child table, 159
        pay history subobject, 154–156
        subobject read list operation, 156–159
    department history child list
        add department dynamic enumeration, 162, 163
        add shift dynamic enumeration, 163
        department history child table, 164, 165
        department history read list, 161, 162
        department history subobject, 160, 161
        EmployeePayHistory, 160
        update column names, 164
    remove fields and actions, 153
        employee fields using appropriate controls, 148
        hiding the internal key field, 152
        remove from read output, 149, 150
        remove from update input, 150
        remove the delete operation, 149
        restructuring the create operation, 151
        review result, 153

Display the employee's home address, employee details screen
    Address Details screen
        Address Details view, 219, 220
        custom code, AddressService, 216, 217
        customizing AddressObject, 217–219
        generate address details view, 214
    address fields
        configuring address fields, 211, 212
        reading address details, 210
    contact tab with address, 213, 214
    custom code, populating address fields, 212
    employee address data object, 209, 210
    populating address fields, 212

Domain Driven Design (DDD), 25, 33, 96

Domain model
    aggregates, 33, 34
    associations between objects, 29–33
    DDD, 33
    design principles, 25
    domain objects, 26–29
    fields, 25, 26
    fieldsets, 25, 26
    presentation model, 40–53
    subobjects, 33, 34

Domain objects
    associations between, 29–33
    defining fields, 26
    module/subobjects elements, 26
    primary key
        composite, 28, 29
        simple, 27
    structure, 26

Dynamic employee title, 204, 205

Dynamic enumeration, 23, 24, 105, 126
    auto-complete for multi-value, 131–133

configuration, 127–129
custom criteria
   implementation, 129–131
customizing criteria object, 135–138
statically displayed criteria, 133, 134
Dynamic view title
   customized view model, 203
   dynamic employee title, 204, 205

E

Edit Address Link, 221–223, 227, 228, 234
Element documentation, 18, 19
Email address parameters, 188
Email address service logic
   EmailAddress table, 190
   email address update methods, 191
   extending EmployeeService, 190
   reading and updating email
      address, 192
Email Address Update Methods, 191
Employee address data object, 209, 210
Employee Address Lookup Link
   employee details view, 233, 234
   reviewing address lookup view,
      234, 235
EmployeeAddressObjectCustomized
   class, 236, 317
EmployeeAddressObject data object, 210,
   211, 220–224, 233
Employee Address Validation, 235–238
EmployeeCriteria data object, 114, 118,
   133, 135
EmployeeCriteria object, 135, 136
Employee list columns, 207–208
Employee list search criteria, 106
EmployeeObject data object, 152, 156,
   201, 208, 209, 225, 240, 241, 249

EmployeeObjectCustomized class, 269,
   315, 317
EmployeePayHistoryList data object, 158
EmployeeServiceExtended Functions,
   262, 263
EmployeeViewModelCustomized
   class, 328
Employee_View_Others permission, 302,
   304, 334
Employee_View_Others_Pay
   permission, 306
EmployeeViewPage partial class, 336
Employee_View permission, 297, 333, 334
Employment tab, 170, 171, 173, 174, 239,
   241, 246, 309, 325, 329
Entity model diagrams, 85–88
EntityModel.edmx, 85
Enumeration types
   dynamic enumeration, 23, 24
   static enumeration, 23

F

Fields from related objects
   person object (*see* Fields from the
      person object)
   person phone subobject (*see* Person
      phone subobject)
   view and edit phone number, 193
Fields from the person object
   adding contact tab, email address, 189
   contact tab with email address, 193
   defining logical types
      name type, 177–179
      person type, 176
   display name fields
      add name field group, 180
      add read output parameters, 179

INDEX

Fields from the person object (*cont.*)
 employee name panel, 182
 populating name fields, 181
 resulting employee name
  panel, 182
 editing name fields
  add input parameters, 183, 184
  custom code, create operation,
   184, 185
  editable employee names, 187
  reviewing editable names, 186
  update operation, custom code,
   185, 186
 Email address service logic
  EmailAddress table, 190
  email address update methods, 191
  extending EmployeeService, 190
  reading and updating email
   address, 192
 view and edit email address
  add email address parameters, 188
  Employee CRUD operations, add
   email address parameters, 188
FromPrincipal method, 286
Full-scale lookup view, 235

G

GenAI agent, 165
Generate CRUD views
 add CRUD operations, 54, 55
 application code, 56–58
 default CRUD operations, 55
 employee object, 54
 search and details views, 55, 56
Generated entities
 AdventureWorks database, 94
 customized DbContext, 99, 100
 custom properties and methods, 97
 EF Core configuration, 99, 100
 EmployeeExtended.cs, 97, 98
 extending, 97
 Find All References, 96
 framework, 98
 human resources module, 95
 navigation property, 97, 98
 sales column on EmployeeListView,
  102, 103
 sales indicator, 94
 sales person diagram, 95
 using enhanced entity, 101, 102
Generation operator, 113, 114
Generation operator enumeration, 114
GetNames method, 119
GetPersonId extension method, 302
Grouping pay properties, 241, 242

H

HasPermission extension method, 294,
 297, 315
Hiding creation links
 adding policies for app
  permissions, 321
 hiding new link, employee list, 320
 reviewing creation links, 322
 updating presentation model, 319, 320
Hiding sensitive data
 hiding sensitive fields, 322–326
 hiding UI panels, 327–331
Hiding UI panels
 marking panels with conditional
  visibility, 327, 328
 visible-flag in custom view
  model, 328–331
History tab, 169, 170

I, J, K

#if DEBUG conditions, 278
IPrincipal interface, 292, 293, 315
IPrincipalExtensions class, 294
Is Between operators, 122

L

Links to Address Details
    create address link, 220, 221
    disabling edit link conditionally, 222, 223
    Edit Address Link, 221
List view
    child subobjects, 83–93
    custom search result fields, 78–83
    generated entities, 94–103
    properties, 69
    refine search result columns, 69–73
    static enumerations, 74–78
Logical types
    name type, 177–179
    person type, 176
LoginAsync method, 278, 283
LoginObjectCustomized class, 280
Login operation, 282, 283
Lookup Result Fields, 231–232
Lookup selection form
    employee address lookup link
        employee details view, 233, 234
        reviewing address lookup view, 234, 235
    employee address validation, 235–238
    generate Lookup View
        changing view title, 232
        configuring lookup criteria, 230, 231
        custom address service code, 232, 233
        Lookup Result Fields, 231
        parameters, 229

M

Manager field
    add employee enumeration
        add custom code, enum, 261
        update the employee type, 259
        update the read enum operation, 260
    adding manager to operations, 257, 258
    Configure UI logic, 266
    grouping manager with position, 258
    Organization tab, 268
    reading and updating the manager
        EmployeeServiceExtended Functions, 262, 263
        update CRUD operations, 265, 266
    refreshing the lookup cache, 268, 269
    review the manager field, 267, 268
Master-detail employee view
    employee details screen, 206
    employee list columns, 207
    unsaved changes, 208
    update employee details links, 206, 207
Master-detail layout
    dynamic view title, customized view model, 203, 204
    master-detail employee view
        Employee Details screen, 206
        employee list columns, 207
        unsaved changes, 208
        update employee details links, 206, 207
Messages class, 236, 296

INDEX

Microservices, 17
Model project structure, Xomega
   application model files, 15, 16
   generators, 11–16
      import from database connection properties, 13–15
   structure, 11
Multi-value control configuration, 123–125
Multi-value criteria configuration, 122, 123

N

Name Field Group, 180–181
Nested structures, 35, 36, 38, 223
Non-employee user, 299, 300
Non-field result criteria, 108
Non-HR employee user, 300, 301

O

Object operations, 37–39
OnInitialized method, 136, 222, 315, 320, 323
OperatorRegistry service, 120
Operators enumeration, 108
   default, 109
   definition, 113, 117
Organization tab, 248, 250, 268, 274
Organization hierarchy
   direct reports (*see* Direct reports)
   manager field (*see* Manager field)
Organization Level criteria, 116
Org level operator, 117, 118

P, Q

Parameter-based policies, 334, 336–339
PasswordLoginServiceCustomized class, 278, 283

Password validation implementation
   PasswordLoginService, 278
   password validation service logic, 278, 279
   removing default username and password, 279, 280
   review email-based login, 280, 281
Pay frequency, 155, 159, 239, 241, 245–247
Pay history child list
   pay history child table, 159
   pay history subobject, 154–156
   subobject read list operation, 156–159
Pay history child table, 159
PayHistory_ReadListAsync method, 306, 308
Pay history subobject, 154–156, 158
Personal info tab, 169
Person phone subobject
   add phone number parameters, 196
   add phone to contact tab, 197, 198
   conditionally required fields, 201, 202
   contact tab with phone number, 202, 203
   person.xom file, 194
   phone number service logic method, 198
      reading and updating phone number, 199, 200
   phone number type enumeration, 195
Person type enumeration, 176, 185
Phone number parameters, 196–197
Phone number service logic, 198–200
Phone number type field, 203, 223
Phone number type enumeration, 195–196
Presentation model
   data objects
      declarations, 41

definition, 41
operations, 43–45
panel/data grid, 40
properties, 42, 43
UI, 40
UI field config, 45, 46
xfk:data-object element, 40
define, 40
navigation
links from a list, 51, 52
links with results, 52, 53
object links to views, 49–51
UI views, 40
attribute, 46
custom view layout, 48
declaring, 46
framework-specific customizations, 47
navigation menu, 47
view model, 47, 48

R

Read and update department, 253–254
ReadAsync operation, 302, 304–306
Read enum operation, 24, 127–129, 139, 142, 157, 162, 163, 259, 260, 268
Reading address details, 210–211
Reading and updating email address, 192–193
Reading and updating phone number, 199, 200
Reading direct reports, 271–273
ReadListAsync method, 80, 101, 130, 232, 304, 311, 312
ReadListAsync operation, 297, 303–306, 310

Read list operation, 54, 55, 69–72, 78, 79, 84, 94, 106, 140, 156, 158, 161, 173, 229, 230, 311
Read operation, 149, 179, 182, 183, 192, 200, 210, 212, 216, 217, 219, 223, 245, 257, 265, 271, 273, 297, 301, 302, 306
Read Output Parameters, 179–180
Realistic security requirements, 277
Refine search result columns
Build context menu, 73
configure column labels, 72
fields, 69
updated results grid, 73
update read list output, 69–71
Removing criteria operators, 111, 112
Removing useless criteria, 106
Responsive layout, 66, 174
Review search/details views
application layers, 58
details screen, 65, 66
search criteria, 61–65
search results grid, 59, 60
sidebar menu, 58, 59
Role-based authorization (RBA), 292
Row-level security
row access in ReadList operation, 303, 304
row access in Read operation, 302, 303

S, T

Search criteria
applied criteria, 64
drop-down list, 61
editing, 63, 64
operators, 62
selection, 61

INDEX

Search operators, 62
Securing business services
    row-level security, 302–304
    securing operation access, 296–301
    securing sensitive data, 305–313
Securing operation access
    adding security error message, 296
    reviewing operation security, 299–301
    security checks in CRUD
        operations, 297, 298
Securing page access
    parameter-based policies, 334, 336–339
    setting view policies, 333
Securing sensitive data
    permissions, 306
    ReadAsync and ReadListAsync
        operations, 306
    review private data in employee
        list, 313, 314
    sensitive data in executive
        user, 308–310
    sensitive data in ReadList
        operation, 311–313
    sensitive data in Read operation,
        306, 308
    unauthorized access protectiion, 305
Securing UI editing
    hiding editing links, 317–319
    making data object read-only, 315–317
Securing UI views and fields
    hiding sensitive data, 322–331
    securing page access, 332–339
    UI editing, 315–323
Service Logic to Update Pay, 242–243
Service model
    DTO, 35
    object operations, 37–39
    service structures, 34

    structures, 35–37
Service operations, 23, 34, 37, 40, 42, 43,
        45, 54, 66, 296, 314
Service structures
    define, 35
    inferring parameter types, 36, 37
    nested structures, 36
    struct elements, 35, 36
ServiceUtil.CopyProperties method, 213
SetAuthPolicy, 336
SetCascadingProperty method, 143
Shift dynamic enumeration, 163, 249
Static enumerations, 23
    defining, 74, 75
    enumeration types, 75, 76
    gender values and descriptions, 74
    predefined values, 74
    update field types, 76
    user-friendly names, 77
    user-friendly values, 74, 78
    values in results grid and search
        criteria, 77
    values on details view, 77, 78
Subobject read list operation,
        156–159, 161

U

Ui:blazor-control config, 124, 132
UI field config, 45, 46
UI-only annual pay field, 241
UI-only shift fields, 249
Update operation, 150
Update department method, 251–252
UpdatePayRateAsync method, 244
User claims
    categories, 282
    Claims IPrincipal Extensions

CurrentPrincipal property, 289
employee check, 289
executive check, 290
Human Resources check, 291
person ID retrievel, 291, 292
enhancing user info, 282
reading user info, 283, 284
reviewing claims in UI, 288
security requirements, 282
user info conversion to IPrincipal, 284
UserInfo from ClaimsPrincipal
Conversion, 286
UserInfo to ClaimsPrincipal
Conversion, 285, 286
UserInfoPrincipalConverter class, 285, 286
Username validation service logic, 278

V, W

View and edit phone number, 193
Visible-flag attribute, 327, 328

X, Y, Z

XAutoComplete Blazor control, 135
XAutoComplete control, 132
Xomega
applications in defense, 277
concepts and development
techniques, 103
criteria framework, 105
Xomega generators
configuration, 12
include in build property, 13
Model Enhancement folder, 11
output path property, 13

properties, 12, 13
Xomega model
defined, 16
domain entities, 16
domain model, 25–34
element configuration, 19, 20
element documentation, 18, 19
global configuration, 20
logical types
configuration, 21
defined, 20
enumeration, 23, 24
external user, 20
inheritance, 21, 22
internal user, 20
physical types, 20
user, 20
modules, 16, 17
separate XSD schemas, 16
service model, 34–39
structure, 16, 17
types of model elements, 16
Xomega.Net, 1–10
Xomega Solution
AdventureWorks, 2
Blazor components, 5
Blazor solution structure, 5–7
configuration, 3–5
home screen after authentication,
9, 10
login credential validation, 9
login field validation, 8
password login form, 7, 8
template, 1–3
wizard, 3, 4
XOptions Blazor control, 124

351

GPSR Compliance

The European Union's (EU) General Product Safety Regulation (GPSR) is a set of rules that requires consumer products to be safe and our obligations to ensure this.

If you have any concerns about our products, you can contact us on

ProductSafety@springernature.com

In case Publisher is established outside the EU, the EU authorized representative is:

Springer Nature Customer Service Center GmbH
Europaplatz 3
69115 Heidelberg, Germany

www.ingramcontent.com/pod-product-compliance
Lightning Source LLC
LaVergne TN
LVHW081346060526
838201LV00050B/1728